CHOCKS & DI...

1st Edition
published in 2011 by

Woodfield Publishing Ltd
Bognor Regis PO21 5EL England
www.woodfieldpublishing.co.uk

© Stanley Newton, 2011

All rights reserved.
No part of this publication may be reproduced
or transmitted in any form or by any means,
electronic or mechanical, nor may it be stored
in any information storage and retrieval system,
without prior permission from the publisher.

The right of Stanley Newton
to be identified as Author of this work
has been asserted in accordance with
the Copyright, Designs and Patents Act 1988

ISBN 1-84683-120-2

Printed and bound in England

Cover illustration by Stanley Newton

Chocks & Driptrays

Experiences of a RAF Flight Mechanic in the UK and Abroad 1946-56

STANLEY NEWTON

Woodfield

Woodfield Publishing Ltd
Bognor Regis ~ West Sussex ~ England ~ PO21 5EL
tel 01243 821234 ~ e/m info@woodfieldpublishing.co.uk

Interesting and informative books on a variety of subjects

For full details of all our published titles, visit our website at
www.woodfieldpublishing.co.uk

Dedicated to the thousands of chaps, both officers and airmen, of the Royal Air Force with whom I am proud to have served.

Also to Arthur Frier, without whose encouragement and hard work in formatting and typing the text, this book would never have been finished.

Also to Lowden Masterton for proof reading so constructively

Plate 1. Blackburn Lincock II G-AALH.

~ CONTENTS ~

Preface .... *iii*
Introduction .... *iv*
Illustrations .... *vi*

1. Early Memories 1
2. First Flight 10
3. Miscellaneous Recollections 15
4. Apprentice at Blackburns 24
5. At the Crossroads 40
6. Square Bashing 47
7. Learning a Trade 54
8. Waiting for the Boat 64
9. A Life on the Ocean Wave 70
10. Passage to India 79
11. Getting my Knees Brown 87
12. Last Days of the British Raj 104
13. Leaving India 125
14. Sind, Sun and Sand 132
15. Mystery and Suspense 147
16. Personalities and Politicians 153
17. Mad dogs and Englishmen 160
18. Pakistan Zindabad! 169

19.	Ships that Pass in the Night	176
20.	Lighter Moments	186
21.	Per Ardua Ad Asbestos	190
22.	Final Year at Mauripur	193
23.	Homeward Bound	203
24.	A Lancaster of my Own	213
25.	Two-Six on the Bamboo Bombers	222
26.	Happy Wanderer	252
27.	An Encounter with the Chief of the Air Staff	266
28.	Final Two Years	280
	Epilogue	*299*

Preface

I started to write this book around 1971, mainly for my own satisfaction and to form a record while I could still remember events and details clearly.

My father-in-law had served in Mesopotamia with the Army in the First World War and also with the Royal Air Force in Iraq, Aden, Egypt and the UK between the wars. He had many interesting stories to tell about NineAcks, Fairey IIIFs, Sir Alan Cobham at Heliopolis and 'Brainy' Dobbs at Henlow. I often asked him to write them down but he never did so, unfortunately and now that he has, sadly, passed on, these stories are lost forever. As a result, I felt a compulsion to finish the book before I, too, pop my clogs.

Not that there is anything in it of great historical, technical or social significance. There are no descriptions of great hardships suffered or battles won, just a miscellany about aircraft and how they affected the lives of thousands of us in those now far-off days.

The title is intended to be evocative of when flying was over for the day and the aircraft, having safely returned, were carefully pushed back into the hangar and bedded down for the night. The last order was "Chocks and driptrays!" and these were placed in position, pitot head covers and wheel covers were fitted and the hangar doors were closed.

Introduction

I was in the house when I noticed the subdued roar, which had been apparent for several minutes, was gradually getting louder. Being five years old, I also realised that this was a different pulsating sound and somehow it seemed to vibrate a responsive chord inside me.

The roar was swelling then and with some fear of what it might be, but with great excitement, I dashed outside as the roar rose to a crescendo, just in time to see a breathtaking sight, the memory of which has remained fresh to this day.

Low across the rooftops, in line abreast, flew several aeroplanes, the centre one being an enormous silver twin-engined biplane, quite dwarfing its companions. Every strut and wire could be seen and the head of the pilot in the nose was quite distinct. Following behind the dignified formation was another, much smaller, biplane, obviously the impudent one, weaving and rolling with gay abandon.

The shadows of the aircraft flashed across the gardens and then were gone.

This was my introduction to another world, the world of aviation, which has ever since seemed to me to have an atmosphere all its own. Even the more mundane jobs I had to do in later years, such as cleaning cowlings and driptrays, seemed more interesting and worthwhile because it was to do with aircraft.

Enthusiastic as I was, I came to realise that aviation would never make me rich, if only because better and more able people were also drawn to it and, wartime excepted, there would always be more people than the industry could absorb. Those that made it in aviation would do it by ability alone.

To be in aviation at all was its own reward therefore, being an indication of some achievement, even if one was the most junior mechanic or airman. Circumstances of bringing up a family have taken me in other directions since the days I am writing about and a flip with the children around Blackpool Tower and trips to Air

Shows and the Shuttleworth Collection are the nearest I get to the real thing.

I buy the odd sheet of balsa and content myself with as much aeromodelling as I can spare time for and hope I won't be too old to fly again when the pools come up. Two things that have impressed me are that there appears to be a great interest in aviation history these days and that aircraft I saw, worked on and flew in, have now passed into that history.

Although my story is similar to that of thousands of chaps of my age, new generations, brought up to accept colour T.V. from the moon as a normal event, have had little except reference books to convey to them what aviation meant to my contemporaries. I hope that this literary effort fills a gap and will prove to be of interest.

Illustrations

The ink sketches in this book were all drawn by me, based on photographs not suitable for reproduction. I included all the details that were shown on the photographs, at the risk of spoiling what artistic merit they may have, because to my mind it is detail that gives them life, interest and authenticity.

1. Blackburn Lincock II G-AALH

This particular Lincock did not have the exhaust collector ring generally fitted, which must have reduced the drag and increased the performance considerably. Stub exhausts were fitted to each cylinder, the upper central cylinder having an extension to pass the exhaust gases over the top of the wing and away from the pilot.

The dummy machine gun troughs, one on each side of the fuselage, were a residual indication that the Lincock was originally designed as an inexpensive, lightweight fighter. It is shown about to take off for a superb aerobatic display.

2. Handley Page W10 G-EBMM / Blackburn Lincock II

The ex-Imperial Airways airliner G-EBMM, reduced to giving 5/- pleasure flights with Scott's Air Display near West Hartlepool, is shown taking on board more passengers with the Lincock parked in the foreground.

3. De Havilland Tiger Moth G-ACEZ

Shown being turned into position by a mechanic on the wing tip, this aircraft was flown by Geoffrey Tyson when performing his renowned feat of picking up a handkerchief from the grass.

4. V.S. Spitfire PR Mk XIX PM 545

One of several Spitfires parked on a huge expanse of concrete at R.A.F. Drigh Road, this aircraft is shown as it was prior to being dismantled for shipment back to the U.K. A number of Vultee Vengeances were parked in the distance to the left. Note the 34 Squadron badge on the fin, the engine cover to keep out desert sand and monsoon rain and the bicycle so necessary for getting around the spread-out Station.

5. Douglas Dakota KN 243

Parked at R.A.F. Chakeri dispersal after a test flight, the engines, propellers and wheels of the Dakota are protected with covers from the monsoon rain and frequent spells of scorching sun. A ladder, used to fit the covers, lies under the wing and, in the foreground, an air compressor stands in the open, protected by its own canopy. The aircraft is fitted with a glider towing attachment, which was used as a lashing point to secure the tail to a concrete block.

6. Avro York MW 102

The personal aircraft of Lord Louis Mountbatten, it is shown as it was photographed on its arrival at R.A.F. Mauripur Technical Site for a Base inspection. Note the Governor-General of India badge under the cockpit window and the flaps partly lowered to discharge the hydraulic accumulator and relieve the system of stress. The nacelle fairings on the flaps are separate and retract into the main portions of the fairings as the flaps are lowered. Note also that the centre fin has no rudder and was added to the basic Lancaster flying surfaces to compensate for the fatter fuselage of the York.

7. Avro Lincoln RF 498 'Crusader'

This aircraft was in transit though R.A.F. Mauripur. The finish is natural metal. Note the Crusader's shield motif. A Lockheed Ventura is parked in the background near to the Terminal Building.

8. Handley Page Hastings TG 503

Seen at Mauripur and about to be refuelled before continuing its proving flight to the Far East. This particular aircraft, modified to Mk T5 standard, is still in existence as a permanent memorial to the Berlin Airlift at Gatow Airport, Berlin. The open hatch, through which a member of the servicing section fell, can be seen.

9. Junkers Ju 52/3M

French Red Cross aircraft shown after repairs to the centre engine which was about to be test-run. The aircraft was staging through Mauripur en route to French Indo-China.

10. Bristol Freighter G-AIFF

One of my earlier sketching attempts, the original photograph showed the aircraft partly obscured by a large field gun and two North West Frontier Policemen standing to attention with their rifles at the slope.

11. V.S. Spitfire Mk XVI TE 206

This illustration shows the aircraft parked under a Lincoln's wing shortly after being pushed inside the hangar. The starting batteries (trolley-acc) behind the Spitfire has also been pushed in for the night and the airman outside is walking over to fetch the chocks.

12. Airspeed Oxford LB 458

This particular Oxford is one of those with its undercarriage fairings hinged to pivot backwards with the undercarriage on retraction. It is shown parked outside the 'B' Flight (South) end of the Flying Squadron hangar at R.A.F. Debden. The airfield is to the left up a gradient and the hangar is the one nearest to the Saffron Walden-Dunmow road

13. Percival Proctor III

The prettiest of the three Percival types at R.A.F. Stoke Heath, this view shows its attractive lines and also the trailing edge section of wing which folded upwards, so that the wing could be folded back. The steps let into the walkway can be seen although the walkway itself is not clear. The walkway had a non-skid finish which looked like carborundum paper.

14. De Havilland DH 88 Comet "Black Magic" G-ACSP

This was drawn from one of a number of photographs given to me by Charlie Isaacson, a Karachi friend. They showed various aircraft in the Mildenhall - Melbourne Air Race on their arrival at Karachi. This particular aircraft was flown by Amy Johnson and Jim Mollison, who had to retire with engine trouble when they reached Allahabad.

1. Early Memories

It was in 1934 when Sir Alan Cobham's Circus, (or Scott's as it was otherwise called) flew over our house in West Hartlepool and landed in a large field to the south of the town, which was still recovering from the depression. Looking back, I am surprised that the circus was as well patronised as it was, although the crowds were nothing like those that attend today's Air Shows. One could, at least, find a clear space at the rope fence. My parents had taken me to the field, probably in desperation, for since the aircraft had flown over, I had talked of nothing else.

The silver machine was the ex-Imperial Airways Handley Page W 10 G-EBMM and it looked very impressive, as it took off and landed, every twenty minutes or so, all afternoon, while a queue of people waited patiently for their turn for a flight. Its short take-off and the ease with which its four-wheeled undercarriage coped with the rough grass field, impressed me immensely. The silver finish made it look solid and heavy and, for those days, it was certainly a big aircraft.

Plate 2 Handley Page W10 G-EBMM / Blackburn Lincock II

I can't remember the exact number of machines there but there were four or five altogether. There was a Blackburn Lincock II G-AALH (the impudent one in the formation) which provided the main acrobatic features and a Tiger Moth G-ACEZ which, amongst other stunts, was used to bomb some 'bank robbers' making their escape in a decrepit old Austin 7, which eventually blew up in a spectacular fashion.

The pilot was, I believe, the renowned Geoffrey Tyson, who could pick up a handkerchief from the ground with a spike on the wingtip. I think he did it at this show but can't with honesty say I remember it.

After each display the machines would taxi back to the fence and it was fascinating to me to watch a mechanic in a white overall grab hold of a wing tip and swing the aircraft round into position, the long grass streaming back with each burst of power from the engine. Eluding my parents' grasp, I slipped under the rope and ran up to an unattended machine and touched it and then went back. No amount of scolding could spoil the knowledge that I had actually touched an aeroplane.

Plate 3 De Havilland Tiger Moth G-ACEZ

From then on the air show fired my imagination and although other childish interests took my fancy, they never superseded an abiding passion for all things aeronautical.

This was the period of the Flying Flea craze and, one day, my father came home with a kit for a model of one. I was still too young to construct it myself, so he made it for me.

It was an advanced kit for its day with a die-cut balsa sheet, preformed wire parts and a pressed metal propshaft bush for the rubber motor assembly.

My father made a good job of the construction and the tissue covering, but it was not doped. Neither of us had experience with flying models, in fact we had a touching faith that it would fly because it was a 'flying' model. Well, of course, it didn't. It hit the ground hard and broke apart.

In the kit were spare sheets of die-cut parts which I broke in pressing them out, so repairs were never done. It was a pity, for it was a very complete kit of a delightful model.

Another model – a toy really – available at Woolworth's was a printed cardboard representation of a twin-engined aeroplane, with little metal free-wheeling propellers attached to the wings by metal clips.

A thread attached to the port wing tip enabled it be swung round in a form of R.T.P. flying, the pilot being both the power and the pole. It was quite instructive, having a form of whip control that I often used before U-control became popular.

The nearest aerodrome to my home was at R.A.F. Thornaby and I eventually persuaded my father to take me to the Empire Air Day Display in 1937. This consisted mainly of displays by Hawker Hart variants, mirror flying – that is – one flying inverted above the other while carrying out manoeuvres, aerobatic displays, crazy flying and the traditional bombing of the 'revolting natives'. There was also a form of radio control by members of the public who, for a small charge, could radio instructions to the pilot of an aircraft, flying high over the aerodrome, to carry out certain manoeuvres. A Vickers Virginia showed up late in the afternoon, flying so slowly that I expected it to drop out of the sky. It looked like a flying plantation with so many struts.

At that time, war was beginning to appear a distinct possibility and to us youngsters I suppose it all seemed exciting, although for the grown-ups who still had clear memories of the Great War, as they called it, it must have seemed a terrible prospect, too terrible for them to really believe it could all happen again. The activities of the Japanese in China, Mussolini in Abyssinia and Franco in Spain, were constantly featured in the newsreels, illustrated magazines and newspapers and they seemed to have more impact on us in those days because the world seemed bigger and more unknown and the dangers correspondingly greater: dangers that were already a reality in other countries and could be here within days, thanks to the effectiveness of new bombers being produced by every major nation.

I remember 1939 as a beautiful summer and, one Sunday, I watched a yellow Hawker Hart with polished cowlings perform aerobatics over our house in Eaglescliffe, where we now lived.

Aeronautical news was obtained by buying and reading from cover to cover, the odd copy of *Popular Flying* for 6d. I avidly read, for example, Arch Whitehouse's scathing article on the crash of the Lockheed XP38. Another magazine, more within my means at 3d, was *Flying*, which initiated my liking for the Hillson Praga.

We busily collected A.R.P. cigarette cards, also a series about naval ships of the world and went to school in buses with blue tinted windows and camouflaged roofs. At the pictures we saw George Formby in '*It's in the air*', with R.A.F. recruiting sergeants in the foyer of the cinema. They had pamphlets, some with a picture of the nose of a Hampden, which I eagerly collected.

In the cobbled High Street of Stockton-on-Tees, the Durham Light Infantry put on a display with a Bren Gun Carrier towing a small gun and limber. The whole outfit shone like a new pin and the carrier pirouetted on the cobblestones most impressively, for it was a new thing then. Little did we know what the Germans had in store for us, for the only manifestations that the Germans existed were the clockwork Schuco toy cars and the tin, toy, pocket battleships etc. in every toyshop.

A small German coaster tied up to the quay at Stockton one day, where I used to call sometimes on the way home from school. It looked very inoffensive, the swastika flag at the stern, although an object of interest, was not at that time an object of notoriety. A deckhand was leaning over the rail and I started a conversation with him. He spoke good English and after a while I asked him if he thought there would be a war. He replied that he hoped not. The conversation ended there when an officer called him and I had the impression that he should not have been talking to me.

Brief though the encounter was, it served to remind me for many years after, that the ordinary German was an ordinary human being and the whole episode seemed to put in a nutshell the situation in Germany.

The war came eventually, yet suddenly, on September the third, a sunny Sunday. My Dad took us to Leven Bridge where there was a pub and a stream, which I enjoyed messing about in. I remember that in the *Sunday Express* there was an article about salvaging H.M.S. Thetis, which eventually sailed again in the war. As eleven o' clock approached we went over to the pub to listen to Neville Chamberlain tell us that we were now at war with Germany.

The main excitement for the first month was that the Army put a searchlight behind the house and then, to my great disappointment, moved it away! During the Phoney War I saw a squadron of Hampdens fly, one at a time, into R.A.F. Thornaby.

During an occasional trip to Darlington when the train passed through Urlay Nook, it passed a large wire-netted compound full of parts of crashed and scrapped aircraft, all with R.A.F. markings. Half of the equipment of the Royal Air Force seemed to be there, which concerned me greatly, for I could see no German aircraft.

Around the time of Dunkirk, my Dad sent for my mother and me to join him in Scotland where he was working at the time.

We travelled up by train, through very wild countryside as it seemed to me. I insisted on carrying my air rifle – which, ironically, was German-made – in case we spotted some German paratroops. I remember a fellow passenger saying gloomily that the country would need something better than air guns to beat the Germans.

It was a beautiful summer and the Battle of Britain was raging, but there was no sign of it up in Ayrshire where we arrived. Prestwick, which was nearby, was a hive of industry however and the beach was as good a place as any to see aircraft as they took off over the town. Tiger Moths abounded and there were two Fokker F 22s based there. They were big four-engined airliners with fixed undercarriages and high wings, camouflaged with training yellow underneath and used as flying classrooms. They took off regularly, low over the town, their big wheels still spinning as they climbed slowly away. A melodious note emanated from the engines.

I was told that they were ex-K.L.M. airliners and had come from Holland before the Germans overran that country.

Another aircraft seen, this time over Kilmarnock and probably from Abbotsinch, was a Blackburn Botha, still secret and not identified as such until later. In spite of its later reputation, it looked impressive as it did a banking turn quite low down. It was painted grey underneath the stubby pointed wings, which enhanced its lethal appearance.

Also at Prestwick were Lockheed Hudsons, one of which beat up the beach along the water's edge at a height of about ten feet, low enough to cause panic among the children paddling, not to mention the mothers!

A further move brought us to Dumfries, where I was able to satiate my youthful interest by walking to Heath Hall Aerodrome.

Heath Hall was where they used to make Argyll cars, I understand, but for me the only interest was the aerodrome. In early 1941 it was a bad winter, as were all the winters during the war that I remember and the only reward for walking to Heath Hall Aerodrome, standing around for an hour in the bitter cold and keeping a sentry company, was to see a Hurricane start up and taxi out of sight somewhere across the snow-covered airfield.

I think about this time, everybody was morally shattered as they realised the predicament the country was in. Rationing was beginning to take effect, the Forces were short of equipment and what they had was largely obsolete and the whole coast of Europe was barred to us. I say "us" for to say "Allies" at that time was merely to rub salt into the wound.

The country seemed to be filled, rather like a lifeboat, with a wide cross-section of European people, Poles, Frenchmen, Danes, Dutchmen, to name a few, all in different uniforms, all with nothing but what they stood up in.

We now had a permanent home at Lochmaben and I was sent to school at Dumfries Academy where, sooner or later, I was ribbed about the Scots beating the English at Bannockburn. Fortunately, a Scottish teacher at my previous school had warned me about this and told me to say "Ah, but we beat you at Culloden!" It worked like a charm with a nationalistic music teacher and to get her own back, she made me sing to the class 'I wish I was where Helen lies'.

Helen was dead, of course.

I regret to say that this good Scottish schooling, and it was good, was wasted on me. This was partly due to the fact that Heath Hall had only one runway and when aircraft took off in a westerly direction they passed over the front of the school! For the next three years my lessons were punctuated with loud crescendos of noise and my attention wandered away from the blackboard to the sight of some venerable aircraft staggering up over the town. These were usually Fairey Battles and, later, Ansons and Whitley IIIs with Tiger engines.

The Battle of Britain being over, two Spitfire Is were on display on the Whitesands at Dumfries, where I used to catch the school bus home. They were the first Spitfires I and most other people, had seen close to and they aroused much interest. They were in good condition, with red patches over the gun ports and were there to show what the *Wings for Victory* money would buy.

The Blitz followed in 1941. We were not affected by German bombers except when they passed over on their way to bomb Clydeside. A dull red glow in the sky could be seen to the North when they had found their target and Clydeside burned.

Around this time, I took up aeromodelling seriously by investing in some Airyda kits at 1/6d each. The Spitfire and Battle were built in quick time and crashed even quicker. Previous to this, I had brought to a fine art the making of paper gliders from notepaper, of scale appearance, with the wing leading-edge stiffened with a fretsaw blade which also helped to balance them. Camels and Nieuport Scouts were favourites and flew well. I learned a lot from them of the theory of flight.

Solids, as they were called, were not my cup of tea because you required the resources of a joiner's shop to shape the wood, balsa being unobtainable in blocks. They were very popular, though, as a means of teaching aircraft recognition, amongst other reasons.

Kits were quite plentiful although the quality varied. I was unable to explore the higher priced range, but the small stuff kept me happily cutting my fingers on the razor blades which were the universal tools of the trade. With practice, the side of one's forefinger next to the thumb took on a serrated and chipped appearance and the skin became calloused. One literally developed a thick skin!

Some of the kits built around this time were: – 'Frog' Heston Phoenix and V.A. Wellesley, both accurate in form and construction, but small, 'Airyda' Fairchild 24 J, 'Tower' Spitfire and 'KeilKraft' Lysander. The Lysander kit was a much-prized acquisition. Being a balsa kit, its sale was controlled and limited to members of some approved organisation such as the A.T.C. and they had to produce a chit from higher authority before they could actually buy it. I was already pestering the school Squadron to let me join, without much success – I was too young – but in the end they gave me a chit to keep me quiet.

Although balsa wood was becoming scarcer, obechi was obtainable as raw material or in kits. I built a 26" Sopwith Camel entirely from 1/8 sq. obechi. It was powered by a clockwork motor and achieved a powered glide, in the hands of a friend, for I lacked the nerve to precipitate its destruction. In the event, it survived to fly again.

At a later date, my father became ill and was in Middlesbrough Hospital where my mother and I travelled down to see him. While in the waiting room, a middle-aged gentleman engaged me in conversation and soon elicited the information that I was very keen on aircraft. I told him about the Camel I had built and he showed quite an interest. He volunteered the information that he had been a Camel pilot and it must have surprised him that I was overcome with awe and respect, as a young man's respect was more often given to Hurricane and Spitfire pilots.

However, I had read as much as I could about the Camel, when the model was built and knew that Camel pilots had been considered a breed apart, on account of its tricky handling characteristics. This had been due, as much as anything, to the rotary engine fitted to it, which created considerable gyroscopic forces, particularly when executing violent manoeuvres. These forces caused the aircraft to deviate from the expected flight path, unless corrective action was taken. This required a skill that could only be acquired by flying Camels and many novices did not last long enough to acquire this skill.

I had read all about this and was therefore much interested to know what his first-hand opinion was of the aircraft. He told me and I suspect that his natural modesty forbade him to say more, that the Camel had not been particularly tricky to fly, provided that the pilot was competent and not a complete novice.

He said that the aeroplane would turn extremely quickly to left or right, but most quickly to the right, because the gyroscopic force pushed the nose down. When I expressed my surprise at its apparent docility, he conceded that the Camel became tricky when it was on its back, when it was likely to become uncontrollable and fall into an inverted spin. The best course of action was to avoid inverted flying, which was rarely necessary anyway, even in a dogfight.

Returning to aeromodelling, an unusual commodity one could buy was camouflaged tissue, quite effective and with a slight sheen. It did not shrink very well, but neither did ordinary tissue, being in the days before Modelspan. The experts used to advise wetting the tissue first and then covering. I got in an even bigger mess that way and became reconciled to the wrinkles.

The flying ability of these scale models left a lot to be desired and it was not until a 'KeilKraft' Achilles kit was built, at a later date, that I started to achieve anything like a worthwhile flight.

Descriptions in magazines of 'out of sight' flights of a minute or more were regarded in the same light as fishermen's tales.

Postcards could be bought in a particular bookseller and newsagents in Dumfries that were a real bargain. They were known as 'Real Photographs' and were of such aircraft as the DH 5 and the Bristol Fighter F2B, amongst others. They had very clear details and I spent all I could afford on them.

I had a shot at building a glider, in our back garden, out of bits of wood offcuts that a friendly local joiner let me have. My mother was persuaded to let me have the clothesline prop, that the joiner had made long and strong, for a main spar. She also gave me an old sheet to cover the wings with. The fuselage was an old orange-box and the undercarriage was an old pair of pram wheels.

It never took off because I couldn't get it out of the garden, or so I claimed. The end came when my mother demanded the return of her clothesline prop. The rest of the structure kept us in kindling wood for some time.

Gliders in 1942 meant square boxes with wings and an unbelievable number of troops packed in the dark of the fuselage. My idea of such a glider was quickly constructed from 1/8" sq. obechi, 1 mm plywood ribs and covered with cartridge paper. It had a tricycle undercarriage with the main wheels set on the wings and was rather ponderous. To get it airborne, it was towed down the length of Lochmaben High Street. It came to an unfortunate end, as the writer nearly did, when an Army lorry came the other way.

2. First Flight

The time came when they let me in the Air Training Corps. Square bashing, or Morse code practice, was something to be cheerfully undertaken, like looking in dress shops with one's girlfriend. Transmitting and receiving Morse code has the distinction for me of being the most useless of my few accomplishments, now that Morse code is no longer used anywhere.

The real incentive was the annual camp at an R.A.F. Station. I was desperate because I had no uniform and one could not go to camp without a uniform. My obvious disappointment must have had some effect because, in the last week before we were due to go, I was given a brand spanking new uniform, literally smelling of newness. To enlarge on this theme, the smells that I encountered in the coming week lent atmosphere which, when I encounter them today, bring back memories with vivid clarity. For example, the smell of the bell tents we slept in, the smell of the tank of greasy hot water we washed our knives and forks in at the cookhouse and above all, the intoxicating smell of aircraft, a masterly blend of petrol, dope, hydraulic oil, grease, jointing compound and rubber.

Heath Hall, I remember, had one runway, a maintenance unit and a training unit for bomber crews. There was a 'Dome' Trainer, which was a building of hemispherical appearance, inside which images of aircraft were projected on the wall-cum-ceiling. The effect, when standing behind a replica of a machine gun, was that of being in a gun position in an old Hawker Hart, or similar, staring into the sky looking for enemy aircraft.

With frightening speed, a tiny dot would materialise into a German fighter, guns blazing away and if you returned the fire correctly, spots of red would appear on the fighter before it shot past you. The realism was completed by loud sound effects and was far superior to the sort of thing you get in amusement arcades.

The Parachute Section was manned by WAAFs who descended on us to fit us with observer-type harnesses and who embarrassed us mightily as they adjusted and tightened the straps. Then followed a lecture on how to check and operate the 'chute, with dire warnings of what would happen (to us) if it was picked up by the wrong handle. Needless to say, somebody (not me honestly!) did just that, later on, in an aircraft and, to complete the job, was sick on the canopy. It cost him five shillings – 2/6 for each misdemeanour – for the extra work he caused for the WAAFs.

The final instructions before we were allowed to fly were for dinghy drill. To facilitate this, an old Anson airframe, lying on its belly, had been positioned beside a static water tank and the idea was to take up crew positions, with the instructor as pilot.

On the command "Dinghy, dinghy, prepare for ditching", we got behind the main spars and sat down on the floor, facing aft, with our hands clasped behind our heads. When the aircraft was supposed to be ditched, the man nearest the door threw the dinghy out, holding on to the line which, when pulled, inflated the dinghy. The hilarious bit was getting in. To avoid jumping straight in and through the bottom of the dinghy, one did a somersault, landing on one shoulder on the inflated gunwale and rolling into an upright position. Thereafter, one moved smartly to the other side to avoid getting the next chap's boots in one's ear. As the dinghy was bobbing about quite violently on the end of the string, it became more difficult to judge the manoeuvre accurately and I nearly fell back into the water, but was grabbed by the seat of my trousers and hauled to safety by the instructor, who was no doubt prepared for the eventuality.

Then it was discovered that the string had broken and the next twenty minutes were spent trying to paddle to the side. Being a round dinghy it would spin on its axis at the slightest urging, but getting it to move in a straight line was almost impossible.

Agonisingly, the days, hours and minutes to my turn for a flight ticked away and finally the moment came when another chap and myself were detailed to collect our parachutes and report to the flights. There, on the apron, stood two Ansons, oil-stained and work-worn, camouflaged green and brown with yellow undersides. They had long greenhouses but no turrets and a door on the 'wrong' side (starboard). Each Anson carried one cadet with the crew on a normal bomb dropping exercise and I was allocated the rearmost seat, which had a good view of the ground behind the wing.

Showing me how to stow my parachute and fasten my seat belt, the crew gave me a cheerful nod and took their seats up front. The door was shut, the engines started and the Anson came alive. The tailplane twitched disconcertingly and the aircraft seemed to bounce as the pilot ran the engines up. Then we taxied out and swung round towards the perimeter track, as the outside world passed by the window at a curious angle.

The Anson taxied at a fair lick, for miles, it seemed, with the pilot dexterously manipulating the two throttle levers protruding from the console. Alternately pushed back in one's seat by an engine revving and forward by the brake being applied, it seemed a quaint means of locomotion.

Finally, we stopped for several unbearable minutes while the pilot did his checks and waited for an aircraft to land. Another run-up of the engines, then throttled back, a hiss of air from the brakes and we swung round on to the runway. The engines opened up in a full-throated roar, greater than I had yet heard and we swung slightly as the pilot corrected the heading. An invisible force pushed me back in my seat, which resisted stoutly, as the tar macadam passed under the wing with increasing speed.

The tailplane rose and the pressure on my back increased and then slackened off as the Anson thundered down the interminable runway. Just as it seemed we were running out of steam and very likely to charge off the end of the runway, now visible and fast approaching, our progress took on a smooth quality and, with a tightening of the chest, I realised we were off the ground.

The end of the runway dropped below the nose and by the time it appeared behind the wing we were surprisingly high. Passing over Dumfries, under the starboard wing, I could see the River Nith and my school, but before I could take it all in, we had climbed over Maxwellton, heading for the wilds of Kirkcudbrightshire and gaining height steadily.

I have no definite idea where we went, but it was to a bombing range somewhere along the coast, over rugged-looking countryside, purple with heather. Anxious to see out of the window on the starboard side, the seat being on the port side, I undid my seat belt and crouched in the gangway, drinking in a vista which, at approximately 10,000 feet, must have taken in most of Galloway.

The bombing range could not be seen when we made our run, though I squinted through the window. At the end of the run, the pilot put the Anson into a steeply banked turn and I found myself forced to my knees. As the turn tightened, my handhold proved insufficient and I sprawled in a ridiculous fashion on the floor, pinned there by centrifugal force and unable even to lift my head.

When the aircraft levelled out, I scrambled back into my seat, feeling very foolish and thankful that none of the crew had noticed.

On the return journey, it was a fast run, losing height steadily. Relieved of its bomb load and with no climbing to do, the speed was obviously much higher and confirmed by the increased draught up my trouser leg from a gap I could see, where the wing joined the fuselage.

"Got your seat belt fastened?" shouted the navigator as the runway came into view.

"Yes," I yelled back, feeling vaguely guilty – did he know that I had undone it earlier?

The runway, a tarmac strip set in a sea of gorse known as the Lochar Moss, looked much smaller than it did when we took off. Looking forward, the runway could be seen through the windscreen as the pilot throttled back and put the flaps down, which caused the Anson to slow up perceptibly with a ballooning sensation.

The glide path steepened and the end of the runway loomed larger, as we slipped through the air, slightly crabwise due to the crosswind. As the ground came closer, the pilot eased back on the control column, the nose came up and we floated down the runway gingerly inching our way down the last few feet. A touch on the rudder to straighten us up, a slight swerve as one wheel touched the ground with a mild squeal of protest, followed by the other wheel one second later and we were down.

The Anson rolled down the rest of the runway with an air of self-satisfaction with a job well done, swaying up and down gently and from side to side, as the pilot corrected with the rudder. At the end of the runway, the pilot applied the brakes intermittently with increasing force and turned off down the taxi track. In no time, it seemed, we were back at dispersal and, with the brakes alternately hissing and squealing, we swung round and stopped. As the engines died away with a rattle, the door opened and an aircraftsman's head appeared.

"Been sick? No? Thank goodness for that!" he said with relief, as he helped me down.

Remembering at the last second not to pick the parachute up by the silver handle but by the material handles at the sides, I walked away, trying to appear as nonchalant as the rest of the crew. The pilot called me back and asked for my logbook, which he filled in.

I thanked him for a good flight and returned to the rest of the cadets. And so my first flight came to an end.

No subsequent flight is as clear in every detail in my memory, although the joy of flying never diminished; rather, it increased as the years passed. I suppose nervousness and a slight twinge of fear, which I undoubtedly felt, heightens one's perceptions and impresses them on one's memory.

My apologies are tendered to those readers who fly to Majorca and other exotic places each year and to whom flying is but an extension of their local transport facilities and used as a matter of course. They well may wonder why I bother to describe a perfectly ordinary first flight, but it was in an 'Annie' after all!

As late as 1971, one flew over the house, rumbling along like a two-year old, with the famous diamond-shaped tailplane proudly bringing up the rear – some 45 years after the first one flew.

3. Miscellaneous Recollections

During the summer of 1942, my mother fell ill and, until she had recuperated, I was sent to Hull to stay with my aunt, uncle and cousin. The school I went to there was a year behind Dumfries Academy and did not advance my education. When I went back to Dumfries I was well behind in my studies.

There were air raids, mainly of a nuisance nature, two or three times a week, but sometimes there was heavier bombing, mainly in the centre of the city and the dock area. The unsynchronised beat of the German engines were apparent, supposedly to confuse the defences' sound detectors, but you knew by that when they were overhead and also when the shrapnel from the anti-aircraft shells rattled on the rooftops.

In spite of this, life went on as usual and I met kids who bragged about how many times they had been bombed out. Walking about three-quarters of a mile to school, I would occasionally see the latest bomb-damaged house from the night before. They seemed to have been quite small bombs generally, but on a bus journey to Cowden on the coast, we passed a field with an enormous crater. It was so deep that the blast from the explosion had gone right over a row of houses on the other side of the road, leaving them virtually undamaged.

At Cowden, my aunt and uncle had a weekend cottage which was due to disappear over the cliff in two or three years or so, due to coastal erosion. The garden was full of gooseberry bushes and we picked them until we were sick of them.

Aircraft flew over continually, mainly Defiants towing targets along the coast out to sea, with other aircraft firing at them.

One day, a Beaufighter came over the village and fired all its guns several times as it headed out to sea. My auntie rushed out of the cottage in panic and called my cousin and me away from the cliff edge. She was not reassured when I told her it was a British Beaufighter and hurried us indoors. She had a point as the Germans had a habit of machine-gunning places like Hornsea and Withernsea just up the coast.

On my return home, I was able to resume my aeromodelling interests. One of the more interesting brands of kits available was the 'Atlanta' series; later named 'Astral', when they started to produce kits for the Hampden, Beaufighter, Blenheim and Stirling, etc. These were rubber driven with the skeins inclined to give greater length and were designed by Mr Towner, if my memory is correct. It was rather unfortunate that the material was obechi and that the rubber provided was the white stranded stuff used in elastic tape, for, if the proper materials had been available, the kits would have been first class. Nevertheless, they were good value for 12/6 and made up into accurate models.

I received a Hampden kit with a very good plan, which I wished I had kept. A lot of use was made of parts slotted together and the model could be assembled almost completely to check how it went together, without using any glue at all.

It was unlikely to fly well and in fact it was never finished, but it brightened a wartime Christmas for me. Since those days, Christmas for me has never been complete without a model kit. They gave a satisfaction that is hard to define, even after I progressed to designing my own, or building from plans and the ingenuity with which they are marked out to use the least possible wood, consistent with grain run requirements, has always intrigued me.

Full-sized aircraft continued to provide an interest. Many strange aircraft were seen from time to time, that the *Aeroplane Spotter* (a three penny publication of great value) failed to provide identification for, generally because they were still secret. One would see a Barracuda, Whirlwind, Manchester, or Albermarle with puzzled concentration and not a little apprehension (was it a Jerry?), for my school friends and I were far more competent at aircraft recognition than French irregular verbs.

The school bus went across the Lochar Moss to Dumfries past a small Robin hangar on the other side of the road from the airfield. There, it was apparent, was where they dismantled aircraft. One day there were Miles Mentors – without spatted undercarriage fairings – looking very dainty, but they soon disappeared. Later, there were Westland Whirlwinds, with the squadron markings

'HE', having their engines taken out, which surprised me as they were only just off the secret list.

I had been fortunate enough to see two Whirlwinds arriving over the airfield. They looked very small, fast and menacing as they crabbed across the sky before banking around into the circuit and landing.

The long 'Queen Mary' trailers often provided a close-up of an interesting aircraft. Such aircraft that come to mind were a Hawker Henley, Hawker Hurricane and a Fairey Battle Trainer.

One day at Lochmaben, an Auster landed in a field beside the Kirk Loch next to the main road. The field sloped down to the Loch and was quite steep. The approach was made across the Loch and up the hill and after landing the pilot turned the aircraft around and got out. I was nearby at the time, so I dashed across to him. He asked if there were any Army units in the vicinity. I told him there was an Army camp a mile or so away on the other side of the village and after telling me not to go near the 'plane and asking me to ensure that nobody else did, he disappeared up the road.

About an hour later he came back, thanked me and went over to the Auster. After hooking the seat harness over the controls to raise the elevators and fiddling about a bit with the engine, he began to swing the propeller until eventually it started. He then got in and let the engine warm up, while he considered the best way to get out of the field. I continued to hang about, although I was late for lunch. Eventually, the Auster taxied down the hill as far as it could, but it must have been apparent to the pilot that the uphill run was insufficient for safety. He therefore taxied back up the hill, not without having to open the throttle wide merely to keep moving, until he was against the hedge. Turning, with the hedge brushing his wing tip, he lined the aircraft up in the direction that appeared to give the longest run and waited while he sized up his chances, one imagined, for the take-off had to be down wind.

Fortunately, the wind was not strong, but the down draught over the hill would not help. Finally, the pilot decided to take off and opened his throttle as rapidly as he could without tipping the aircraft on its nose. Aided by the slope, the Auster gathered speed and, as I watched goggle-eyed, it hurled itself down the hillside, bouncing and swaying over the hummocks until only the wing was visible over the curve of the field. At the moment when it seemed inevitable that it was going to plunge straight into the Loch, the Auster staggered into the air, ruffling the surface of the water with its slipstream. Miraculously, the Auster kept going, gathering speed across the Loch until at the far side it did a steep climbing turn over the village and disappeared into the distance.

Another Loch at Lochmaben, the Castle Loch, was the scene of a further incident. At the southern end of the Loch stood the ruins of a castle, known as Bruce's Castle to my friends and me, which stood on a peninsular, at the tip of which was a small island. Two hundred feet or so of shallow water lay between. It was an ideal place for adventurous games and with the aid of an airbed the scope was increased.

On this particular day, we were going to the island and were ferrying our equipment and supplies on the airbed, towing it behind us as we paddled across. It was beautiful weather and the sun glinted on the ripples of the greeny blue water.

Two Tiger Moths were flying around and these were so commonplace that we did no more than glance at them. They had spotted us, however, for they commenced to circle around the area, until we were halfway across where the water was at its deepest.

Our attention was now divided between the aircraft and the necessity of avoiding a deep pothole that we knew existed there, when one of the Tiger Moths swooped down towards the lake, closely followed by the other. Our attention was now fixed on them, for they were headed directly for us and it was apparent that we were the objects of their attention.

The two aeroplanes sped across the Loch, dropping lower until their wheels were not more than five feet above the water. Closer they came, wings rocking slightly and our interest changed to consternation for they gave no indication of commencing a zoom upward. We stood there, too surprised to move, as the aircraft hurtled over our heads, the wheels missing my companions by inches. Our heads swivelled like stopcocks, after the manner of the men in the Shell advertisement ("that's Shell, that was!!") and watched the two Moths climb steeply away and bank round. Not content with scaring seven sorts of sweat out of our pores the first time, we saw, with trepidation, that they were coming round again.

My companions and I were fully clothed apart from the boots strung around our necks, but I made a mental note to plunge under the surface of the water if it proved necessary. However, the intrepid airmen must have realised we were not troops on exercises for they cleared us this time at about ten feet.

The Tiger Moths were camouflaged halfway down the fuselage with trainer yellow below and they had blind flying hoods folded back on the rear cockpit.

Twice more they beat us up, by which time our courage had returned sufficiently for us to wave to the crews who, to our joy, waved back before climbing away and setting course for base. As we watched them go, we almost felt sorry for the Germans when their turn came for a beating-up.

German and Italian prisoners of war were a common sight as they worked on local farms, usually on their own. Italians particularly were allowed great freedom and one was able to attend the birthday of his nephew, a friend of mine, whose family ran the local ice cream parlour and chip shop.

At about this time, I became a regular subscriber to the *Aeromodeller*. I had bought the odd copy since before the war, but now it became a compulsion. Finances were always precarious and a regular order for the *Aeroplane Spotter* left little of my pocket money for other commitments, but by cycling the eight miles to school and saving the bus fare, I somehow always managed to raise the tenpence that *Aeromodeller* cost. Deliveries to the shops were a bit erratic in wartime and, without a standing order, it was necessary to call at the shop each day for up to a week around the time it was due, to make sure of a copy.

It was a good magazine for wartime, with Rupert Moore paintings on the covers and convincing articles on the making of air wheels from bicycle inner tubes, or harnessing that unemployed Brown Junior petrol engine to drive your bicycle (assuming you were all right for petrol and inner tubes!), to recall some of the more unusual ones. Bicycles, in fact, provided raw material for many aspects of modelling, from the manufacture of lathes and drills to prop shafts and elastic bands. Valve tubing was used to sheath rubber motor hooks and valves, cut down, made brass bushing. All this was absorbed religiously, including the more technical articles by Col. C. E. Bowden and Dr. Forster. They might have been writing about Rolls-Royce engines, so remote did the possibility seem of owning a miniature petrol engine and, in any case, one could not actually fly a model under power, so all the arguments, for and against, were rather academic.

Gliders were a popular feature, ranging from the Ivory Gull to the Fighter Glider (both still in the MAP plans as well as several others from that era), including plans for the Horsa glider which had detachable wing tips to conform with the law. This laid down precisely what the maximum wingspan for a glider had to be – 7 feet, I believe.

The lending library provided books which are collectors' items today. *Pilot's Summer* by Frank D. Tredrey was a favourite of mine, about a student instructor, at the Central Flying School, flying Crabs (Avro 504Ns) and a particular sentence has always stayed in my memory. The author was describing the practising of various manoeuvres while reciting the appropriate 'patter' and while doing so, he thought "why shine the seat of one's trousers on an office stool, when one could be doing aerobatics and be paid for it!" or words to that effect and a very profound thought too!

Another book that I had out so many times that I was able to copy a lot of it into an exercise book was the 'Flying Flea' by Henri Mignet. The mental pictures he conjured up, of a doped and varnished creation of fabric and wood waiting to fly wherever you wished to go, or of camping in the corner of a meadow with a sleeping bag under the wing of your eager aerial mount, captured my imagination. I knew, of course, that the flying of Fleas in this country (Britain) was banned, due to an aerodynamic fault in the design that did not become apparent until several people had been killed. I still believe, however, that this was due to the fact that people were building and flying them who had no appreciation of the machine's limitations, for others who presumably did, including Mignet himself, came to no harm. One British person in Egypt flew one for several years after they were banned in Britain, making regular flights between the Canal Zone and Cairo.

The Flea was a very unusual aircraft in several ways and worthy of a short digression for those who may not be familiar with it.

The aerodynamic problem was caused primarily by the system used for controlling the aircraft about the lateral axis. In a normal aircraft, elevators are used, but the Flea had a fixed tailplane (or rear tandem wing, as it really was). The mainplane, or front wing, was therefore hinged about the spar and its position varied by cables from the trailing edge which were connected to the control column.

When the control column was pushed forward to dive, the trailing edge was allowed to rise, by air pressure on it, as the cables were paid out. Conversely, when the control column was pulled back, the cables pulled the trailing edge down, increasing the angle of attack and, therefore, the lift.

As you may know, the sum of the total forces acting on a wing are said to act through a point known as the Centre of Pressure (CP). On the Flea, the CP was behind the wing hinge so that the trailing edge would always tend to rise, but be restrained by the cables. The pilot therefore had to exert a constant gentle pull on the column to keep the Flea flying at a constant height and if he let go, it would dive. Adjustable spring loading of the column was the answer to that.

A factor, which Mignet allowed for in the design, was that the CP moves forward with an increased angle of attack and if the angle was increased beyond a certain degree, the CP would move ahead of the hinge point. As built by amateurs, slight variations in dimensions could easily cause this.

The immediate result would be for the wing to tip up and the trailing edge to crack down on the pilot's head. Later Fleas had a strut linkage to avoid this, but this did not effect a cure for the uncontrollable dive that followed, unless the pilot knew what to do.

The fact was that by the time the CP had moved forward by that amount, the wing was well and truly stalled: i.e. the smooth airflow over the wing had broken away and the lift was lost. Now a wing can be un-stalled by either (1) immediate application of maximum power to overcome the increased drag caused by the turbulence, although height may not be maintained, or (2) accepting that the stall must be followed through by a vertical dive, which relieves the wing of the necessity to maintain lift. The dive realigns the airflow with the wing chord and the stalled conditions of turbulence disappear.

The power of most Fleas was marginal, although some people tried to cure this by fitting car engines complete with radiators, which couldn't have helped matters much, so method (1) was no use. Method (2) was the only way, but whereas in a normal aircraft, pulling back on the column will not usually hinder the un-stalling of the wing, doing so in a Flea left the wing at the same relative angle to the airflow as it had been before and it was therefore still stalled and would remain so all the way down to the ground. A pilot would consequently have to overcome his natural instinct to pull back and, instead, push forward first before pulling back gently.

It was a tricky system to put in the hands of amateurs and the ban on Fleas undoubtedly saved lives, but in the right hands I believe it was safe enough. The Flea created a craze that the authorities must have been worried about and when the opportunity arose to kill it off, they took it.

There may have been some other factors involved, of course and all the foregoing is my own opinion entirely. Nevertheless, with the demise of the Flea, so died also the hopes of thousands who had thought, for a brief but glorious period, that private flying was within their means. Mignet wove a spell in his book that lost nothing in the translation from the French. It contained, apart from an exposition of his theories and practice, full constructional details that anybody could understand and was not an expensive publication, which must have helped its popularity.

In the library at Dumfries (the adult section – to which I was admitted on sufferance) where these books were borrowed, many a lunchtime was whiled away browsing through the selection on aircraft engineering. A book on aerodynamics was doggedly studied and being the first useful application for mathematics I had found, my maths teacher must have wondered at the sudden interest I started to show in the subject, albeit, rather late in the day.

Other books on aeronautical engineering, including an illustrated manual on the routine servicing of the Luton 'Minor', 'Major' and 'Buzzard' by Latimer Needham, gradually forced me to realise that a prosaic job when I left school had no attraction, compared with a job in aviation. All thoughts of worldly returns from such a job were not even considered. I should have had my backside kicked of course but, in wartime, who knew what the future had in store, or what the best thing for a fifteen-year-old boy would be?

A letter, in response to an advertisement, brought by return of post an illustrated brochure for the Chelsea College of Aeronautics. It looked fine and the subjects covered were all that I found absorbing. The snag was in the fees, which were quite beyond my family's means and though there may well have been some scholarship scheme in operation, I knew my limitations in this field and so I regretfully gave up the idea.

The death of my father precipitated matters, however and so it came about that, a few weeks after Christmas 1944, I walked through the gates of the Olympia Leeds Works of the Blackburn Aircraft Company Limited for my first day as an apprentice fitter.

4. Apprentice at Blackburns

The Olympia Works were scarcely as I had expected an aircraft factory to be. There was no airfield, or background noise of engines running up. In fact, there were no aircraft either, that is to say, no aircraft in a complete state. They did make parts there, however and the aircraft atmosphere was not lacking.

The factory itself was rather quaint and was built back from the road up to a wooded hill, every bit of available ground being utilised. I knew very little of Blackburn's history and most of what I learned was gleaned from older employees, but it would have been nice, looking back, to have learned more. Not that I had much time to visualise BE 2cs and Kangaroos cluttering up the place.

Blackburn Aircraft Limited had started in Leeds around 1909 and had moved to Olympia before the First World War, where there was a disused roller skating rink. This provided a ready-made building ideally suited for the construction and erection of aircraft, having a curved roof with an uninterrupted span. Here the Blackburn enterprise was based all through World War One and into the middle 1920s, when the main activities and administration were moved to Brough. The tide of great events passed Olympia by and it was closed for a while, but reopened to cope with the contracts for the expansion before World War Two. There had been a small field further up the road near Roundhay Park where, in Olympia's heyday, the aircraft used to be taken in a dismantled state and reassembled for test flights before delivery.

The small hangar that was there, before the field ceased to be used, was removed and re-erected in the factory next to the main gate and, at the time that I worked there, it served to house the Despatch Department.

On one side of the skating rink was an extension which housed the stores and, upstairs, the Jig and Tool D.O. and other administrative offices and on the other side was the Press Shop with a central glass roof around which, upstairs on three sides, ran the Swordfish Shop. The Time Office and switchboard were at the front. To the rear, separated by narrow roadways, were the Fabric and Dope Shops, Sheet Metal Working Dept, Canteen, Cost Office, Pattern Shop and two or three Fitting Shops. The skating rink itself was now the Machine Shop and Tool room with a large inspection View Room and there was no trace of the wooden floor that used to be there.

I had brought with me a pair of white overalls, because the illustrations in all the technical books I had read showed mechanics in white overalls. I was under the impression it was the right thing to wear and was not prepared for the hoots of laughter from the other apprentices and workmen. "Where's your paintbrush?" they quipped. Somewhat nonplussed but not discouraged, I put them on anyway and eventually lived it down.

I was sent to the training school and instructed in the gentle art of using a hacksaw and file on chunks of mild steel, which eventually took the forms of an engineer's bevel and a square.

There was a senior apprentice who was often in charge of us in the absence of the Apprentice Supervisor, Mr Wolstenholme. He had taken his Higher National Certificate, which he passed with distinction and seemed to be destined for great things, which he certainly achieved. He eventually became the Project Engineer at Hawker's on the Harrier jump-jet fighter.

His name was John Fozard and he was also an aeromodeller. His patience with unruly fifteen-year-old brats like myself was exceptional and he was the sort of person you could rely on to sort your problems out if you went to him. He had practical experience which doesn't seem to matter today. His last job was scraping three surface plates, one of which was for the works manager, one for Mr Wolstenholme and one for himself.

I nearly finished his promising career before it had started. I had been given a job which involved drilling a hole in a fixture using a very long drill. I started the drilling machine and then noticed that the 'skilly' (soluble oil) was not coming through to lubricate the drill. I nipped around to the back of the machine to start the pump, not realising that the arm which lowered the drill had been moved sideways into the automatic feed position. Before I could get back to the front of the machine, the drill descended too quickly, hit the fixture and broke into several pieces. One long jagged piece of drill flew across the workshop and embedded itself in the blackboard behind John, luckily missing him by two or three feet.

Perhaps my white overalls helped to pick me out as it was the only thing about my work that was distinctive, for I was selected, after a couple of months, to go in the Drawing Office. My duties were those of an office boy, although I was given a spare drawing board to practise on.

At that time, the Firebrand IV was going into production and was still secret. One of my jobs was to file all the drawing prints of components and keep them up to date by scrapping old issues and producing the up-to-date issues for the draughtsmen when required.

The draughtsmen and one draughtswoman – Mrs Warburton, working with her husband – were a great bunch. One, Mr Kirk, was a model engineer and made me an oscillating steam engine, for which he only charged me 15/-. It was a prized possession of mine.

Another gave me a photo of an Arrow Active, which was designed and built in Leeds and which he had something to do with. Others gave me photos and books of aircraft, realising, I suppose, that they would be in appreciative hands.

There was a planner, whose name I can only recall as Sam, who gave me a copy of a famous photograph of a Fairey Flycatcher which he was flying over H.M.S. Eagle at the time. All in all, I was at least amongst people who could understand youthful enthusiasm, even if their own had worn rather thin.

The office was purely a Jig and Tool D.O. but the work was very interesting. Each morning I had to do the rounds with prints, mod sheets and miscellaneous paperwork for the various departments, which gave me plenty of opportunity for getting to know people and to see what was going on.

I saw Mr Robert Blackburn but once, when he came unannounced to see Mr Hartley, the Works Manager. He seemed to be an unassuming but business-like man and when I first heard that it was Mr Blackburn who had gone into Mr Hartley's office, the name didn't click for a few minutes because he seemed to be just one of many that beat a path to the offices each day.

"Not *the* Mr Blackburn?" I asked, when invited to take him a cup of tea. An amused nod was the response and thereafter, for the duration of the visit, I watched him through the glass of the partition, when I could, with respectful awe.

Looking back, it surprises me that a factory of that size could be run as effectively, as it certainly was, by so few management.

Under Mr Hartley, the Works Manager, there was the Chief Draughtsman, Mr Horsley, a kindly, dapper man with a clipped moustache and Mr Kellington in charge of the Time Office.

Mr Wolstenholme was the Apprentice Training Superintendent, a gentle man with great patience, in charge of a large number of apprentices who, if not in the Training Section, were scattered throughout the works. There was no other management that I can recall.

With the expansion of the aircraft industry before the war, Blackburns must have been fortunate to have people of the right calibre to run the new factories at Abbotsinch, Dumbarton and Sherburn-in-Elmet, producing Bothas, Sunderlands and Swordfishes respectively. Additionally, other aircraft were built, such as the Barracuda. All the aircraft for the Fleet Air Arm supplied from America passed through the hands of Blackburn Aircraft Limited for modifying to F.A.A. standard. The Company was also a major supplier of Aircraft General Spares (AGS) parts, the nuts and bolts, etc, that were to be found in all British aircraft.

It is to the credit of the few members of management that were available, that so much efficient work was achieved in such a short time. I find it difficult to understand why, with the aid of management techniques, computers and so on, modern management have made such a hash of British Industry in later years and I put it down to the fact that, today, there are too many whiz-kids who don't like to get their hands dirty and not enough who have learned their job from the shop floor up and got to the top by sheer talent and hard work.

The factory had made a lot of parts for the Fairy Swordfish, most of which had been made by Blackburns and the shop in which it was done still carried the proud name, although the contracts were finished. Now, the shop made torsion boxes for the undercarriages of Barracudas and bomb carriers and, in conjunction with the rest of the factory, was once again making parts for a Blackburn design. The Firebrand was a not inelegant single-seat low wing monoplane with a Bristol Centaurus radial engine and it carried a torpedo. We made the fin, rudder, tailplane, elevators and flaps and also the back end of the fuselage, known as the monocoque extension.

The flaps were unusual for those days, being very large and like a scaled-down wing of irregular shape which moved backwards and downwards as they were extended, on rollers set in a track. In the trailing edge of each flap was another flap of the split type, which I think was perforated.

The Firebrand was a Naval aircraft and, of course, the wings folded. The complication of designing a wing to fold upwards and backwards while carrying flaps of that size must have been considerable.

My own part in the production of this advanced and, at the time, secret aircraft, was to draw a drill and file template for a trim tab rib on the elevators. These trim tabs were the only fabric-covered components that Olympia made. The rudder and elevators were metal skinned and were mass balanced. These mass balances were brass castings, their weight was surprisingly considerable – about 40 lb. each at a rough guess – and were shaped to fit inside the horn balance areas.

The noise in the shops was fantastic. One's ears were assailed by the scream of pneumatic drills and the staccato hammering of the riveting guns, all operated by women who were extremely skilled through much experience. They put in thousands upon thousands of rivets in the process of skinning a component and it was rare for any to be faulty. They worked in teams, clipping the sheets in position and drilling through the internal members using holes already in the sheet as a template and afterwards riveting on the outside, with a reaction block held on the inside. These components were held upright in special jigs.

At side benches worked girls, old men and apprentices, making the smaller parts and using drilling and filing templates, or other jigs.

The women were a remarkably capable bunch. I remember one, who was shortly due to get married, having her leg pulled by an apprentice, who said something that annoyed her. "If you don't shut up, I'll sort you out!" she threatened. Of course, he said it again, whereupon she grabbed him and, before he quite knew what had happened, he was lying face down on the floor with his arm twisted behind his back and the girl sitting heavily on him. A gasping apology was soon forthcoming, then she released him and he slunk back to his bench, red-faced and embarrassed by the guffaws of his mates.

Lunch times were moments of opportunity for me to acquire scrap materials that might be useful in model building, or to make contact with some craftsman to get a difficult part produced. I managed to persuade one highly skilled tinsmith – he did the double curvature skinning on the control surfaces – to manufacture the complete cowlings and petrol tank for a six feet wingspan Tiger Moth I had embarked on, to my own drawings. They were beautifully made and were prized for many years, although the model had to be abandoned due to later events.

For this Tiger Moth, I tried covering it with the boiled remains of tracing linen, for which purpose every unwanted tracing in the drawing office disappeared. It was not a success and the cost of clear dope was prohibitive, but I persevered and tried using red dope, unofficially supplied by the fabric shop. This was full-sized aircraft dope, thick and heavy and it seemed to need a lot to get the wrinkles out of the linen, by which time the structure had warped. I think now that the weave was too open in the material, which was put on too slack and the overall result was of a model of an aircraft covered with lino.

Four-wheeled trolleys with pneumatic tyres were used a lot in the factory, for transporting parts and materials and these would provide a diversion for the more adventurous apprentices. By sitting on the front and holding the handle out ahead, they were easy to steer and the lads would pile on for a coast down the hill from the KL fitting shop, turning right at the Cost Office and speeding along the narrow roadway that led past the Training Section.

This activity I enjoyed immensely, until the day we turned the corner at high speed and saw, coming towards us, the Apprentice Training Superintendent, Mr Wolstenholme, talking chess with his friend. To cries of "Look out!" and "Toot toot!" we shot past him as they both leapt, with unexpected agility, to either side. Using great presence of mind, the apprentice doing the steering did a sharp left hand turn towards the canteen, scattering workers who were just leaving. The truck was steered towards a patch of grass and rapidly abandoned; melting into the crowd, we made our devious ways back to work.

I was never identified as a culprit in this incident, but the fun and games were eventually stopped when one inexperienced 'driver' failed to negotiate the Cost Office turn and carried straight on into that part of the wooden building where the ladies powdered their noses! Stopping only to pull free the unfortunate apprentice, we disappeared from the scene, with the screams of the women and the noise of splintering wood still echoing in our ears.

From then on, the carts were strictly out of bounds and the direst threats issued to deter us from using them again.

We had a full hour for lunch and when somebody said that there were some old aircraft in the wood at the back of the works, no time was lost in looking for them. The woods were out of bounds, but a well-beaten path led into it over the barbed wire. The aeroplanes turned out to be only a few yards from the fence and exactly how they got there, I do not know. Both were minus their wings and rather bashed about. One was a Blackburn B-2 and the other an Avro Cadet. I spent many pleasant lunch hours, sitting in the cockpits of one or the other, daydreaming, or practising flying. I had a 'Teach Yourself to Fly' book and, with the aid of a bit of imagination, practised all the necessary motions for taxiing, take-off, climbs, turns and all the other manoeuvres described therein, until I was quite certain I could fly safely, given the opportunity.

It was a very enjoyable way to pass the time, in that sunny glade, in the spring of 1945, when at that very moment, Germany was being hammered into the ground and fighting back desperately.

Most evenings, to the north of Leeds, the sky would be filled with the angry roar of hundreds of aero-engines, as the bombers circled and formed up for yet another onslaught on Germany. Looking back over sixty years, the destruction created in cities such as Hamburg and Dresden appears quite reprehensible to people who consider themselves civilised, but the fact is that at the time – after five weary years – it was with exultation that the majority of people learned of each new pounding of the Fatherland, for they knew that the war, at long last, was nearing its end. The fact that the Germans continued to fight in spite of the terrible blows, I think, drew reluctant admiration, but they and we, knew that they had only to surrender for the bombing to cease. They chose not to and for good measure, commenced the intensive use of the long awaited 'Secret Weapons', the VI and V2.

We didn't get many V1s in our part of the world. These particular flying bombs were launched by aircraft over the sea and near to the coast. When in bed one night, I heard one but it kept going out of earshot, to my great relief. There was no air raid warning, as it happened. It was a vicious weapon and had it been used earlier in the war, its effect, psychologically and materially, would have been much greater. Much the same could be said of the V2 rocket, a forerunner of frightfulness to come and against which there was no defence once it was on its way.

My view of the war was broadened by transferring to the local ATC Squadron, which was under the wing, so to speak, of Blackburns and officered by people from the Company. The Headquarters were at the end house of a cul-de-sac of rather grand houses, in the garden of which, there was room enough to park a fully complete Hawker Hart and a wingless Blackburn B-2. The Hart was for airframe instruction and the B-2 for engines. It was reputed that they taught prop swinging and actually ran up the B-2 engine, although I never saw it done personally. I wondered what the neighbours thought of that!

Quite frequently, on a Sunday, a trip would be arranged to some R.A.F. Unit. One such trip took us to Pocklington, a typical wartime bomber station, with gaunt Bellman hangars set in a bleak plain near York. The place seemed busy in a quiet but purposeful way. There were a lot of aircrew walking about in battledress with whistles in their lapels and many had ribbons under their brevets, the diagonal dark blue and white stripes of the D.F.C. and D.F.M. frequently catching the eye.

The aircraft were Halifax IIIs and the ground crew seemed pleased with them. These were the latest versions of the Halifax with rectangular type fins and rudders and smooth Perspex nose and extended wing tips of rounded shape. A far better looking aircraft than the earlier Marks and better aerodynamically (swing at take-off and landing had been one problem cured), the Halifax had blossomed into a reliable and well-liked machine. They now had Bristol Hercules engines which somehow suited them more than the Merlins previously fitted.

We were taken to the hangars to look over a Halifax, one that looked new and fresh and had a strong "new aeroplane smell". It had been on a raid the previous night and was pulled into the hangar to fix a snag. When we saw it, all work had been completed and the ground crew showed us round with pride and also with eagle eyes to ensure that we didn't fiddle with anything!

The entrance was at the rear on the port side and an effort and lifts up were needed by the smaller boys to climb in. The first impression was of darkness and a surprising lack of room. There was a multitude of black boxes and other strange-looking equipment, some of which the sergeant explained to us and some of which he was, not surprisingly, extremely reticent about.

Groping our way to the flight deck over the main spar, we passed the pilot's seat in which, of course, we all had a turn to sit. This was on the port side with the walkway on the starboard side.

Below the pilot was the cosy-looking cubby hole of the radio operator and, in front of him, that of the navigator, packed out with black boxes, work tables, Anglepoise lamps and dark-coloured curtains over the little windows.

I can't remember exactly where the flight engineer sat, but it was probably on a collapsible seat in the walkway, as in the Lancaster.

Still further forward in the nose was the bomb aimer's position with a single Vickers gun poking through the Perspex and, below it, the bombsight, switch panel and the hand-held pushbutton bomb release switch, on which we gazed with some awe, thinking of the destruction that little object had precipitated only 12 hours previously.

There were some cigarette stubs in the special ashtrays which helped to sharpen the remembrance that only a short time before, in this very aircraft, men had sweated and used their wits to survive and, through those windows, had witnessed the ultimate in mass destruction at that time, what is now described as a firestorm. The matt black finish on the flight deck seemed appropriate.

This aircraft had come back unscathed, but not all did. One of the Squadron's aircraft was still on its belly in a field having just failed to reach the runway.

On one of these visits and I think it was to Pocklington, although Melbourne was another place we went to, we were given a trip in an Oxford. This was painted in the usual trainer yellow, brown and green camouflage and looked quite dainty. It carried two cadets sitting on seats perched on the wing centre section, one facing forward and one facing back.

The pilot, naturally, made for Leeds to give us a view of our home town, but it was very overcast and all I saw as we flew into a clear patch was the half completed Tower of Leeds University, on which all work had stopped during the war.

Another time we went to an operational Control H.Q. manned almost entirely by WAAFs and located at a big country house. They showed us the Ops. Room with the big map on the table, but as radar was still top secret, they could not explain much and the implications of a lot of it were lost on me.

From this room were controlled, as we now know, the AI equipped Beaufighters and Mosquitoes that defended the north-east coast of England against enemy bombers, air-launched V1s and the intruders that followed our bombers back to England and then attacked them as they were preparing to land.

The WAAFs must have been very bored, isolated in that lonely mansion, bored enough, at any rate, for our visit to prove a welcome diversion, to judge from their reception of us. Perhaps I am being most unfair to them, but reception of the ATC by most people was rather less enthusiastic. Anyway, those gorgeous girls in blue swept us into the dining hall as soon as it was open, watched with amazement and some impatience while we got outside a large-sized dinner and then ushered us into the 'Snogging Room'. It was a very enjoyable dinner hour and the first time I had really noticed that there were other things in life besides aircraft!

On yet another trip, a few weeks before VE day, we flew in a Dragon Rapide, or Dominie, as the R.A.F. version was known. These were used as flying classrooms for radio operators. The fuselage was wide enough for seats on either side with worktables and frameworks for mounting the radio sets and a narrow gangway up the middle. This led to an opening in the bulkhead, beyond which the pilot sat in solitary splendour in the centre of the nose which tapered sharply. The view enjoyed by the pilot must have been one of the best provided by any aircraft.

We flew down the Humber Estuary, over the Brough factory and airfield and on to Hull.

At about three thousand feet, we flew past the city and the devastated areas were quite appallingly obvious. I had spent some months in Hull two or three years earlier, as previously related and became familiar with bomb damage and knew that Hull had suffered badly, but the full extent, thus revealed, made me gasp. Hull never seems to rank with Coventry, London, or Liverpool as a victim of the bombing in the minds of the public. Perhaps the blitzes that Hull suffered were not as concentrated as some others, but the town suffered bombing, both heavy and light, day and night, over a longer period of time than possibly any other in Britain. After five years of war, the damage was considerable and no part of the town had escaped. In the centre, near the docks, there was an area approximately a third of a mile by half a mile, as near as I could judge, which was completely devastated and most of it was quite flat.

Considerably shaken by this evidence of the destruction wrought by the Germans, I could not refrain from looking out of the other windows in turn, half expecting to see the sinister outline of a Dornier 217 emerge from a cloud, bent on yet another hit and run attack, not an unknown thing, even at that stage of the war.

Finally, VE day came and went. I don't remember the hysterical celebrations that the history books and newspaper articles recall, possibly because I was rather young for that sort of thing and I don't remember anything out of the way at work. The workforce at Blackburns had been forged by war into a team that was, I think, a happy one and the older people probably realised that the whole purpose of their jobs was evaporating and, with it, security of a sort that they had not known before the war. They were not wildly excited by any means.

What I do remember was seeing, when I cycled to and from work, the blue uniforms, white shirts and red ties of war wounded men from the hospital at Chapel Allerton, men without arms or legs, men on crutches or in wheelchairs, but all cheerful as they went out for walks.

But the whole war was not over yet, there were still the Japanese to sort out. The Allies had been making good progress in Burma and elsewhere and now that all the forces in Europe, released by the German defeat, were available to concentrate on Japan, nobody expected the war to last more than another year. In the meantime, Firebrands were in good demand and work went on as usual.

The outstanding events of that year of 1945 – for me! – were the ATC annual camp and the Battle of Britain display, both at Church Fenton. For the annual camp, I was allowed a week's leave of absence, with pay, from work and off we went in a coach provided by the R.A.F.

With the end of the war in Europe, Church Fenton had a curious atmosphere of anticlimax, all armed to the teeth with Mosquito 30s and nothing to do. These Mosquitoes had A.I. bulges on the nose which, surprisingly, did not spoil the appearance of the aircraft and, indeed, made them appear very purposeful in their day camouflage. We had a good look at them and marvelled at their smooth finish and their small, snug, almost cramped, cockpits packed with equipment and instruments. They were new aircraft and the sickly sweet smell one had come to associate with them was there in full strength. We ranged the aerodrome, from the radio workshops to the control tower. There was not a great deal of flying going on and one day, lounging over the rail at the control tower, we were idling the time away when a Lancaster called up asking for permission to join the circuit. We perked up interest on hearing this and soon spotted it doing a wide slow ponderous circuit in the distance quite low down.

He started his straight approach to the runway some miles away and as his grey silhouette slowly grew larger, an Oxford, which had appeared on the scene in the circuit, took a short cut and proceeded to land in the path of the approaching Lancaster. Realising that the controller was unaware of the presence of the Oxford, we dashed along the balcony into the control room and told the startled chap what was happening. He immediately grabbed a Very pistol, loaded it with a red cartridge and leapt out onto the balcony and fired into the air.

The flare curved away over the runway in front of the Oxford which was just touching down. The pilot immediately opened his throttles, took off again and banked away from the runway. The Lancaster carried on imperturbably and touched down a few seconds later. The Oxford was then given a green and landed normally.

When the pilot reported to the control tower he received a first-class dressing down but, in spite of which, he showed little concern which incensed the controller all the more. I don't know how it ended, but I believe a report was made to some higher authority.

We had all hoped for a flight in a Mossie and I believe one or two senior members did fly in them, but the rest of us were taken to Sherburn-in-Elmet, a few miles to the south, for our flip. Sherburn-in-Elmet, the home of the Yorkshire Flying Club for many years, had, during the war, been expanded and used by Blackburn Aircraft Ltd. as a repair depot, where they had a factory. We were taken to the airfield and dropped on the far side. The sun beat down and the factory buildings shimmered in the distance. Nearby were parked a few Barracudas and Tarpons (otherwise known as Avengers), with men working on them. There was also a small hangar with an earth floor. After talking to some men working on a Barracuda and finding out that they did not think much of that aircraft – they preferred the Avenger which surprised me, having been brought up to believe that British was Best – we decided to seek some shade in the little hangar.

It was unoccupied, except for an aircraft gathering dust in a dark corner, which I recognised as a prototype Firebrand from drawings I had seen. It had a small cockpit hood and full depth fuselage behind, being a Mk II or III with yellow underside, a yellow letter P in a circle on the sides of the fuselage and was fitted with a Napier Sabre engine.

As we were investigating this discovery, we heard somebody calling us and, upon returning to the rest of the cadets patiently waiting outside, we saw that the aircraft we were waiting for had arrived.

It sat on the grass with the propeller flicking over, with a strong resemblance to an eager fox terrier panting in the hot sun. It was a Blackburn B-2, a type that I thought no longer existed in airworthy

36 ~ *Chocks & Driptrays*

condition, but it looked brand new in its glossy camouflaged finish with civilian registration letters G-AEBJ underlined with red, white and blue stripes. The B-2 resembled a Tiger Moth but had side-by-side seating in a metal fuselage with attractive strakes down the fuselage which extended on to the engine cowling.

The first cadet already had his parachute adjusted and fitted while waiting and he now climbed into the B-2 and sat in the right hand seat. A few moments elapsed while he fastened the Sutton harness. This was a harness common at the time, first used in the First World War. It consisted of four webbing straps, each with a row of big brass eyelets. One of the lap straps – the master strap – had a pin sticking through an eyelet from the underside which could be moved to another eyelet if required. The other three straps, two across the shoulders and the remaining lap strap, were then crossed over the pin so that the pin protruded from the eyelet on the top strap. In the top of the pin was a hole, through which a spring clip was passed. By pulling out the clip the harness could be released quickly in an emergency.

The cadet then donned his helmet and, while he was still fastening it, the pilot opened the throttle and, with a wiggle of the rudder, the B-2 ran smoothly across the grass and climbed into the air. They flew out over the countryside in a wide left-hand turn and ten minutes later they came floating in to a gentle landing. With a burst of power the B-2 turned round and taxied to the waiting cadets.

The next cadet was soon installed in the cockpit and so it went on, until eventually my turn came.

The pilot wasted no time, for I was still trying to fasten my helmet when the aircraft took off. Before I succeeded, the slipstream had whipped it off my head. Fortunately, the lead was plugged into the socket, so by hauling on it, I got the helmet back and finally succeeded in fastening it. A pair of goggles was attached to the helmet and, although the cockpit was quite free of draught if one bent forward, goggles were necessary if one sat up straight. They did, however, take some getting used to. By this time we were doing a wide left-hand turn over the countryside of East Yorkshire when the pilot's voice sounded in the earphones.

"Put your right hand on your control column and hold it lightly," he said.

Gingerly, I did so and noted with some surprise that the pilot was not holding his. Feeling very much in charge, I kept the control column stationary while the aircraft flew steadily on. It began to feel all rather tame and, on an impulse, I decided to move the column slightly to see what effect it had. It had more effect than I bargained for and the aircraft rocked to one side. A muffled curse pierced my ears.

"Don't do that!" said the pilot as he straightened the aircraft up.

Feeling duly chastened, I apologised and after a few moments he told me to have another go and not try any tricks this time.

Needless to say, I obeyed to the letter and I found that though the aircraft rocked a bit going through the bumps, it levelled itself up without any action on my part. My principal worry was that the pilot might think I was causing it, but he seemed satisfied.

In no time at all, we were back at the airfield and the grass came rushing up to meet us. The B-2 touched down like a feather, bounced gently over the uneven ground and taxied over to our starting point. All too soon it was over, but it remains one of my most treasured memories and it is gratifying to think that G-AEBJ still exists as a much cherished possession of Hawker Siddeley Aviation at Brough to this day.

The admittedly rather rosy view I came to during that week of life on an R.A.F. camp had a big influence on me. We were in wooden huts, called billets and billet life with good company was enjoyable. After tea in the big dining hall with the hard bench seats and washing our 'irons' (knife, fork and spoon) in the big tank of hot water outside, there was a choice: going to the 'Astra' cinema, the NAAFI, the several quiet rooms where there were back copies of Tee Emm, which featured Pilot Officer Prune, to peruse, or going down to the village. Some of the cadets decided to try out the local brew and arrived back rather the worse for it. Others went to size up the local talent and related unlikely stories of their achievements. My first step as a profligate was to buy a packet of 20 Players which I smoked one after the other until I felt sick.

All too soon, camp was over and it was back to work, until the holidays. A paid holiday of one week was the entitlement in those days, but I had little money and nowhere to go. I was now 16 years of age and my pay had gone up from 15/6 to 26/- a week, enough to allow me to spend a bit more on aeromodelling. A 'KeilKraft' Ajax was sufficiently successful, when flown in Roundhay Park, for a passing Squadron Leader to stop and enquire if I would build him one for £3. Overcome with this chance of riches, I borrowed the money from a friend for another kit, built it and returned the following week. Sure enough, the Squadron Leader was there and following a satisfactory test flight, he duly proffered the £3. At the sight of the money, I felt as if I was taking candy from a kid and gave him £1 back.

The existence of a large lake at Roundhay Park was not to be wasted. Floats were made and fitted to the Ajax which was quite successful until the balsa longerons became soggy and collapsed. At that time, an amphibian was available as a kit, which I bought. I can't remember the name, but it was rather neat. The wheels would swing up or down, restrained by threads and elastic bands. It had a high polyhedral wing with tip floats and the propeller was fitted to a nacelle mounted on a pylon, with rubber threaded through the nacelle back to a hook on the fin. With the aid of stretch-winding and a freewheel device added and as light a construction as I could manage, it gave a lot of fun and lasted for some time.

For the record, other models built were a Spitfire (with a retracting U/C operated by the rubber motor through a sliding tail hook, thread, bellcrank and rubber bands and which succeeded beyond my wildest dreams), a Kirby Cadet 40" glider, a Three-Footer all-balsa glider (which once did 14 ¼ minutes in a thermal) and a couple of 'KeilKraft' Victory Gliders, each modified to have a single undercarriage wheel set in the fuselage and also knock-off wings, which were passable models of an American Schweizer glider.

5. At the Crossroads

With the dropping of the atom bombs on Hiroshima and Nagasaki and the collapse of the Japanese Empire, bringing the war to a close, it became apparent that the huge war effort, of which we at Blackburns were a part, would wind down. The effects were not immediately felt at the Olympia Works until the New Year of 1946. There were tales in the papers of aircraft being made in one factory and being towed to the other side of the airfield to be broken up and of radio sets, brand new, being thrown down disused mine shafts to keep people in employment.

The economic facts of life, which were of great concern to those older than myself, did not worry me in the least and I continued to make the most of all that aviation offered.

The Battle of Britain display in September 1945 at Church Fenton was an occasion when my ATC Squadron attended. Our duties were to guard the aircraft and keep the crowd behind the barriers. Many types of aircraft participated, including a Warwick (a larger edition of the Wellington), a Lancaster, a Spitfire and others.

A high performance sailplane did loops and stall turns down to a low altitude, but the glider that I found most interesting was an Airspeed Horsa which was towed up by a Halifax. Released above the aerodrome, it did a couple of circuits and then commenced its approach. It was still at a considerable height when it put its big 'barn door' flaps down and plummeted towards the ground at an incredibly steep angle. It was, quite literally, hanging on its flaps until it levelled out very sharply and touched down immediately. After an extremely short run, it stopped and was towed away by a vehicle.

Back at work, I found some literature about the construction of the Blackburn Botha. It appeared that the wing spars consisted of tubes and a special means had to be devised to rivet the rest of the wing structure and skin to them. This consisted of an ingenious type of dolly passed up the inside of the tube for the reaction type of riveting used. This meant that solid rivets of greater strength could be used, instead of pop or Chobert rivets normally used in such cases.

I pulled the leg of a planner, who had been with Blackburns a long time, about the qualities of the Botha and he was quite upset. There had been nothing wrong with the Botha, he said, except for the fact that it had been underpowered, because the engines with which it should have been fitted had been kept back by Bristols for their Beaufort, which was a rival to the Botha. He was very bitter about it and I hastily dropped the subject.

One day, a photograph circulated round the office. It was a Luftwaffe reconnaissance photograph which looked fairly recent, but did not show the newly built KL block. Around the border was information in German about the direction of North, the altitude at which the photo was taken, etc. The factory was not easily distinguished amongst the surrounding urban area but the Germans had it neatly positioned in the centre of the photo and must have taken care to find it.

That autumn, I was required to attend Leeds College of Technology for the first year of a course in Mechanical Engineering and for which I was allowed a day off work each week. In the workshops all the lathes were driven by overhead shafts and belts and it was rather fearsome doing some turning with a big belt clacking away at one's ear. There was a big lever hanging down to switch the belt from the idler pulley to the driving pulley and it took some courage to operate it. All the machines at Blackburns had individual electric motors and it was a revelation to find out how the other half of the engineering world functioned at that time.

The only other noteworthy thing was the discovery, on the top floor of the workshop block, of some engines, including a rotary of the Gnome-Rhone type, but I did not get much opportunity to study them.

One day, I cycled to a scrapyard along York Road to look at the remains of two old Blackburn aircraft. Their gaunt outlines presided over heaps of lesser junk and I took them to be Swifts. Thanks to Mr A. J. Jackson's excellent book, I now know them to have been Velos. They had no fabric and only one had a complete structure.

The woodwork was weathered to a dark grey colour and the fittings were rusty or otherwise corroded. They must have been erected after arriving at the scrapyard, but to what purpose was beyond me. They were large aircraft with tailskids the size of shovels; with their days of glory long past they presented a depressing spectacle.

It was many years before I began to appreciate that an aircraft's shape is invariably a compromise between conflicting structural and aerodynamic requirements and theories and that attractive lines were usually a result of good original design. It was always possible, of course, to make the structure and the aerodynamics suit the attractive shape, but doing this rarely made for a successful aircraft because the designer ran into a lot of trouble with complicated structures, excessive weight and drag and unsuitability for its intended job. The only way open was by combining those practical features which were pleasing to look at, but which did not impair the overall design. I think that De Havilland, before and during the war, took this as far as they could. This can be seen particularly well in the shapes of the tail surfaces of the various Moths and their airliners. De Havilland's rudder and fin shapes were almost a trademark.

Aircraft have an advantage over most other mechanical creations due to aerodynamic requirements which could unintentionally confer an attractive outline. These requirements, being of primary importance, justified the use of expensive and involved structures by the principle that what you lost on the swings, you more than recouped on the roundabouts.

Cars, for example, may have been well designed and eye-catching and even beautiful in the Twenties, but deliberate attempts to stylise then in the Thirties did not, in itself, make them better cars. In many cases, the styles hindered the design and were not in any way a result of mechanical requirements. Styles became exaggerated to the point of vulgarity and quickly became dated. What was beautiful and desirable yesterday would be grotesque and unwanted tomorrow and, because this kept sales going, this fashion process became a permanent feature of the car industry to the present day. I wonder how many can feel real pride of ownership in such a car? It is little wonder that the vintage car movement flourishes.

This rarely happens with aircraft. An aircraft recognised as beautiful in the pre-war days still appears so today and even if it was never beautiful, it is still seen to be attractive; obviously old-fashioned, perhaps, but never ugly, unless it started off that way. The quality of its attraction must lie in its design and not in some passing fad of a styling department.

Another frequent cycle run was to Yeadon to see the Lancasters produced at the huge Shadow Factory. Later there were Yorks, Avro XIXs and other marks of Ansons to gaze at over the fence. The fact that Ansons were still being made was, I thought, very remarkable.

A local garage proprietor, Arnold G. Wilson, had bought an Auster J.I and this return of private flying to Yorkshire was much publicised in the local press. The news item, although not significant in itself, helped to keep my aviation hopes alive as the life of the Olympia Works drained away with increasing rapidity.

I was transferred back to the training section for three or four weeks and then to the Swordfish shop. As the work was completed, more people left, until only the supervisors and apprentices remained. The more promising of the senior apprentices were offered jobs at Brough, but the rest of us, in due course, received our notices. It was not a surprise, but I had done nothing about finding another job and, somewhat belatedly, I weighed up the prospects.

Two of the draughtsmen, Mr Hooton and Mr Nelson, had started a part-time business repairing cars and I had done some work for them in the evenings. Upon being made redundant, they went into it full-time and branched out making kitchen cabinets. They offered me a job with them and, looking back, it was a good opportunity because they did very well as time went on. But aviation had me firmly hooked and I turned the offer down. Instead, I wrote to Avros at Yeadon, who offered me a job. I elected to take a holiday for a fortnight, on unemployment pay, to catch up on Technical College work before I started and during this time I received another letter stating that Avros had to withdraw the job offer due to circumstances beyond their control. As it happened, the Shadow Factory was also closing.

This knocked the bottom out of my hopes and in increasing desperation considered the model trade. "Astra" kits were made in

Leeds and, on impulse, I set out to find the factory. It turned out to be a converted chapel, all boarded up, with no sign of life, so I gave up that idea and instead, with memories of the Squadron Leader's £3, investigated the market for ready-built model aircraft.

Canvassing the local model shops for orders, I found that I would have been working long hours for very little money if the work had materialised at all. To work for myself might have been more profitable, but I had no means of financing myself. The unemployment money was 15/- per week, not a princely sum by any means, even in those days, but very welcome and I attended twice a week at the Juvenile Employment Bureau with the other lads.

The fellow behind the counter took a dim view of us and exhorted us to take one of the jobs he had to offer. It appeared that the majority wanted to be lorry drivers' mates, for which there were no vacancies, but no persuasion on his part could budge them. In the meantime, I learned that the R.A.F. were advertising for men in the ground trades which seemed unlikely in view of the fact that the R.A.F. must, in the nature of things, be contracting too. But I went along to the Recruiting Office and sure enough, it was true. I could sign on when I was seventeen and three months, said the sergeant and they would send for me when I was seventeen and six months. This meant that I had another five months to wait, so that was no good. I resolved to wait a week or two for them to forget my face while I adjusted my birthday. I had to get a reference from my Squadron C.O. and this seemed as good a place as any to start.

"Funny!" said the C.O. as he flicked through his card index, "I can't find your card. When did you say your birthday was?"

"The twenty-seventh of November 1928," I said, looking him in the eye.

"Hum!" he said, going through his cards again. "Ah! Here it is. That's odd, your date is down as 27th April 1929."

"Very odd," I agreed, as I felt myself turning red in the face. "Very well," he said, "Leave it with me."

With an uncomfortable feeling that I had well and truly burned my boats and that there was nothing else to do but go through with it, I left and eased the dryness in my mouth with a cup of tea in the canteen, served by the prettiest girl in Leeds.

Back at the Youth Employment Bureau, the clerk was getting worried.

"You'll have to take a job," he said. "It's no good you kicking your heels all day when you should be working." I nodded. "Look," he leaned confidentially over the counter, "I've got a job here, just what you want."

"What is it?" I asked.

"Lorry driver's mate!" he said, triumphantly.

"I don't want it," I croaked.

"You don't want it!" he shouted, almost jumping over the counter with rage.

After he simmered down, I explained that I had a job lined up that I was pretty confident of getting within a fortnight.

"What is it?" he asked. Worried that my true age might be divulged, I replied that I wanted to keep it to myself for now, for if the others got to hear of it, they would all be after it.

Rather doubtfully, he accepted my argument and paid out my dole with the reminder that if I didn't succeed, I would have to take any job offered in a fortnight's time.

As soon as the time was ripe, I presented myself before the Recruiting Sergeant and intimated that I wanted to join up. "You want your head looking at, you mean!" he said. I wondered if he got commission on the bodies he recruited, but thought it unlikely that he would forego money for the sake of my head. He was probably right, but as a recruiter he would have no feeling for aircraft and would not understand.

"Why don't you wait until you are called up?" he asked. "You can always sign on then, if you want to."

"I might end up in the Army," I replied, "and, anyway, I've decided that this is what I want to do."

"Well, it's your life," he said, reaching for a form. "Name?" I told him. "Date of birth?"

"The 27th of ...." My mind went blank as I tried to remember the date I had fixed on. Was it October or November? A quick mental calculation saved me, as the Sergeant fixed me with his beady eyes.

"November 1928," I stammered.

Chocks & Driptrays ~ 45

The paperwork completed, he told me to report the following week for a medical, which I did and a week after that I boarded a train for Warrington with orders to report to R.A.F. Padgate.

6. Square Bashing

The train steamed into Warrington station and disgorged a motley crowd of young civilians of varying ages and descriptions, all carrying attaché cases. An R.A.F. lorry with benches in it waited outside the station and we all climbed in. Shortly after, we rolled into Padgate Camp to encouraging cries of "You'll be sorreee!" and were dropped outside some billets.

My first view of Padgate reminded me of a P.O.W. camp and did nothing to dispel the feeling that the Recruiting Sergeant could have been right after all. Row upon row of grey wooden buildings stretched as far as the eye could see, interspersed with roads and drill squares and straddled with overhead pipes and cables. Squads of recruits were marching everywhere with N.C.O.s barking at them incessantly, even to the cookhouse at mealtimes. My meditations were cut short as we were ushered into the billets to grab a bed and dump our baggage and out again to be issued with bedding, eating utensils and a meal ticket. We were then taken to the cookhouse for an indifferent tea. The tea itself was of a strange brew and reputed to contain bromide. We were returned to the billet to settle in and it was then that I found my sheets had disappeared. An appeal for advice only brought forth a suggestion that I should swipe somebody else's and as everybody by now was alerted and keeping a wary eye on their own, I took a walk down the road wondering what to do.

A passing sergeant asked me, "What's the matter, laddie? Can't you find your billet?" I explained that it was my sheets I had lost, resigning myself to the fact that the pay for my first week would be forfeited to pay for them. He led me to a bedding store, produced a key, went in and came out with a pair of sheets, which he gave me together with a little lecture on keeping my eye on my kit at all times.

Much relieved and much wiser in the ways of the world, I returned to the billet. We were left in peace that evening and I stayed in the billet, half expecting my kit to disappear if I turned my back.

The evening activities at Padgate appeared to be blancoing, judging by all the webbing belts hanging out of the windows to dry and boot polishing and brass cleaning. It was evident that this would be our lot too, wherever we were posted, but I was not sorry to learn next day that we would be at Padgate for only a week.

In the following days we were subjected to further medicals, intelligence tests and form filling. We were each given a number and told to memorise it, issued with identity tags and had our photographs taken. Then we were taken to the stores for our kit.

In rapid succession they handed us kit bags and proceeded to fill them with everything an airman needed to sustain himself. I was intrigued to hear, as the list was read out, "Housewife, one, airman, for the use of" but it turned out to be a little white bag of a different sort, tied up with tape and containing needles, thread, darning wool and a thimble! On then to the tailor, who sized us up wearing our ill-fitting uniforms and expertly marked with chalk where the alterations should be before collecting them in. In due course they were returned to us, but the final results were scarcely to Savile Row standards.

We were allowed out of camp wearing our uniforms to sample the delights of Warrington, before we left, but the town looked very drab and our new boots hurt our feet, so apart from a sense of freedom it was not an auspicious occasion.

The next morning we were lined up on the Square, with our accoutrements inexpertly assembled and ill-adjusted.

The Warrant officer in charge viewed us with a disapproving eye and endeavoured, without much success, to form us into some semblance of order. We were informed that we were going to 2 R.C. Cardington, near Bedford and he managed to convey the impression that he was not sorry to be able to unload us on that establishment. Shortly afterwards, the lorries came to take us to the station and the troop train.

In those days, Cardington had its own station up a branch line and, in the late afternoon, we arrived. From the station, the camp stretched up the hillside, at the top of which, dimly through the mist, appeared the brooding shapes of two enormous airship hangars. After roll calls and the settling-in, I found myself in All Flight, Hut 408, at the top of the hill. Our recruit training would last for twelve weeks, instead of the eight weeks for the conscripts and it seemed a very long time.

Cardington, however, appeared less forbidding than Padgate and much more interesting. There was the airfield, although no aircraft used it except for the balloons of various sorts floating serenely above the camp.

During June and July of 1946 we did not have particularly good weather, which was perhaps just as well, as we were soon plunged into a round of exhausting activities which would have been unbearable in really hot weather.

Much has been said about the merits, or otherwise, of 'Bull' and for those dragged from a cosy civilian life against their will, as were the conscripts or National Servicemen as they were later called, Service life must have been a nasty shock to say the least, made bearable only by the comradeship of their fellow sufferers. Such antipathy did not affect my Flight to any degree and when those who had second thoughts were advised to drop out, there and then, before the attestation ceremony took place, because it would be too late afterwards, nobody did.

All I remember of the ceremony itself is the phrase "the King, his Heirs and Successors", repeated several times through the recitation that we were required to mumble.

The stringent requirements of discipline and 'bull', as it affected me, were no deterrent. The ATC had prepared me to some extent and I found that the best way of coping with it was to get down to it. It was no use kicking against it and so I learned to clean the soles of my boots as well as the uppers and to polish the back of my cap badge as well as the front!

It was an invigorating existence each day. There was no hot water to wash and shave in, but this did not bother me so much as I had not yet started to shave. I had hoped to avoid this chore until I got to a more civilised place, but the square-bashing life must have accelerated my development, for one day, Sergeant Long (who was quite short) inspected my chin and accused me of not shaving. I admitted this and he said that I would be put on a charge. It never got that far however, for I was spoken to in a fatherly way by W/O Manning, who suggested that until my beard actually started to grow, a quick run-over with a dry razor would suffice to remove the fluff. As a matter of fact, I don't think a single member of the Flight was ever actually put on a charge, although fatigues for some minor infringement were a normal event.

Our drill instructors, W/O Manning, Flt Sgt Evans, Sgts Long and Grey and two Corporals (whose names I can't remember) were some of the finest NCOs it has been my privilege to know, fair but firm, sometimes sharp but never vindictive and they did not expect us to do anything that they could not do themselves. Always smart and efficient, they taught by example. They would stand no nonsense and when on parade they acted accordingly, but after working hours they would occasionally join us for a yarn and a joke. They were in sharp contrast to some of the NCOs of other Flights whose attentions we could not always avoid, but fell foul of, on more than one occasion. Our NCOs, however, never let them take matters into their own hands and went out of their way to shield us from their over-zealous retributions,

We had, like any other Flight, a couple of chaps who could never do anything right, but they were not made to suffer unduly.

Good-natured humour worked better and it was the rest of the squad who were told off for not helping the offender and not making sure he was correctly turned out. It was almost impossible not to smile at some particularly funny remark if it was not directed at oneself, but Sgt Long would have none of it. "What are you smiling at, Newton?" he barked. "Think it funny, do you? Well, laugh this off! Report to the cookhouse at eighteen hundred hours for fatigues!"

Cookhouse fatigues meant washing dirty and greasy cooking utensils and plates, cleaning and polishing the dining hall and preparing vegetables. Somebody had to do it and this was one way of supplying the labour. The blow was softened by having a supper of fried egg, or sausage with mash, if the cook thought you had earned it.

The fresh air and the exercise caused us to be always hungry and we took it in turns to volunteer for fatigues, the advantage being that, as a volunteer, one could leave early, having purloined all the bread, butter, apples, cheese and anything else handy that one could stuff inside one's denims. Back in the billet, the loot would be distributed and leisurely eaten while lying in one's pit, listening to Cheerful Charlie Chester on the radio.

The weeks slipped by and as fresh recruits moved in to replace those that passed out, we gradually became the smart efficient airmen the system was intended to make us.

The days were filled with drill, obstacle courses, P.T, firing practice, bayonet drill, throwing grenades (highly dangerous, I thought), more drill, lectures on R.A.F. history and organisation, weapons training, unarmed combat, gas warfare and kit inspections.

One day we were taken to nearby Cranfield for air experience, but for some reason we never flew. Cranfield was then the home of the Empire Test Pilots School and there was a large variety of interesting aircraft, all beautifully finished and polished. Spitfire 21s and 22s, Spitefuls, Tempest IIs and Vs and a Vampire were there that I remember and I felt that if the end result of my R.A.F. training would qualify me to be entrusted with the maintenance of aircraft like these, then I could have done worse than join up.

In wet weather, we would practise our drill in one of the airship hangars. They appeared so large that it was said that each hangar had its own weather inside. They certainly creaked and rattled, expanding and contracting as the sun shone fitfully on them.

Shouted orders were made quite unintelligible by the echoes so the drill sessions were not very successful, but I found them interesting for it was an opportunity to study the buildings that once housed the R 100 and R 101 airships. It required little imagination to envisage their huge shapes and the ghosts of those who died in the R 101, who made this place a monument to their lives' work.

The hangar we were in housed large piles of packing cases and aircraft spares including Tempest wings and the other hangar contained balloons of various sorts. Outside, parked around the airfield was the residue of Britain's wartime balloon barrage, powerful winches mounted on lorry chassis in their hundreds and trailers with hydrogen cylinders everywhere.

We were required to attend church parade most Sundays and many hours I spent in Cardington Church, gazing at the backs of the heads of the officers in front and the W.A.A.F. officer's hat and beyond them to the R.A.F. ensign on the wall, the only thing left intact from the wreckage of the R 101.

One or two of the Flight were sufficiently attracted to the life of a drill instructor and the attainment of Corporal's stripes thereby, to volunteer for a further eight weeks training to become one.

I was tempted, realising that I had much further to go to achieve my goal of becoming a Flight Mechanic Airframe. I was now 3500621 A.C.2 Newton S.L. ACH/GD u/t F.M.A. and the lowest of the lowly in the ranks of the R.A.F. The desire to work with aircraft proved too strong for such temptations, however. It was rather surprising to find that I was almost alone in having such aspirations – others preferring to become cooks, firemen, storemen, drivers, etc.

We all had our own reasons for signing on and all were different. One had been in the Navy, one in the Army, a couple of Geordies had been miners, one – whose dad was a bookmaker – tried hard to explain to me the mysteries of odds and starting prices and betting systems. Some had joined because they had no family, or were divorced, one did it for a bet, but most did it to get a trade which would stand them in good stead when they returned to civilian life.

Some already had good trades or professions, one being a schoolmaster, so the 3/- per day (later 4/- per day) pay of a recruit was not the inducement. Whatever the reasons, the fact was that men from many different backgrounds could live and work well together and it was an exhilarating experience.

Due to bad weather the passing-out parade was held in the dance hall, when I received a silver medal for being the highest scoring marksman. This was sheer chance, as we had, early on, learned to poke a pencil through the bull and quickly paste over the erring bullet hole before the sergeant came round the butts to check the score and not due to superior merit. I received no acclaim, only a few mutterings of "Fiddle!" but as I had only doctored other people's targets and not my own, I was not unduly put out.

The Flight photograph was taken and a day or two later we were sent on leave. Feeling fitter than I have at any other time in my life, I thought nothing of walking into Bedford loaded down with my complete kit and took the train to Leeds.

Full of youthful cockiness, I looked up my old mates, visited my old Squadron and flew what remained of my old models, in Roundhay Park. As my leave drew to a close, I received orders to proceed to No 2 School of Technical Training at R.A.F. Cosford, near Wolverhampton, for my F.M.A. course.

7. Learning a Trade

Cosford in 1946 was a very large camp with about 8,000 men, not including the civilian Maintenance Unit and a great many activities went on there. Flight Mechanics, both Airframes and Engines, P.T.I.s and Junior N.C.O.s were trained on courses there and there were also some Australians waiting to be repatriated. Redundant aircrew were everywhere, mainly Air Gunners remustering to ground trades, which did not seem to go down well with them.

For the first time, I was with called-up men and there was a different attitude to Air Force life, which at first I found rather disconcerting. I was allocated to Pool Flight and did general duties around the camp for a week or two until the next entry was formed. Settling into our permanent billets, we got to know each other and I found that there were several other regulars, which was a relief. There were plenty of after-work activities, such as a cinema, model club, roller-skating, etc. and, because of the P.T.I. School, the more athletic activities were well catered for. It was here that I first met the curious Service phenomenon concerning sport.

Professional sportsmen were eagerly sought after as P.T.I.s and were encouraged to share and develop their expertise and, if they were, for example, footballers, they could expect to devote most of their Service life to that sport. Many famous names passed through Cosford and the standard was undoubtedly very high.

The course was preceded by the usual Service preliminaries of parades, roll calls, form filling and an F.F.I. (Free From Infection) medical inspection for which we were shepherded into a big room, lined up for the medical inspection and subjected to the inevitable lecture on clean living.

The School was comprehensively equipped with aircraft of all descriptions and glimpses of them had whetted my appetite. We were issued with notebooks and our five months course commenced.

It was undoubtedly the finest training one could receive anywhere and we were taken, stage by stage, through the various departments. Two books by A.C. Kermode, *Flight Without Formulae* and *The Aeroplane Structure* were our text books as we ploughed through these subjects, learning about aerofoil sections, dihedral, incidence, the control of aircraft, graduated horn balances and mass balances, all this being demonstrated by films, working models and actual aircraft. Such aircraft as the Auster, Hurricane, Spitfire, Tempest Mk V, Typhoon, Mosquito, Beaufighter, Tiger Moth and Meteor stood around or were mounted on trestles, all painted aluminium with numbers ending with 'M'.

The Hurricane was bigger than the Spitfire and we were allowed to climb in and sit in the cockpit, which seemed very roomy, compared with the Spitfire. The seat was on top of the surface of the wing centre section and seemed quite high in comparison.

Some aircraft, like the Meteors, were original prototypes and of great interest. All, we were told, had been airworthy when they came to Cosford, having flown in, but the attentions of the pupils had caused some deterioration to most of them.

The nature and purpose of frize ailerons, slotted flaps, trim and balance tabs were explained to us and the mysteries of rigging wire-braced structures occupied some time. Progressing to hydraulic and pneumatic systems, we learned of Dowty live line pumps, dual relay valves, Heywood compressors, hydraulic accumulators and the rest. It was the Tempest hydraulic system that we studied and the Dowty live line pump that it used was an expensive-looking work of art.

It consisted of radial cylinders rather like a rotary aero engine with the pistons protruding. The extremities of the pistons were fitted with slipper pads which slipped around a ring which was held eccentrically by a spring plate. As the cylinders went round, the pistons moved in and out and pumped oil. This oil operated whatever was required, flaps, undercarriage, etc and when the operating jack or ram came to the end of its travel, the backpressure acted against the pistons of the pump, preventing them from moving and in turn causing the slippers to press against the eccentric ring. This forced the ring to take up a concentric position, overcoming the force of the spring plate, the strength of which controlled the maximum pressure of the system. The spring plate was ingenious, as once it bent it exerted less pressure, thus relieving the system of strain until the next selection was made.

It was surprising how much noise a hydraulic system could make, the squeak of a hand pump and bang of an automatic cut-out being typical. This was due, they said, to oil being incompressible and providing, in effect, a solid connection between the different parts of the system. Much later, on the Fitters course, we learnt about liquid springing in which oil did compress, which was a bit confusing.

In the fabric shop, we were given wooden frames to simulate a component and taught how to cover it with fabric. This was pure unbleached Irish linen which we cut to shape and stitched round, using special stitches on the edges and boom stringing in the middle. The frames were completed by applying red dope and doping serrated fabric strip over the stitching and stringing and finishing off with a further doping scheme. After awarding marks for workmanship the instructor then, to our dismay, proceeded to cut holes and slits in them which we had to repair by darning and herring-bone stitching, finishing off with serrated patches, cut out with pinking shears. The art of balloon seams, covering on the bias, using a sewing machine, Woods frames, materials and specifications were gone into in great detail, not to mention high speed finishes, wooden aircraft finishes and using a spray gun.

On again to the fitting shop: drilling, filing, tapping, bending, wire-rope splicing and swaging, A.G.S. parts and locking systems being the order of the day.

We learned how to make repairs to stressed skin and tubular structures. Around the shop were Hurricane wings and fuselage frames, all extremely patched. Wielding an axe, the instructor chopped indiscriminately at these, causing damage which we had to assess and repair according to the Repair Scheme.

We were kept hard at it and it was a relief to finish each day and relax by pursuing our individual interests. I built several models at Cosford; a 'Frog' Vanda which was not very successful, being heavy with coloured dope, a 'Drome' Gladiator which invoked memories of flap hydraulic troubles by an instructor who had worked on 'Glads' and, best of all, a 40" wingspan 'KeilKraft' Polydi with a hardwood propeller which I laboriously carved. This model was flown from the square regularly and would fly in a high, wide circuit up over the Hinaidi hangars and down the length of them, turning over the P.T.I. billets across the road. With the propeller flicking over in freewheel, it would drift in over our own billets and touch down again on the square. Once, it failed to make it and caught on the roof of one of the hangars. Fortunately, it was near the doors and, after a nerve-wracking climb up the framework supporting the overhead door track, it was soon retrieved.

The New Year came and went and it was not until the middle of January 1947 that winter really came, a winter that people still recall today.

We were now in hangars near the airfield, learning about inspection schedules and paperwork such as filling in the Form 700, which was the aircraft log book and carrying out various inspections of some Beaufighter IIs with Merlin engines. These were heavily-built aircraft, probably too heavy for Merlins, although the undercarriage looked none too strong. There was a big rack of oxygen cylinders behind the observer's seat which effectively blocked off the tail section unless you were small enough to squeeze past. It was possible to hide behind them for a quick snooze, which I did one day. When I awoke, everybody had gone and all the lights were switched off. Eventually finding my way out, I made my way to the billets to find I had missed tea too.

In the Beaufighter, the pilot sat in the middle of a roomy cockpit with the cannons under the floor and a good view forward. Behind him was the entry hatch with an extending ladder. A curious feature of the published silhouettes of the Beaufighter, when they first came out in the *Aeroplane Spotter*, was that the nose and tail were depicted but the centre of the fuselage was omitted, presumably to hide the fact that there was no gun position and, instead, there was a small blister window for a second crewman who, the Germans might guess, was there to operate the radar.

The hydraulic system was so designed that, if some of it was shot away, parts of it might still function.

As the days passed, the weather became bitterly cold, the great freeze-up had started and it became impossible to work on the aircraft. There was no heating and, in desperation, the instructor swung a big thick rope round and round, not to beat us, but for us to jump over as it came round in order to keep warm. In the end, all instruction ceased and for a few days we were taken out on route marches along the roads around the camp. I distinctly remember icicles forming in my nostrils from my condensing breath, the cold was so intense.

After work, things were little better. There was a shortage of fuel and the heating pipes in the billet were only kept warm enough to prevent the heating system from freezing up. Luckily, our billet was only half occupied and all the spare 'biscuits' (three of which per bed served as a mattress) were used, in conjunction with the double bunk beds, to make igloos along the walls to trap what heat there was and into which we crawled to sleep.

In the end, we were sent home for a week, subsequently extended to a fortnight.

The weather was no better when we came back but, as March wore on, it improved slightly and the entry progressed to a hangar on the airfield to learn flight duties.

Here, in addition to further lectures, we learnt to swing a propeller, picket aircraft, operate a catalytic aircraft heater, refuel aircraft and help to start the engines. Our fellow Engine Mechanic trainees were the ones who sat in the cockpits, to my envy and ran them up. For this purpose, there was a hangar with a dozen or more Spitfires, each with its wings crudely hacked off, outboard of the undercarriage legs, in order to save hangar space. They were probably weighted in the tail to compensate for the loss of the weight of their wings.

Opposite the hangar, on the other side of the perimeter track, was an early Halifax with the old triangular fins, chin type bomb aimer's windows and Merlin engines. It was in the process of being broken up for scrap and the engines were removed by the simple expedient of burning though the bearers and letting the engines drop to the ground. This aircraft was a veteran of many raids, proved by the many bombs painted on the side of the cockpit and it was sad to see it go.

After the freezing weather came the gales and one morning we turned up at the airfield to find a scene of destruction. Two or three Tiger Moths used for teaching prop-swinging had been blown onto their backs with the concrete blocks to which they were tied hanging down over the wings. Another aircraft, an Oxford, had been blown backwards, dragging its concrete blocks with it, until it finished up with its tail down in a ditch. It was an object-lesson in the necessity for picketing aircraft down securely when out in the open.

Through the windows of the classroom along the side of the airfield hangar could be seen Spitfires of various marks, IXs, XIIs, XIVs, XXIs, XXIIs and XXIVs being towed past by tractors, all resplendent in new coats of paint and decorated in the national markings of the countries to which they were destined. These aircraft were handled by the civilian Maintenance Unit.

Walks around the countryside were often interesting. Several smallholdings possessed sections of Horsa glider fuselages converted into hen houses etc. but still with camouflage finish and roundels. Once we went to look at Tong Castle, a mile or so up the road. It was really a ruined stately home and only the façade remained standing. I was intrigued to see that the inner face of the wall still had wallpaper pasted to it and I found it to be a sad spectacle, for it had once been somebody's treasured home.

Behind the camp was an area given over to the Junior N.C.O.'s Course and through the hedge two aircraft could be seen.

Risking the barbed wire, my pal and I climbed over to investigate and found that one was a very early Hurricane Mk 1 with fabric-covered wings and the other was a Defiant. I seem to remember that on the Hurricane the openings for the wheel wells were joined, whereas the later Hurricanes that I had worked on had separate wheel wells.

At the west side of the camp, by the railway bridge, was a dump of old aircraft – strictly out of bounds, the sign said – but it was no deterrent. It was mostly stuff discarded by the School, judging by the patched old Hurricane wings and fuselages and the like, but in the corner was an aircraft I could not, for a time, identify.

At first I thought it was a Gladiator, but closer inspection showed it to be a Gauntlet.

Knowing what I know now, these and other aircraft at Cosford were priceless relics and would have been the ingredients of a first-class aircraft museum, but even if I had thought of it, I had no money to buy them, even at scrap prices and nowhere to keep them. They have long since vanished and, too late, I have learned that a thing that is cheap and commonplace today may very well be rare and valuable tomorrow and that its true value should be judged accordingly.

Finally, at the end of the course, we went before a Trade Test Board for our abilities to be assessed. Those with high marks could be sent on a further course to become a Fitter IIA at R.A.F. Locking. We had a 'Ballard' questionnaire and were then interviewed in turn by the Board, which consisted mainly of elderly Flight Sergeants who plied us with questions about AGS parts, the workings of various components and what action we would take if the aircraft was found to be unserviceable in some way. The first thing one did with regard to the last item and the only answer that they were really after, incidentally, was that one immediately entered details of the defect in the Change of Serviceability and Repair Log of the Form 700 for the aircraft, thus making the aircraft officially unserviceable (u/s) to fly.

It took two days to interview us all and eventually our fates were made known. Only one person had made the grade to go on the fitters' course and a few were put back for a month or a fortnight to brush up their abilities. The rest of us were passed and remustered as AC2 FMAs and transferred to Pool Flight to await our postings.

During the course I had a mysterious illness, if it could be called that. I was shaving one morning when I noticed that the flesh under my jaw looked unusually puffed out, but there was no pain or discomfort and there was nothing to make me aware of it until I looked in the mirror.

Reporting sick in those days was an ordeal and there was some truth in the saying we had, that you had to be fit to report sick. Relieved that that I was not suffering like some of the others on the sick parade and half expecting to be accused of malingering, I was not prepared for the interest that the M.O. showed in my case.

He prodded and probed and asked if it hurt when I swallowed. "No," I said and he retired, baffled, to consult his colleague.

"Well, Newton" he said on returning, "I think we'll put you in the isolation ward for observation."

I was rather put out by this turn of events and said that I felt perfectly fit, but it was to no avail and I was despatched to the hospital immediately.

When I arrived there, the Sister gave me a pair of pyjamas and told me to get into bed, which I did, still protesting. Apart from meals, I saw nobody for the first day. Making the best of it, I slept.

Next day, the orderly came in and scolded me for disarranging my bed, which she tidied up and tucked in tight at each side. She then opened the window, letting in a strong draught which blew through a gap between the sheets on my left side, round my feet and back out of the gap on the other side. She was followed by the Sister, who informed me that the M.O. would be making his rounds shortly and that I was not to disarrange my bed, or get out of it, but to lie to attention when he came!

"How are you? Good!" barked the M.O. before I could say anything. "Keep him in bed, Sister."

With a cursory look at my chin, he left. As soon as he had gone, I hopped out of bed and shut the window, the temperature being around freezing point, but it was no use, the orderly came back and opened it again, uttering dire threats. Matters seemed to be improving when the Sister came in with a packet of Sweet Caporal cigarettes, by courtesy of the Canadian Red Cross and put them on my locker. "These are for you" she said.

"Thanks very much, Sister," I replied. "Is there any chance of acquiring some matches too?"

"Oh, you mustn't smoke them!" she exclaimed, as she swished out of the room.

Fortunately, on the third day, it was a different orderly who came to attend to my needs, rather less cast-iron in nature and she reluctantly obtained some matches for me. As there were no ashtrays, it was necessary to lean out of the window while smoking and thus dispose of the smoke problem at the same time. At the sound of footsteps, the cigarette would be dropped outside and I would dive into bed. After the danger passed, the cigarette would be retrieved with some agile contortions.

By this time, my chin had returned to its normal size and I let it be known that I wanted to be discharged. A couple of days more, they said, just to be sure. But they let me get up and dress and they issued me with a white shirt and red tie – standard rig for the war-wounded!

On the last night, they wheeled into my room a chap suffering from acute bronchitis, or worse and who kept me awake all night with his coughing. It was with great relief, next morning, that I was told to get dressed and report to the M.O. at the Sick Quarters. The M.O. turned out to be a woman who sympathetically reviewed my case and checked that I was fit. I was already suffering from incipient flu brought on by my enforced hospitalisation, but managed to conceal this.

"I think you should have some sick leave," she murmured. "Will fourteen days be enough?"

This, I realised, would mean that I would be separated from my mates in the entry and relegated to a later one and I did not like the thought much. I explained that if I had seven days, I would only be relegated to the next entry, in which I had several friends and I would prefer this.

The lady M.O. put down her pen and considered this proposal. Having an airman refuse fourteen days sick leave was obviously a new experience to her and I had an uncomfortable feeling that she was considering that my mental health could do with some observation too!

"Oh, well, if that is what you want!" she said finally, in a tone one reserves for fools.

In due course, then, I returned to join my new entry and complete my training. I never regretted my decision, for this one entry – every man jack – was posted to India.

Finally, before this description of life at Cosford is complete, mention should be made of a coach trip, run by the Cosford Model Club, to the Midland Area Rally at Walsall Airport. Considering that this was in the days before R/C, control line flying, or even model diesel engines, there was an enormous crowd and, of course, gliders and rubber-powered models predominated. There was, in fact, an example of an early diesel engine, fitted in a large, plain, but well-made model with 'OWAT DIESEL' printed along the top surface of the high wing. The owner appeared to have some trouble in starting it, as it would fire but die away each time. This engine appeared to have no compression adjustment, which was an undoubted handicap, but the spectators, of whom I was one, found it very interesting.

Through the windows of a hangar with the name Helliwell on it, which was near at hand and investigated by the curious, could be seen a Globe Swift – a recently imported American light plane of pleasing appearance – and a Harvard Mk I with its fuselage side panels removed and undergoing overhaul. It had a fabric-covered fuselage, which was not so on the Mk II.

8. Waiting for the Boat

The next posting, as it turned out, was to the P.D.C. at Burtonwood, near Warrington, but first we were sent on embarkation leave. My pay was now 6/- per day, but even with the ration money added to it, I had difficulty making it last for the 28 days. There was not enough to buy new civvies, having outgrown my old ones, but as I was now a fully-fledged Flight Mechanic and full of swank, I was quite happy in my uniform.

There was an air show at Sherburn-in-Elmet, to which I went thus attired. There was a lot of the usual stuff, but two interesting participants were a Miles Aerovan and a Miles Messenger. The Aerovan was a metal one and showed off its slow-flying capabilities. It had two retractable supports at the rear of the fuselage to steady it when loading, but one had broken, through somebody forgetting to raise it before flying.

The Messenger was beautifully finished in cream with red lettering, being very smooth and glossy without a blemish anywhere. The contrast with the drab camouflaged aircraft surrounding it was very marked. It was a private owner's dream – but not for privates or AC2s!

The wind was quite strong towards the end of the day and was blowing from the direction of the spectators that still remained. The departing aircraft were taking off over their heads and the effect of the wind was noticeable by the extra height that the planes gained before they passed over the crowd barrier. That the sales team with the Aerovan and Messenger were aware of this fact became apparent when they taxied out for the departure takeoff.

At a distance of no more than a hundred yards from the barrier, the two aircraft turned and faced the crowd. I watched, spellbound, while removing myself from the danger area, as they both ran up their engines. By the time the sound of their engines came back up-wind as they were opened up for takeoff, the Messenger and Aerovan rose off the ground in quick succession, like big birds of prey, with their large Fairey-Youngman type flaps drooping for maximum lift. Higher they went, rocking gently with each turbulent gust until they crossed the barrier with a good seventy feet to spare, to my relief.

I arrived at Warrington Station for the second time, being the nearest to Burtonwood. I smugly surveyed the new recruits with the air of a veteran and my mind dwelt on the thought that at least a quarter of the young men of Britain must have passed through the station's grimy portals. Picking out the transport for Burtonwood, I slung my kit aboard and after an interminable wait for more customers, we finally reached our destination.

Burtonwood was a rather different sort of camp from those of my previous experiences. To start with, it had been a major base of the American 8th Air Force, of wartime fame and although it had been well anglicised by the time I got there, it had features that only time would erase, like the matey toilets – no doors or even walls – just a line of thrones! Or the flat washbasins 4' by 6' with eye level taps. In the cookhouse and also in the Stores, were big wall paintings of a flag-waving nature. An enormous portrayal of the 8th's famous badge hit one in the eyes, the sort of thing only the Yanks would think of doing when the order was given—"Sgt. Karinsky, get that goddam wall painted!"

Life at Burtonwood was far from demanding and provided that we attended two parades a day – 10 a.m. and 2 p.m. – the rest of the day was our own. At these parades, roll-calls were made for the various drafts to distant parts, Rhodesia, Malaya, Germany, Egypt, Iraq, Malta, etc. Each day we waited to have our names called for the draft to India, as we knew it to be and each day we returned to our billets unwanted. The easy life was marred to some extent because few of us had any money left. Burtonwood had not yet received our 'docs' (documents) from Records and, as a consequence, we could not be paid.

Perhaps this was deliberate, to discourage the gambling that many billets engaged in to pass the time. One could not gamble without money at such a camp, as a man foolish enough to give credit might find his debtors gone in the night and he certainly did not know when he would be paid, if at all. So when the cash ran out, which in my case was almost immediately, we carried on with the brass trouser buttons with which R.A.F. trousers were amply endowed! As I never wore braces, trusting instead to a leather belt, I could afford to lose six buttons before feeling any anxiety! Needless to say, the shortage of trouser buttons was only exceeded by the shortage of safety pins.

The situation was not too bad during the day, as the long hard winter was well past and now the weather in that month of May was beautiful. Day after day, the sun shone out of a cloudless sky and the inmates of each billet dragged their beds outside and lay on them, hour after hour, until they looked like lobsters.

My thoughts turned, amongst other things, to aeromodelling, but Warrington was very backward in this respect and all that was available to a man of my means was a Tempest II kit by Frog. The fuselage was in two halves, of a brown paper composition trimmed and glued together, with pre-cut balsa wood parts for the tissue-covered wings. It had clip-in undercarriage legs similar to the Frog Interceptor Mk II, which was appearing in the shops about that time.

To digress, for the benefit of posterity, the Interceptor first appeared before the war and was a high mid-wing model of an attractive freelance fighter. Rubber driven, through a gearbox in the nose, it had a beautifully formed aluminium body, stiffened paper tail surfaces with a printed finish and knock-off wings also of printed paper of folded construction to give a reasonable aerofoil section, maintained by an aluminium rib at each wing root. Two holes in each rib lined up with two dowels passing through the fuselage. These dowels had a small slit at each end to enable the wing panel to slip on easily yet securely, but to knockoff without damage. A four-point clip-on undercarriage and smart black wooden propeller completed the model. I was lucky enough to have had one.

The box that it came in had a geared winder, which engaged the propeller when the assembled model was placed in it. On each side, in separate compartments, was a bottle. One had lubricating oil and the other rubber lubricant.

These models were examples of first-class engineering, rare in the model industry and were not cheap. They could be easily damaged by Junior's hot sticky fingers but, used sensibly, they were surprisingly durable. The Mk II was similar, but given a more modern appearance with a teardrop hood over the cockpit and the U/C moved to the wings in a similar manner to the Tempest.

To return to the Tempest, it was not a very successful flier, due to the coloured dope making it heavy. However, it was used to try an experiment on board ship which I shall come to, later in this narrative.

We could hear engines running up on the airfield where there was a Maintenance Unit, but I had had my fill of aircraft for a bit and didn't venture up there.

Money was non-existent in the billet when we decided to have a night out, by hook or by crook. Somebody suggested visiting a pawnbroker, so we turned out all our most valuable possessions and took ourselves off to the sign of the three balls. Most had cameras or watches to hock and some of the more affluent had both, but I had only my silver medal for shooting. A mate cheerfully lent me his cigarette lighter to hock as well, a brotherly act I am happy to record, as I'm also glad to record that he got it back in the end too!

Such was the everyday spirit of the billet and pocketing the 5/- I got for the two items, we set course for The Ship hostelry, where beer never tasted so good, followed by a dance in the hall over Burton's the Tailors.

With a large, floating, R.A.F. population in the town, I think parents tended to keep an eye on their daughters and the reputation of our predecessors, the Yanks, still lingered on to make them wary. There were certainly remarkably few girls to be seen about. Still, there were enough to go round at the dance and I must say they were very nice, those Warrington lasses.

Eventually, we were paid and redeemed our chattels. Flush with money, we tried to relive our high life, but girls were scarce. One day, somebody suggested we should go to Widnes, where the girls were avowed to be fantastic. Shaved, showered and shampooed, we climbed aboard the bus for Widnes that afternoon, with high hopes.

The chemical works, we found out too late, were the only fantastic thing in Widnes, unless you included the smell of them! Birds there were none and the pubs, to which we turned in sorrow, did nothing to dispel the air of gloom which hung over us. Sadder and wiser men, we returned to camp and retired to bed with the guffaws of those who had remained in camp ringing in our ears. It was my introduction to practical jokes.

Days passed and we seemed to be a permanent part of the camp. I knew little of India and what news there was of the place seemed to be of riots and famine, but I was too young to worry about it. The more knowledgeable among us asserted that we would not go there because India would be getting her Independence soon. It came as something of a surprise, therefore, when our names were called out on parade. India it was, they said and get your 48 hour leave passes made out for a last chance to nip home to say cheerio to the folks. Reawakened from our lethargy, we complied and piled on the train. I spent the last of my money that weekend and, having returned to my usual state of perennial poverty, hitch-hiked back from Leeds, walking the whole way from Salford to Warrington in the early hours.

Next morning, we were hustled through the stores and kitted out with various strange items which we stuffed into a new kitbag, identified with two blue bands around it, for which I had to buy a new handle and padlock. There were khaki drill tunics with red kitehawks on the shoulders, shorts and slacks, thick woolly vests and aertex pants (the reverse of what I already had, so that I now had complete sets of aertex and woolly underwear), a clasp knife with a thing for getting stones out of horses' hooves, mosquito boots, shoes, a sandfly net, a bush hat, long woolly socks and sunglasses with leather on the sides like blinkers. They were short of pugrees in the stores, whatever they might have been and a few other things, so they were listed on a deficiency chit, which we were warned to safeguard at all costs. On the reverse of this piece of paper were the mysterious words "Kitting East of the Brahmaputra" and a further list of strange items. Apparently "East of the Brahmaputra" meant Burma.

The rest of the day and the next day, were spent sorting our kit out and marking them with our Service Numbers and marking our kitbags with our Draft No. '2677' and 'ARUN CAS' (short for Arundel Castle, the ship on which we would be sailing). The last night of each draft was traditionally a bit of a riot and to our surprise the sergeant in charge allowed us out of camp with the proviso that we were to be back at 20.00 hrs., on our own responsibility.

We rolled back at the appointed hour, some carrying their mates, singing and laughing, rolling and reeling, with nobody missing, strangely enough and we went back to the billets for the last time to collect our kit. Windows were broken and beds overturned in a final fling of exuberance by the more inebriated airmen, before they could be sobered up under a cold tap, after which we paraded, rather unsteadily, to collect our rifles. The waiting lorries were loaded up and the tailboards secured and we trundled out of Burtonwood down to the railway station, singing at the tops of our voices all the choicest Air Force songs that we knew.

9. A Life on the Ocean Wave

We awoke next morning, June 19th 1947, to find that the troop train was entering Clapham Junction in the early morning sunshine. It was the first time I had seen London and I looked out of the window with curiosity, feeling rather surprised that there was anything left to look at after six years of war. In fact, London looked remarkably substantial, but remarkably dowdy too. There was the occasional gap in a row of terraced houses and a gutted office or factory block here and there, but, with bumptious northern pride, I considered that Hull had suffered worse, size for size.

After a tardy change of locomotive, we were on our way again to Southampton, eating our packed breakfast, after washing and shaving as best we could. The close confines of the compartment made a walk along the corridor an apparent relief from the aches and pains of prolonged sitting, but it was full of people coming and going, struggling their way past the queue for the toilet and washbasin. Thanks to the foresight of an early waker, we had finished our purifications before the rush, so now we sat fidgeting, watching the countryside of England flash past the window and then the fact struck home, the fact that we had known all along, that this was the last of England that we would see for two and a half years. Some were noticeably quiet, now that the time for departure was imminent. The sight of the Vickers Supermarine works at Eastleigh Aerodrome signalled that we were nearly there and, shortly afterwards, we squeaked to a halt at the dockside terminus.

Grabbing our kit and rifles, we clambered down to the trackside on hearing the shouted orders. Looking about me, I could see a train further up the track, with colourful Pullman coaches that had brought passengers for a large liner that loomed up behind a fence of dockside cranes.

The salt air, the cries of the seagulls and the indeterminate smell of a large seaport – the scent of oranges predominated – on a bright sunny day, gave me a great feeling of exhilaration. This was a glimpse of the world of the affluent globetrotter and I liked it, but I was to find that travelling on a troopship was rather different.

We were shepherded over the railway lines and across the quayside to the Arundel Castle and over the gangplank with 'Union Castle Line' on its side in bold letters, struggling to carry the two kitbags and a rifle across our shoulders. Stepping off the gangplank into the ship, a strange world seemed to enclose us. There was a continual humming noise, as from ventilators and dynamos and a stronger smell of oranges.

While our eyes became accustomed to the artificial light after the strong sunshine outside, we were led to our mess deck down a companionway into the bowels of the ship. The mess deck looked like an illustration I had seen of a gun deck of HMS Victory, a curving floor from one side of the ship to the other with headroom of seven to eight feet, reduced in places by pipes, ducts and cables wending their way around or between the girders of the deck above. The floor was covered with a smooth red composition, rounded at the side and corners to avoid dirt traps and was very clean. Bolted to the floor were long tables and benches at right angles to the sides of the ship, with a clear space in the middle partly occupied by neat mounds of what looked like rolled-up tarpaulins.

Depositing our accoutrements and kit bags into receptacles overhead, we were next taken to the armoury and handed in our rifles, after which we were allowed on deck to take our last view of England.

There were very few people on the quayside to see us off, but one chap – one of the affluent ones at Burtonwood – let it be known his mum and dad were motoring down to see him off, so we scanned the quayside and, sure enough, there they were, car and all, scanning back at the rows of faces looking down at them from on high. No amount of waving or calling could attract their attention and we suggested that he should get permission to go ashore which, rather to our surprise, he obtained.

I felt vaguely envious, but was nevertheless glad that all my goodbyes were behind me, as I surveyed the scene, along with hundreds of other chaps, mainly Army, crowding to the rail.

A Tannoy announcement bellowed at us, instructing us to spread over the deck and not crowd to the side and I realised that the weight of bodies were the cause of a slight list of the ship. I took myself off to the other side and found that the view was much less interesting there. Nobody else took much notice, despite repeated entreaties.

Then the siren boomed, making everybody jump and the gangplank was pulled away, the mooring ropes were dropped and almost imperceptibly a gap appeared between us and the quayside. The deck shuddered gently beneath our feet as the propellers began to turn and, slowly gathering speed, we slipped down the Solent, passing other ships moored at the quayside.

The huge liner we had seen earlier was the Queen Mary, resplendent in a new post-war coat of paint, in black and white, with three enormous red and black funnels. Strangely enough, she did not look as big as I thought she ought to look, until I compared her with the ships in front and behind, both being obviously large liners themselves. It was then apparent that she really was huge and at the same time, the longest ship in existence, being even longer than the Queen Elizabeth which, as it turned out, we had a glimpse of through a forest of cranes, being refurbished in dry dock.

The Solent was familiar, from the accounts which I had read, as the scene of some of the Schneider Trophy races and I looked out over the water hoping to see Calshot Castle. Finally we came level with it, looking deserted at the end of a low spit of land and lying offshore a squadron of Sunderlands lay slumbering at anchor with the sun reflecting off the ripples of the water. They looked rather dingy and neglected, their war work well behind them. One flying boat looked rather different from the rest and I saw that it had six engines. It was in fact a captured German flying boat, a Blohm und Voss 222. It was impressively large and I felt glad that it was now floating peacefully with its erstwhile enemies. The Germans rarely did anything by half measures and this flying boat was proof of that.

The Arundel Castle swung away to port, to round the Isle of Wight on the east side and gathered speed. Behind us lay Gosport and Portsmouth, with Ryde on the other side of the water. In the gathering haze of Spithead, a lone Swordfish flew low, practising torpedo dropping. The old stringbag looked slow and vulnerable, but it was probably Blackburn-built and the first I had seen.

The Tannoy barked again, instructing us to attend Boat Drill up on the boat deck (the one above the promenade deck) where we congregated, grouped according to our various messes. The boat deck was normally out of bounds, being reserved for officers and married families, but for once, here we were, altogether, with nobody, nobody, the Tannoy said, excused for any reason whatever. I was reminded of a picture I once saw of the troops drawn upon the deck of the sinking Birkenhead. The sound of children crying, as they were fitted with the strange-looking lifejackets, added poignancy to a scene invoking thoughts of historic maritime disasters like the Titanic and the Athenia and I hoped that things were better organised on this voyage!

The lifejackets, made of cork-filled canvas painted white, resembled two hard and uncomfortable pillows, joined together with a hole in the middle for one's head.

Cords passed under one's arms and were tied in a certain way, which necessitated helping each other to get them right. After instructions – and inspection by the Captain, no less – we returned to our normal routine.

The ship headed out into the English Channel and the slight pitch and roll became more apparent. It was surprising how many of my pals became incommunicative and glassy-eyed. It was quite a shock to see how their ruddy, healthy, faces had acquired what really appeared to be a greenish hue. The coastline of the Isle of Wight disappeared into the haze, but not all the chaps lining the rail were there to see this last glimpse of England.

The first meal on board ship was appreciated by only a few of us, therefore and exhortations to try the beautiful white, freshly baked bread (what a contrast to the gritty, dry, dirty brown National loaf we had suffered for years), the genuine butter and the strawberry jam with real strawberries, merely produced a rush to the nearest porthole.

After tea, we had a quick lecture on the hammocks, as the rolled-up tarpaulins turned out to be and after a quiet evening sorting out our personal effects and finding a spot to hang the hammocks, we turned in.

They say that hammocks are very comfortable and so they may be when you get the hang of them but, on our mess deck, a lot of people finally gave up trying to get into them without dislodging the blankets or falling out the other side and, instead, they made the best they could of sleeping on the floor, the benches or the table.

I persevered with my hammock, adjusting the strings at each end until it hung right, neither forming a tube around me, nor tipping me out at the slightest movement.

The blankets were the next difficulty. To make a normal bed was no use, as the act of getting in the hammock upset it all.

The correct technique, as I discovered several nights later, was to lay each blanket in turn on the hammock with the surplus width lying all over each side alternately. Then, hanging from the pipes and beams by hands and feet, one carefully manoeuvred over the hammock and gingerly lowered oneself into it, being careful not to dislodge the blankets.

Once safely in, one reached out on each side, again alternately, for the overhanging blankets and pulled them over one until, with the last blanket in place, the result was like a cocoon.

The only way to extract oneself from this cocoon was to reverse the process and any desperate need to go to the toilet in the middle of the night presented more than the usual difficulties, as the only light was a pilot light by the companionway. I found this out on the one occasion I felt the need was justified.

Carefully unwrapping myself from the embraces of my hammock and feeling for a stout pipe above my head, I gathered my strength and raised myself up in a bid to lift my legs over the side. My legs landed in the hammock of the chap next to me, fortunately without waking him up and I had to force a gap between my hammock and his and gently lower myself down – right on to the face of a body lying on the floor below.

Muffled curses rent the thick atmosphere – muffled because my blankets had followed me down and had enveloped the unfortunate fellow. Stopping to apologise and to dump my blankets back in the hammock, I debated whether to go on or not, but it seemed to be as much trouble either way, so I groped my way like a moth towards the pilot light softly illuminating the way out.

But my troubles were not over. I realised too late that the ship was rolling from side to side, quite gently but enough to make me lose my balance, as I tripped headlong over more recumbent forms and banged against a bench on which was yet another body.

Our corner of the mess deck was well and truly awakened by now, on account of the cries and curses that arose and I beat a hasty retreat, accompanied by suggestions that I should tie a knot in it and other coarse suggestions.

It was a relief to gain the security of the stairs and the fresh balmy air of the Bay of Biscay blowing along the upper deck was very welcome after the fug of the mess deck. The ship was swishing along seemingly unattended, with the occasional white wave breaking and thrashing past into the darkness. I found it very soothing, if a bit chilly and lingered for a while until the desire for sleep became irresistible, so I completed the mission and returned to the mess deck.

With the light behind me, it was easier to see where I was going and, creeping carefully and slowly past the once more snoring humanity, I finally found my hammock. Now the problem was getting back into it! It was in the middle of a swaying line of other hammocks all close together and in order to force a space to remake my bedding, I had to push away not one, but four or five others as the boat rolled. My only desire by now was to settle myself down to sleep somehow and I remembered the old tale of the doss house where, for a penny a night, the down-and-outs leaned over a rope stretched across a room and slept like that until the morning, when they were awakened by the rope being cut.

As a solution, the idea did not appeal much. Groping for a handhold above me, I heaved myself up, felt for the hammock with my toes and gingerly lowered myself in. The blankets were heaped anyhow, but I pulled what I could over me and, despite the cold tarpaulin of the hammock against my back, I dropped into a sound sleep.

The Army did most of the chores on board ship and ours were limited to taking turns as Mess Orderlies, which involved cleaning the mess deck each morning and collecting the food from the galley for our own mess table. The Ship's Warrant Officer (SWO) made it plain that he didn't like the R.A.F., but wasn't sure how far his authority extended to us. He gave his own men a lashing with his tongue every time he appeared on the mess deck and they stood blank-faced, taking it all without a murmur.

He usually ranted on about the state of the mess deck, but his words to us were limited to remarking, sarcastically, that he required us to make more effort to smarten it up. He did not expect the R.A.F. to be capable of coming up to Army standards, but our mess deck was like a farmyard.

At this, muted cries of "Baa!" and "Moo!" arose from the rear ranks and the SWO's face changed rapidly from white, to red and then to purple; we waited apprehensively for him to explode.

His waxed moustache quivered with fury for ten long seconds and then, to our surprise, his façade of overbearing omnipotence seemed to crumble. He mumbled something to the effect that we would be reported to our superiors and, turning on his heels, stamped away up the companionway.

The only supervision we had that I knew of was an easy-going sergeant and we heard no more. Our mess deck had, in fact, been spotless. We were not picked on again, but often had to witness, with a feeling of awkward embarrassment, some unfortunate squaddie catch it in the neck.

The ship's Captain, on his inspection rounds, was preceded by the SWO, who was adorned, on these occasions, with a red sash and a bugle. As the SWO came down the companionway onto our mess deck, a few seconds before the Captain, he raised the bugle and, looking like an overweight cherub, blew a long, unmelodious blast, at which we all stood to attention. The Captain, with an expressionless face, paced the deck with an eagle eye, retraced his steps, gave a curt nod to the SWO and then they both left by the companionway to inspect the lower mess decks.

Apart from inspections, meals and mess duties, we had to spend the day on deck. This was not too bad as the weather was fine and the sea was calm and we had plenty of time on our hands.

We received an issue of 'Waverly' cigarettes -- in tins of fifty. After the dried-up Woodbines I usually smoked, these cigarettes were perfection indeed, with sealed-in freshness. To open the tins, there was a blade in the lid which was rotated to cut the seal. Other brands of cigarettes in tins were available for sale, including—Woodbines! But what Woodbines! Full-sized, full-flavoured and fresh and one more contrast with the austerity we had come to accept in Britain.

I found a gusset plate forming a triangular shelf above the deck, between the bridge superstructure and the bulwark on the port side of the ship and there I sat for most of the day in the sunshine, reading a book and smoking luxuriously. It was forbidden to flick the dog-ends overboard, as they might have been blown back through an open porthole and set the ship on fire, but an empty tin made a commodious ashtray.

The Bay of Biscay did not live up to its reputation and the Arundel Castle steamed on its stately way south to Gibraltar, accompanied by soaring seagulls that stayed with us all the way from Southampton, living on the scraps thrown overboard from the galleys.

It occurred to me that the constant wind, which blew along the decks, due mainly to the motion of the ship, might be useful for tethered flight using the Frog 'Tempest', the only model small enough to bring with me. It was impossible to tow it up as a glider, as the decks were too crowded, so we secured strong thread to a wingtip and, with the rudder bent to keep the model pulling outwards, lowered it over the side.

The wind took it and lifted it upwards and outwards until it stalled, when it swooped down again towards the ship's hull, missed it by inches and climbed up again to repeat the manoeuvre. Finding this too hair-raising, I quickly pulled it in and adjusted the elevators. This only made the flight even more hair-raising and a nasty clout against the ship's hull resulted.

U-control (as control-line systems were called in those days) might have been the answer to this, but I had not heard, at that time, of the revolutionary new way of flying models and Jim Walker would have been taken to be some relative of Johnny Walker.

We moved to the stern of the ship and tried towing the model. The turbulence was terrific, judging by the model's antics and, eventually, it proved too much for the thread which snapped, precipitating the Tempest into the boiling wake of the ship. The possibility of stopping the ship and going back for it was lightheartedly discussed, along with other possibilities, like tossing a particularly obnoxious member of the Military Police into the sea to retrieve it. Indeed, one beribboned member of the Army swore that more service policemen had gone missing that way on dark nights during the war, than had been lost in action.

A short digression now to discuss Service Police! They, of all people in the Service, were a race apart, heartily loathed in the main and particularly by those airmen who fell foul of them. Considered to be as thick as two short planks and fit only to catch some poor erk and charge him for having his coat collar up, it was generally believed that they would shop their own grandmother.

It was a puzzle to me, for ten years of my service, how they could train people to act in such a way, but it was so and one has to admit that the Police did their job thoroughly, regardless of unpopularity.

To be fair, I did meet some very decent policemen, but I always had the feeling that they would revert to nature at any time, so it was always as well not to give any opportunity for them to do so.

We woke up one morning to find that the ship was stationary and, rushing to the porthole, we saw that we had arrived at Gibraltar. The Rock looked most impressive.

We were out in the harbour and could not see much of the town itself. We seemed to be the only ship of any consequence there and the place seemed to be quite sleepy.

The only activity came from the occasional launch, ploughing a creamy furrow out to the ship and returning to the shore. We were not sorry when we slowly turned round and headed out to sea again.

10. Passage to India

The ship turned east and entered the Med, as it was invariably called. The temperature was rising daily and the order was given to change into K.D. which produced some laughs as we put on the creased clothes, smelling of musty stores. The tailoring was non-existent and there was some doubt as to whether the trousers were long shorts or short longs. In fact, to avoid the shorts rubbing their calves, many people had to roll them up above their knees.

The Army fellows seemed to be less exuberant than us, many being older and wiser. Talking to us about our respective pay, they were not made any happier to learn that we youngsters were getting a shilling a day more than they were, in spite of their greater length of service.

The days passed and, apart from a fleeting glimpse of Pantellaria and the coast of Tunisia, we saw no land until Port Said appeared over the horizon, apparently sticking out of the sea.

Entering the channel leading to the Suez Canal, the ship passed long breakwaters and dropped anchor in Port Said. Here were a lot more ships, all waiting their turn to negotiate the Canal, as it was not wide enough for two streams of traffic. There was a lot of talk at that time of duplicating the waterway to keep up a continuous stream of ships going through, for it was then, as now, the cross-roads of the world. By 2010, work is due to be completed to increase the depth of the canal, opening it up to fully-laden supertankers with a draught of 22m (72ft).

Back in 1947, Britain controlled the security of the Canal Zone and trade was flourishing, to judge by the shipping queuing up. Across the water of the harbour was a large French liner bound for French Indo-China, that then unhappy land, now called Vietnam. We found this out by calling across to a number of French nurses who were grouped at the stern of the ship. They did not seem to understand English, which was probably just as well, but schoolboy French extracted this information and a fair amount besides.

We were still in Port Said when we turned in and awoke to find ourselves moving along the Canal. It was strange, looking out of the portholes, to see land so close, with lorries moving up and down the road that lay along the bank and to spot the occasional camel. It must have been equally strange to be on land and see large ships moving through the desert.

My impatience to see everything was not helped by being Mess Orderly that day and, by the time I got on deck, we were passing the 1914-1918 War Memorial – in memory of the Canadians, I believe – which was a very striking structure of four columns set together on a plinth. It towered over the Canal and the surrounding desert of white sand.

At intervals along the Canal we passed what looked like landing stages and, occasionally, two-storied buildings with signalling masts in the adjoining grounds. They were probably something to do with the organisation of running the Canal.

Progress along the Canal was quite rapid, although it must have been a tricky job steering the big ship round the slight bends.

We noticed that a rather tatty native boat was hanging in some davits, with an Egyptian sitting in it and we debated amongst ourselves what he was doing there. It seemed to us that he was hitching a lift to Suez and a few aggrieved customers of the Port Said bum-boats felt like getting their own back by tipping him out and making him swim there. Wiser counsels prevailed, but not before the Egyptian gentleman, dressed in a striped galabia and with a red fez on his head, had suffered a few anxious moments. He got a bit agitated, judging by what he said, although he spoke no English.

The bum-boat men of Port Said had spoken English fluently. In fact, a very dark-skinned fellow went one better and announced that his name was Jock McGregor, conducting his business all the while in a broad Scottish accent that could not be faulted.

We had been warned about the bum-boats and the danger of buying thin-skinned fruit and also alerted to the necessity of inspecting the goods before passing down the money.

The bum-boats' technique was to surround the ship, shouting and displaying their wares: watches, lighters, knives, fruit, shawls, rugs, cameras, etc. and pestering the passengers to examine their goods. This was achieved by throwing a plaited line up to the deck, which the passenger would catch and thereby haul up a woven shopping bag with the goods in it. The haggling would commence and the basket might travel up and down several times with each offer and counter-offer, until a deal was concluded.

They were sharp, those bum-boat men and in dealing with Servicemen, preferred to have the money before parting with the goods, which was understandable. Some of the lads were not above receiving the goods and throwing the bag and line down into the water, or even cutting the line attached to the bag with the knife being sold to them and keeping both!

This happened to 'Jock McGregor' and the resulting stream of foul language in his perfect Scottish brogue was so admired that his customer relented and returned the bag, together with the money. British money, even small change, was quite acceptable.

A friend was much taken with a bright, shining, knife with a handle in the shape of a figure and dug deep in his pocket to pay for it. He had owned it for no more than half an hour when he dropped it on the deck and the blade broke off. Overcome with rage, he picked up the pieces and hurled them in the direction of the bum boats.

The ship sailed serenely on, passing Kantara and Ismailia, but I only saw glimpses of these places through portholes and the open part of the lower deck, because of mess duties and mealtimes.

At mealtimes, we – the mess orderlies – had to queue at the galley for each course and carry it in containers to our table and we had an arrangement whereby the next day's mess orderlies helped us out by keeping a place in the queue until we had eaten our course. This meant that the whole meal could be finished more quickly. Some tables took up to an hour and a half to complete a meal and they were rather late latching on to the system. When, finally, they did, the system degenerated to the level of a hectic relay race. There was a mad dash from the galley with the food containers, a quick serve-up at the table, the orderlies would gulp their meals down and return to the queue to relieve the stand-ins before their meals went cold.

Day by day, the pace became more hectic and, rush as we might, being furthest from the galley, our table's usual position in the queue, gradually moved to the rear. The queue would wind along the passage, up the companionway, around the forward hold, up a further companionway and the end of the queue was usually to be found on deck. It became less of a light-hearted physical activity and more a case of the survival of the fittest.

Much to our relief, we learned that the Army were getting off at Port Tufik (or Suez, I never did find out why there are two names), so we made the best of it.

The Arundel Castle stopped in the Bitter Lakes to let another convoy, travelling the other way, through. We lined the rails and had a grandstand view of the procession of ships which passed close by.

After a quick run down the final stretch of the Canal, we entered the Red Sea and, shortly after, anchored off Port Tufik. Here the Army disembarked, including the Ship's Warrant Officer we were gratified to see and none of them looked very cheerful. It was now very hot indeed and the land shimmered in the heat. The airlessness, together with the heat, made the mess deck almost uninhabitable and I wondered if it was possible that the heat could increase. No wonder that the normal trooping season to India was October to March. Why were we being shipped out at this irregular time of year?

Once we got under way again, we stuck tubes, made from cardboard and anything else we could get hold of, out of the portholes to catch the air that blew past with the motion of the ship.

Fresh water for washes and baths was rationed and we were encouraged to take showers using salt water and salt water soap – which was like a block of sandstone and about as useless.

A day or two later, a mountain range appeared to starboard and the ship turned towards it. No information was ever given out about where we were heading that I can recall, so it was a bit like a mystery tour. We did get, via the ship's loudspeaker system, the total nautical miles that the ship travelled each day – over 400 every 24 hours, I think – so that the winners of the ship's sweepstake could claim. I suppose you could say we were certainly moving.

We came closer to the barren white-hot mountains and then we saw a small port, which we headed towards. It must have needed quite good navigation to find it.

The ship nosed into the harbour and a small tug, scruffy and ancient-looking, helped us to turn round and close up to the quay. The secret, if there was one, was now out, for on the stern of the tug, under its name, were the words "PORT SUDAN".

It looked a God-forsaken place, purely a port to serve the great hinterland and nothing to be seen but cranes, warehouses and railway tracks.

Stevedores swarmed aboard and opened the hatches. They were fearsome-looking fellows, genuine 'fuzzy-wuzzies', and the large mound of frizzled hair of the foreman stevedore was skewered by a long stick. This he used to idly scratch his head while he leaned nonchalantly over the edge of the hold, which we could see was opened up like a mineshaft to the very bottom of the ship.

He led the sing-song with which the stevedores punctuated their work and the sound welled up from the bowels of the vessel. "Aah ee yah nah HAH! Kaah ee yah baa HAW!" or something like that, repeated over and over again.

Only he wore something remotely resembling European dress. This was an incredibly stained and decrepit bush jacket, scarcely recognisable as such, but undoubtedly his symbol of authority. The others were all in native dress, much as they must have looked at Omdurman and to see them swarming about the ship gave me an apprehensive feeling.

Competently and quickly, they removed the cargo and replaced all the gratings which covered the hold at each deck level and, finally, the hatch cover.

As soon as they had left the ship, the moorings were slipped and we headed out to sea again, well on our way to India.

In another day or so, we dropped anchor in Aden Harbour. This place looked even less hospitable than Port Sudan, if that was possible, although fragments of the town stretched around the waterside. Altogether, Aden did not look very inviting so it was not really a disappointment not to be able to go ashore, although we were getting a bit bored with shipboard life,

Nevertheless, conditions had been much more pleasant without the Army. Mess deck inspections had been much less of an ordeal although standards had not dropped, as the mess deck was easier to keep clean with practice.

Also, we no longer had a mad rush at mealtimes as we now ate in the Main Dining Saloon in style. The food was prepared by the Union-Castle chefs instead of Army cooks and our digestion improved as a result.

There was more room on deck, too and the voyage seemed more like a pleasure cruise than it had done previously. We even had a free issue of a bottle of beer each day,

We now had meal tickets which were punched at each mealtime and I kept mine in a breast pocket of my bush jacket, together with my paybook.

While in Aden harbour, I was leaning over the rail, not realising that the flap of the pocket was unbuttoned. All at once, the meal ticket and paybook fell out. Luckily, we had been watching the refuelling activities and the lighter was alongside. The ticket and paybook fell on to its dirty deck, missing by a few inches the murky green water lapping around it, where some revolting-looking flat fish sported.

An Aden boatman, with whom we had been trading insults, saw them fall and retrieved them. Realising that he had me in a spot, he then demanded an exorbitant sum for their return. I had little money but would have given him some to get them back. However, I could not have met his bill and he refused to hand them over for less.

Fortunately, the sergeant on duty at the gangway could speak Arabic very forcefully and managed to browbeat him into handing them over, albeit reluctantly. Conscious of my luck, I thereafter always, instinctively, fastened my pockets, preventing further loss and possibly being put on a charge for being improperly dressed.

Refuelling over, the Arundel Castle weighed anchor for the final run to Bombay.

We headed out into the Indian Ocean and, for the first time on the trip, the sky clouded over and the sea had a swell on it. This gave the ship a different motion, which caused some people to be sick. The weather became more humid and the mess deck became unbearable at night, because the portholes had to be kept shut to stop water coming in from the extra large waves. This happened once or twice and it took some effort to get rid of the water that slopped up and down the mess deck with the pitching of the ship.

A bunch of us had an attempt at sleeping on the promenade deck, risking the occasional spray. We were joined by some civilian Indian families who, I had not realised before, were also on the ship.

The fresh air more than made up for the hard deck, but the main snag was that we were awakened at 4.00 a.m. and given five minutes to move before the crew washed down the decks with a large hose. Failure to do so meant retreating before an advancing tide of water along the deck, frantically clutching bedding and hastily gathered up clothes.

A mate and I finally plumped for sleeping in the hold. This was more pleasant than it sounds, for the lower deck had an open section just by the hold and one could look out over the sea on both sides through the open grill surrounding it. At each deck level was an open-grid removable floor, through which one could see the decks below.

The only snag to sleeping here was that if small articles or coins were dropped accidentally, they would fall through, deck by deck, to the bottom. I lost the small change out of my trousers that way.

In the meantime, the weather had deteriorated. Heavy black clouds scudded overhead, although it did not rain and it became very humid and warm with a strong wind. The swell of the ocean became enormous, coming up on the ship's stern from the starboard quarter, if that is the correct terminology.

From the stern, where I spent some time, the scene was very impressive and rather frightening. An enormous wave, stretching from horizon to horizon, would loom over the stern and appear to be about to break over and engulf, the ship. Strangely, it would appear to subside as the stern lifted and the ship, small against the enormous sea, accelerated down the mountainous slope. The wave would overtake us, the crest passing along the length of the ship causing it to lurch awkwardly, before commencing a tail slide down into the next trough. It was probably an optical illusion, due to the motion of the ship, but we seemed to be doing 4 knots forward and 3 knots backward.

Every fourth or fifth wave was even more breathtaking and it seemed to be a miracle that we could survive them, yet, very little water broke over the ship and most of that was spray.

The saloon was in the middle of the ship and the movement was less noticeable there. The main indication was the tea in our mugs, tilting first one way and then the other. Periodically the saloon would go dark as the waves travelled past, submerging the portholes and causing a sensation that we were going under.

Once, at night, we passed another ship, well lit up and apparently smaller than the Arundel Castle. It would disappear for minutes at a time and then reappear, climbing at an incredible angle, rock over into a dive and disappear again. Conditions must have been very uncomfortable for its passengers and crew.

Imperceptibly, the waves became less mountainous and shafts of sunlight broke through the high banks of cloud occasionally. We knew that land was just over the horizon and excitement mounted under the matter-of fact attitude that we tried to adopt.

India, to me, was schoolbook stories of John Company, Rajahs and the North West Frontier, the films of Sabu and the Drum and newspaper reports of famines, riots and floods. History lessons had taught me about Clive of India, the East India Company, the Moguls, the Battle of Plessey and the Indian Mutiny.

Now that we were nearly there, what would it really be like? I neither knew, nor cared much at the time, whether the British Raj was coming to an end or not and I little realised that I was one of the last R.A.F. drafts to British India, perhaps the very last on a traditional troopship.

In telling of my own experience of the R.A.F. in India, I may depart, for a period, from my theme of aviation, but I feel that to portray those historic days as I saw them is important.

11. Getting my Knees Brown

Late one evening, land appeared and several tall buildings soon became prominent on the skyline. For the last time, we slung our hammocks and slept. Early next morning we awoke to find that the ship was moored at the quayside in busy Bombay Harbour.

After a quick breakfast, we all filed down into the deep hold to collect our two-ringed kitbags and then to the armoury to collect our rifles.

At the appointed hour, on the 4th of July 1947, we lined up on deck for roll call and then filed down the gangplank on to the quay. With a last look at the rust-streaked, lilac-painted hull that had been our home for seventeen days, we struggled with our kit some two hundred yards across railway tracks to the waiting lorries.

We had been greeted by a horde of Indians, who offered to carry our kit – for money, of course. One or two men, who still had money to throw around, took up the offers, for it was no easy job on one's own, but they were brusquely ordered to keep on carrying their kit themselves. The coolies, as they were called, became rather peeved and demanded payment for having shouldered their burdens. The airmen paid up, for the sake of peace and plodded on,

We climbed on to the lorries, the tailboards were raised and off we went through the streets of Bombay. The lorries were covered and not much could be seen over the tailboards. We travelled north for several miles and finally stopped at a pleasant seaside suburb, outside some long, low, bungalow-type billets.

We climbed down and were ushered into the nearest billets. These were shady, cool and whitewashed, with electric fans quietly flicking round. This was Worli transit camp, through which all R.A.F. personnel came to and left, India.

I bagged a bed next to those of my 'oppos' by dumping my kit on it and trooped out with the rest, to deposit my rifle in the armoury across the road. This building had around it the only barbed wire that I saw at Worli.

The dining hall, at which we arrived later for lunch, was further up on the same side of the road as the armoury. The camp staff insisted on calling lunch "tiffin" and in fact their English was liberally mixed with a lot of words I couldn't understand.

Then it was time for the ritual of 'arriving'; that is, taking a piece of paper around all the various departments or sections, sick quarters, pay accounts, stores, Station Headquarters, etc. We were checked for having the correct jabs and vaccinations and promised some pay in a day or two. It gave us a chance to get to know our way around and it was quite one of the most unusual R.A.F. stations that I had ever seen.

Along the sea front were some large and imposing houses, one of which was S.H.Q.; another was Station Sick Quarters and I think yet another was the Officers' Mess. The sea front had a high wall, the other side of which was a very rocky beach, which we were ordered not to go on. Peering over the wall, we could see that it was not very inviting and the sight of a large and gaily coloured lizard did not make it more tempting. India has the only poisonous lizards in the world and I have often wondered if that was one of them.

The coast road ran north, past the houses with the sea on the left, with another road forking off to the right behind the houses. Along this road on the left were our billets, strung continuously up the rising ground, with access from the road via stepped paths.

On the right were the cookhouse, armoury and some other buildings. At the road junction was a small conglomeration of shanties, known as Tin Town. There was no clearly defined boundary to the camp and Indians walked unhindered through it.

In the camp were many time-expired men waiting to be repatriated to the U.K. in the *Arundel Castle* and they seemed to be very much a breed apart. They looked very brown and lean and their speech was quite incomprehensible, being well spiced with strange slang and Hindustani words. To them we were 'Moon men', on account of our white faces and knees; hence the expression "Get your knees brown!" meaning, "Get some service in!"

I saw two airmen, squatting in true Indian fashion, on the low, wide windowsill of a billet further up the road. One had an organ, of a type common in India, being a small oblong box with a keyboard along the front and a bellows along the back. It was played with one hand and the other hand operated the bellows.

As I watched, they commenced to play the organ and also to sing some Indian music, which they did extremely well. The Indians walking by stopped to listen and their appreciation was such that they joined in the singing too and to my astonishment, in no time at all, they were swaying and singing up and down the road.

For a quarter of an hour, the two airmen played encores and requests and, when their performance was finally over, their audience responded with rousing applause!

Next day, true to their promise, we received our pay or, more precisely, R20 of it. Rupees twenty, as it was quaintly called by some, or twenty chips, as it was irreverently called by others, was enough, they said, to squander in Tin Town.

Straight down to Tin Town we went and, sure enough, we could have spent it all in ten minutes. Tin Town consisted mainly of stalls selling photographs of all subjects (pornographic, riots, funerals, ships, film stars, etc.), cameras, lighters, watches, silks, ornaments, jewellery, carved objects in wood and ivory, etc.

Resolving to save most of my money for the rest of the week we would be at Worli, I nevertheless had a hard time resisting temptation.

We were told of a standing invitation for us servicemen to visit Breach Kandy, which was a Club with its own lido further down the coast, nearer to Bombay. It had an irregularly shaped outdoor swimming pool, an indoor pool and clubhouse, well-kept gardens with lots of palm trees and around the outdoor pool were tables and chairs with gaily-coloured sunshades. We found the place by some devious route one afternoon and enjoyed ourselves very much.

Encouraged by this little jaunt and finding that the parts of Bombay that we had seen so far had been very attractive with good wide roads, smart blocks of flats and plenty of palm trees, we looked forward to visiting the city centre. The weather was very humid, with the sun shining fitfully from a sky full of lowering clouds.

The monsoon was due any day and I believe there was a sweepstake in Bombay based on the time that it officially started. However, it kept dry for the week that we were there.

We walked to Maliksmee Station to catch the train to Bombay. To see trains coming and going with people hanging out all over them, even standing on the running boards, was a revelation.

Fortunately, we weren't required to do that. We bought second-class tickets, which got us slatted wooden seats, so the compartments with upholstered seats must have been for first-class passengers.

We had asked for tickets to the centre of Bombay, so when the booking clerk gave us tickets to Bombay Central Station, we took them, although he did ask if it wasn't Churchgate we wanted. Feeling confident, we said "No!"

In due course, the train rolled into Bombay Central Station, huge, dark and deserted; we gave up our tickets and strolled out into the sunlit city. It didn't look like the European quarter at all, in fact it was quite obvious that it wasn't. It was very sleazy with small stalls in the streets and large tenement buildings, with string beds, called 'charpoys' hanging from windows and balconies. There was a lot of litter lying around.

We decided to ask our way, but nobody could understand us. Finally, we found a policeman dressed in K.D. tunic and shorts, turban and chaplis (sandals) and carrying a lathi (a stout stick). He seemed to size up the situation, although he, too, spoke no English. Indicating a nearby bus stop, he said "Churchgate" several times, so we nodded and waited for the next bus. When the bus arrived, we chanted "Churchgate?" to the conductor, who nodded and we piled aboard.

The bus was a double-decker of typically British appearance, so we took our seats on the top deck and started to enjoy the journey, which took us for miles around the suburbs of Bombay for only a few annas each. We had such an interminable journey that we began to think that we had gone past the stop we wanted, but every time the conductor came upstairs, he motioned us to remain seated.

Finally, he bounded up the stairs, beaming and called out "Churchgate!" I hope that we gave him a tip. I can't remember, but he may have refused it anyway. I found that many Indians were like that, particularly those whose livelihood did not depend on serving or otherwise attending to the needs of the British and they usually refused any such gratuity with great dignity, saying that they were happy to be of assistance.

Arriving, at last, at Churchgate, we found it to be rather a letdown. There were many impressive offices, banks, hotels, flats and public buildings, but the restaurants and bars were rather expensive to fellows of our means. (At an exchange rate of thirteen rupees and four annas to the pound, we had only been paid the equivalent of thirty bob and that was fast dwindling).

The feature of Churchgate that I disliked most was the beggars. Some were exceptionally hideous and I learned later that, in India, begging was part of the caste system. In other words, a beggar was born into the job and the more he was deformed, naturally, accidentally, or deliberately by his parents, the better head start he had over the other beggars competing for 'baksheesh'. It took a strong-willed, hard man to walk unconcernedly past these wretched specimens of humanity uttering their piteous cries.

Others – tongawallahs and various shady characters – drawn by our 'new arrival' appearance, plied us with offers of the services of their sisters, or the ladies of Grant Road. We politely refused their blandishments, retreated into a large circular-shaped restaurant and ordered a beer and snack for each of us. The price was exorbitant, so we made the meal last until we were virtually shown the door. It was rather a posh place and I think our presence was thought to lower the tone of it.

Finally, we wended our way to Churchgate Station and bought our tickets for the return journey to Maliksmee. By this time it was dark and the smoke from thousands of little cooking fires and the smells of a thousand different things, played like an orchestra on our nostrils. Once in the dimly lit and uncomfortable compartment on the train, we shared our remaining cigarettes and willed the train to start, which it did with commendable promptitude.

Arriving at Maliksmee still left a few miles to travel to get to Worli and we elected to walk despite the attentions of a driver of a horse-drawn victoria. This chap followed us patiently, badgering us all the while about the dangers of loose-wallahs setting upon us and such-like probabilities. Finally, he played his trump card and told us that there was a riot going on ahead.

As his price had been steadily dropping and we had been getting more tired the further we went, we were finally persuaded that a ride in his victoria had a lot to recommend it. A quick whip-round produced enough for the fare and we leapt aboard the ancient carriage. The driver whipped his tired and skinny horse into a heartening gallop, while anxious heads peered at the dimly-lit road ahead.

There was neither sight nor sound of a riot, of course, but we were not sorry to roll back to our billets in style and comfort, though it had cost us the last of our money.

The days ticked by and I was beginning to enjoy the lazy life; there were no fatigues or duties, apart from the odd roll call to make sure none of us were missing in the fleshpots of teeming Bombay.

It is always disconcerting to be winkled out of comfortable circumstances, any time now I could expect to have to put my training to good use and earn my keep. I had now been in the Royal Air Force for over a year and in all that time, I had done nothing that the long-suffering taxpayers back home might have appreciated. However, I was no longer a burden on them, as we were now in the pay of the Government of India.

On the evening of the sixth day, our names were called out on the parade held on the road outside the billets. We were told to fill our water bottles and eat a light breakfast, or none at all if we were prone to airsickness, for in the morning we would be flown to R.A.F. Drigh Road, near Karachi. What a strange name, we thought and we had a look at a map somebody had brought with him.

Bright and early we were up, water bottles filled and lightly breakfasted as instructed and on our way to Santa Cruz Airport by blue-grey Bedford buses. There, awaiting our arrival, were several drab-green Dakotas. The organisation was very good and, with little delay, we were each handed a packet of 'K' rations as we boarded our aircraft.

These Dakotas belonged to a famous squadron – No 31 – that was well known all over the Indian sub-continent and had done valuable work in Burma during the war, I was told. The only markings on the aircraft, apart from the wartime roundels and serial numbers, were the individual letters underlined with a bar, both in white, I think.

Being the aerial equivalent of cattle trucks, there were no concessions to comfort. We scrambled up the short ladder hooked on to the edge of the floor at the doorway and up the steep smooth floor of the interior to the front, where our kitbags were stacked and lashed down to swivel eyes, located at various points and set in the floor.

The seats were down each side, rather like railway luggage racks and were no more than collapsible webbing affairs, supported by some dural tubes. I grabbed a portion of seat next to a window and, together with the others, sat awkwardly, due to the slope, waiting for takeoff.

For the few minutes left, I looked around me at the interior of the Dakota. It was a leftover from the war and probably a veteran of the Chindit airdrops and the Hump. There was a cable running down the middle of the cabin, overhead, for paratroops to clip their parachutes release lines to and two lights by the doors labelled 'Ready' and 'Drop'.

The fuselage structure of formers and stringers was unadorned by any panelling and it looked rather delicate. The skinning was inscribed in a regular pattern with the material trade name and a number and appeared to be over-sprayed with a translucent green lacquer.

Although the construction was starkly utilitarian, looking at it with my professional eye, I could see from a close examination of the riveting and the various members that it was of a very high standard indeed.

The rectangular windows each had a small hole about two or three inches in diameter and fitted with a rubber ring like a large grommet, presumably for ventilation or to poke a rifle through for defence.

Then the door was closed and fastened and the engines started. Each engine started with a rattle and a bang or two and picked up with a sound like a dustbin being filled with tin cans. Blue-grey smoke blew back in the slipstream as the plane shook tremulously, until the engines ran smoothly and the smoke disappeared.

Minutes later, we were speeding down the runway and climbing laboriously up into the cloud-laden sky, setting course for Karachi.

It was a tedious journey and chilly too! The holes in the windows were fine on the ground but, in the air at seven or eight thousand feet, they let in a draught every time the pilot moved the rudder. This was no joke when one was wearing K.D. and many attempts were made to bung up the holes with the empty tins of bacon and eggs from the 'K' rations. The tins were just too small and, invariably, they were sucked out and went rattling down the side of the fuselage, probably causing dents in the tailplane on the way.

Those people who decided to walk about and get warm that way were soon discouraged by an irate crew member, who poked his head around the door to the flight-deck and yelled at us to sit down and keep still, because the pilot was getting fed up with having to adjust the trim of the aircraft.

The constant roar of the engines discouraged conversations, so we watched through the windows as best we could, by twisting in our seats, as the dusty land of India edged out from under the wing.

Once we flew over a large town with a rectangular street plan, which somebody thought was Baroda.

Gradually, the cultivated and populated areas became sparser and finally were left behind us as the aircraft flew, with unflagging determination, onward across an extremely large and featureless desert. I could not see out of the other side of the aircraft, but the view was probably of the Indian Ocean, for long fingers of water began to appear under the wing, cutting the desert into a complicated pattern of mudflats.

There was no vegetation of any sort and I was beginning to think that nobody could possibly live there, when a very small fishing village came into sight. It was, however, the only one that I saw and a more god-forsaken spot I could not imagine.

We read books or magazines and dozed uncomfortably until a change in the note of the engine roar indicated that we were near our destination.

The desert looked much the same, but the water had retreated and in its place were sporadic rashes of buildings, some large, some small, some in lines and some in huddled disorganisation, with ribbons of roads connecting them and tracks in the sand leading nowhere in particular.

One building was much larger than the others and, with some amazement, I saw that it was similar to the two airship hangars at Cardington. It was, in fact, the hangar erected at Karachi Airport to house the R 101 for when it completed its first major voyage to India which, instead, terminated tragically at Beauvais in Northern France.

Unused as an airship hangar, it had stood for seventeen years and still stands, I expect, as a monument to the propensity of British Governments to invest large sums of public money on white elephants that fail to fly profitably for one reason or another – Brabazon, Princess, TSR 2, to name but three.

The setting sun was bathing the bare and inhospitable-looking landscape with a reddish glow, as we landed and taxied up to a large concrete dispersal area at the nearby airfield of R.A.F. Drigh Road.

Darkness came quickly as we wended our way, once again struggling with our kit, to some remote transit bungalow situated in one of the 'lines' of bungalows strung out across the desert. There were no roads away from the Technical Area and in the dark we took most of the evening getting bedding and finding the toilet facilities.

The bedding arrangements looked rather rudimentary, the bed itself – known as a charpoy – being nothing more than a wooden frame on four legs with a woven string mesh stretched across it, tensioned at the foot by a cord lacing. Over this was laid a mat-like covering, called a dhurri, followed by a blanket, two sheets and another blanket on top if required. The pillow was round and so hard that it was more comfortable to sleep without it. As you might imagine, the bed was extremely hard and uncomfortable altogether and if an airman stayed in bed too long, he was likely to be covered with 'diamond rash'.

To cover the subject of charpoys in its entirety, in the ensuing years we got used to sleeping on them, so much so that when I eventually slept on a mattress again, it was many weeks later before I could expect to get a goodnight's sleep.

Charpoys frequently became infested with bed bugs and every few weeks a coolie came round the billets with a tank of D.D.T. strapped to his back. The tank had a pump arrangement, similar to a toilet chain over his shoulder, which he pulled with one hand as he sprayed the charpoys, stood out on the verandah, with the other. Unfortunately, the D.D.T. usually failed to kill the bugs, but it certainly made them very naggy!

For the next few days we would be bitten from head to foot until their usual homes in the crevices between the strings became habitable once more. They normally never bit me and I preferred peaceful coexistence, so I made sure that the bearer saw to it that my bed was left unsprayed, although this was against all the regulations. When the bugs multiplied to the point of overcrowding – I don't know what they lived on – dropping the bed about three feet on to the concrete floor would dislodge most of them very effectively.

But this was in the future, when I had become inured to the wild life of India. To moon-men like us, the lessons we had drummed into us about not eating thin-skinned fruit, drinking only boiled water, etc, were gospel to be obeyed to the letter and all animal life, from microbes to camels, was suspect. The old hands said that a bite from a camel could give you syphilis.

This feeling was reinforced when we went round with our arrival chits next day. Waiting in the Sick Quarters to be attended to, we relieved the tedium by inspecting the various specimens preserved in jars of alcohol that were displayed around the room.

There were scorpions, snakes, lizards, insects and other nasty-looking exhibits – all of a dangerous nature – and I became rather apprehensive about the chances of surviving my tour.

R.A.F. Drigh Road had a Maintenance Unit – No. 320 – to which we were posted. It was a large unit and I never discovered the full extent of the work carried on there. Parked on the other side of the large apron were some Vultee Vengeances left over from the war. There were some Tempest IIs in the hangar adjacent to the one I worked in and various Spitfires were dotted around.

Half a dozen of us were placed in the charge of an L.A.C. rigger, who seemed to be the only person who knew what needed doing or, indeed, how to do it.

We were expected to dismantle Spitfire PR XIXs and prepare them for packing and despatch back to the U.K., apparently. One of these, parked outside, was PM 545, an ex-34 Squadron aircraft, looking rather shabby in spite of its silver finish with matt black anti-dazzle in front of the windscreen and a squadron badge on the fin. It was very dusty after standing there for a week or two, exposed to the desert winds.

We wheeled a selected Spitfire into the hangar, inhibited the engine and removed the five-bladed propeller. The aircraft was then jacked up and trestled and the undercarriage retracted.

Now came the laborious bit, for the wings had to be taken off, or rather, pulled off. The Spitfire main spar consisted of a rectangular hollow section tube, top and bottom, into each of which were telescoped several progressively smaller section tubes. In this way, the strength was built up at the root end.

The fuselage root fittings, on each side, consisted of a plate each side of the top and bottom spars, through which fitted bolts passed. The top and bottom spars were thus clamped between the plates. I seem to remember there were three bolts in the top spar and four in the bottom. Using multiple bolts meant that the size could be kept small, so that the holes spaced along each spar would not unduly weaken it. These bolts proved to be far from easy to remove.

A single, smaller bolt nearer the trailing edge took care of the backward and twisting loads of the wing on the fuselage.

Theoretically, there should have been little twisting load because of the 'D' spar of the mainplane formed by the thick skin of the leading edge back to the hollow sections, top and bottom and the web between. The root fitting did not have this stiffness because there was a gap between wing and fuselage, normally covered over by fairing panels, but the one small bolt was enough to take care of this.

With the bolts removed, the wing had to be carefully manhandled outwards. It was no mean weight to just hold level, without having to pull as well, even for six men.

We were supposed to have some Sikh airmen of the Royal Indian Air Force working with us, but they spent most of their time making rings from dural and Perspex.

They were well built, impressive-looking men, unsmiling and somewhat truculent, I sensed, because of impending Independence. I would have left them to get on with their pastimes, but not our suntanned, skinny L.A.C.

"Hey, Singh!" he would bellow, "Put those trinkets down and give us a hand here!"

"You can make as many rings as you like, when we are on the boat," he encouraged them and, like sullen children, they obediently ambled over and took the weight of the wing.

I once mentioned to him that I would have left them alone for fear that they turned nasty, but he told me that the Sikhs themselves had their worries, for they were, at present, in the heart of what would be a new alien country – Pakistan would be its name – and they did not know what their future would be. It seemed certain that if they were still at Drigh Road when Independence came to Pakistan, their very lives would be in danger.

I shook my head in amazement at the goings-on in this strange land and consoled myself that we would all have left India in a month or two.

Plate 4 Vickers Supermarine Spitfire PR XIX PM 545

Had I known what the future would hold, I would have been more concerned, not just for myself, but for the luckless people of India, whom I came to like very much indeed.

We were moved to permanent billets in a line of stone-built bungalows with cool verandahs and red tiled roofs. My own billet had two bearers, Ramzan and Johnny, who attended to our needs and to whom we paid two rupees a fortnight out of our own pockets.

They made our beds, fetched our cigarettes, laid out our clean K.D. and sent our dirty clothes to the dhobi-wallah who washed and starched them. This was a routine service paid for by the R.A.F. and it took a couple of days to get them back. The results were not always satisfactory and most people patronised the 'flying dhobi' which meant that we had to pay, but our clothes came back the same day, beautifully washed, starched and pressed. We merely told the bearer which we wanted and it was done.

The K.D. was marked with an individual 'dhobi-mark' in ink by the bearer. This ensured that we would get our own garments back from the dhobi-wallah. Mine was a diagonal cross with a dot in each corner.

The bearers took charge of our K.D. as soon as we stripped off after work for a shower, going through the pockets to remove everything and putting all that was needed in the pockets of our fresh K.D, laid out on our beds. They would refill cigarette cases from the tins of 50s kept in our lockers and the lighters too if necessary.

Shoes were expertly cleaned and socks darned, by those willing chaps. There was a lot of competition to become a bearer, but good bearers like ours had to be treated with consideration, or they would be enticed away by another billet that was fed up with mediocre service.

It took some getting used to, having somebody to attend to your every need after being used to doing it all yourself and some chaps even had to argue with the bearer in order to be able to attend to their own chores.

There were no extra charges by the bearers, who seemed to be quite put out if a British Other Rank (B.O.R.) did them out of a job by, for example, cleaning his own shoes.

Sooner or later, we all succumbed to the system established by previous generations of the British in India. Today, British people seem to be almost ashamed that this 'exploitation' of Indians in their own country was an accepted thing.

I would say in justification that it was an expense that a low-paid airman could ill afford if he had a family or dependants to support and no mean sacrifice on his part in order that an Indian man and his family might have comparative security and the independence of a steady income.

It was a purely business arrangement between a number of airmen in a billet and the bearer, but if the arrangement was mutually satisfactory, my experience was that usually the bearer became more of a friend, reliable, loyal and honest.

The charwallah came round the billets regularly in the afternoons and evenings, dispensing char and wads from an urn with a padlocked lid and a battered tin trunk. These two containers were carried around suspended from the ends of a pole balanced over the charwallah's shoulder.

Many were the arguments that we had with the charwallah over the level of the tea in our tin mugs, for which he charged two annas. Some said that the level should be the same distance from the rim of the mug as the width of a two annas coin, which was of a rounded square shape. Certainly, my mug was never filled to that degree and as we drank several cups a day of the brew, it worked out to be rather expensive.

There was no N.A.A.F.I. in India for some reason and all such services as the canteen, the tailor's shop, the watchmaker's shop and the barber's shop, were supplied and controlled by a contractor.

He was usually a mysterious figure in the background, (you could never get hold of him to lodge a complaint, not that he would have taken much notice of an AC 2), but he had a firm grip on the financial side and it was obvious that he was not running a charity.

Some contractors even made their own lemonade and a most expensive way of drinking flavoured tap water, with the barest minimum of fizz, it usually turned out to be. Beer cost little more, but was a dear commodity for all that. Drinking as a pastime left little money for anything else.

I again considered the possibilities of aeromodelling, but at Drigh Road they were not good. There was no model club that I could discover and no model shop in Karachi, a city I visited a couple of times.

I did find an emporium which sold aircraft timber and plywood however and, as we had every afternoon and evening free, I spent a lot of time planning a light aircraft based on the B.A.C. Drone. This was not as easy as I had thought and as it seemed that we would be leaving Drigh Road sooner than originally expected, I shelved the idea.

Further down, between the lines of bungalows, was the fuselage of a scrapped Mosquito and somebody, knowing my desire to get my hands on some balsa, suggested that the Mosquito might be a source of supply. Armed with a saw and a knife, we attacked the plywood sheath, stripping it off with difficulty.

Underneath was the balsa, laid in staggered blocks about ¾" thick, 2" wide and 2'-0" long, to the best of my memory. Most of the blocks were damaged in the process of prising them out, but enough was obtained to start the construction of a glider based on the Three-Footer.

The wood was extremely coarse and hard and its light weight was the only thing that I could recognise as being that of balsa. It was more fibrous and of a darker colour than I expected and very difficult to cut with the clasp knife that the R.A.F. had kindly provided me with, (it was the only time that I actually used it).

Having laboriously carved the components, I had to find some sort of adhesive and thick red dope was the nearest to cement that I could find. This proved to be woefully weak, the model disintegrating at the slightest opportunity, but the problem was solved by doping fabric strips of aircraft linen over the joints, although the wings flapped a bit after a time.

It did not fly well, mainly because of its weight and after some futile perseverance, it followed the parent fuselage on to the scrap heap.

Drigh Road could boast of an indoor swimming pool, dimly lit, narrow and shallow too, as I found out when I dived in and hit the bottom, but it was the best amenity there was and very popular at that time of year.

The monsoon did not break in Sind and the weather was very hot and sticky. During the day, the wind blew grey scudding clouds north across the desert and the sun shone only when the wind dropped in the evening and at dawn, but it never rained. Some years it never rained at all, apparently and I wondered at the size of the monsoon ditches that straddled the camp and why they should be necessary.

Discipline was in evidence at Drigh Road, probably due to the fact that only a year had passed since a strike at various Maintenance Units in India including, I understand, Drigh Road. Some had described it as a mutiny, but it was really just a well-organised strike to protest at the slow rate of repatriation to the U.K. after the war.

One result was our being sent out to India, even though the days of the British Raj were numbered, so that repatriation of the old hands could be speeded up.

We paraded early each morning, for an hour or more and were inspected rigorously. It was then that I found out what a pugree was. Around each of the bush hats that we all wore should have been a khaki band with several folded layers and with a red, white and blue ribbon on one side. Most people went to the camp tailor (dhurzi- wallah) and had them made up at their own expense, but having one listed on my deficiency chit made me reluctant to spend my own money. The stores had none, so I went on parade without one.

The Station Warrant Officer eyed me severely, as being improperly dressed, but my chit worked like a charm and I was sent off the parade and told to keep out of sight until it was over.

Now that Independence for India was due in a few weeks, a slight feeling of edginess became apparent on the Station and many thought that the Karachi mob, freed from British rule, would get out of hand and Drigh Road would be attacked. The possibility did not seem to be very real to me, after all, one could walk unmolested around Saddar, the European shopping district. "Ah, yes," said the old hands, "but that's only a small part of Karachi. You wouldn't walk unmolested in some other parts of the city."

The official population of Karachi at that time was around 250,000 so I realised that I had scarcely penetrated the outskirts on my occasional trips out of the camp, across the railway line to board an ancient single-decker bus that bounced its way down the narrow sand-strewn road that led across the desert to the cantonment and Saddar.

Here there were single-decker motorised trams and crowded shops and some British servicemen's wives haggling over fruit, or rolls of cloth, in what seemed to me to be fluent Urdu.

There were many fine buildings: Frere Hall, the Union Jack Club with an outdoor swimming pool, the Y.M.C.A., the Locomotive Institute, the Roman Catholic Church and the Church of Scotland, to name but a few.

Beyond this, the city extended further south and west. In many ways Saddar was like a pleasant provincial town with a luxurious cinema, the Paradise, which had double seats for courting couples at the back.

Certainly, the 'powers that were' thought it a possibility that we would be attacked, so we were issued with rifles, but no ammo, for night manoeuvres; for it was at night that an attack would most likely occur.

Off we trudged along the monsoon ditches out into the dark desert. Stumbling and cursing our way across the rough ground, strange animals, reptiles and insects watched us approaching and scurried away. I took care not to fall over and perhaps put my hand on a scorpion or silver krait.

It was on account of these creatures that we wore our mosquito boots, which were like shoes with khaki canvas extensions up past the ankles, into which the bottoms of our slacks were stuffed, presumably to stop mosquitoes biting our ankles.

The Sergeant leading us had soon had enough of this carry-on and, at the earliest moment that he could reasonably do so, he led us back to the camp and the armoury. Arriving back at our billets, our hard string charpoys had never seemed so inviting.

12. Last Days of the British Raj

I was settling nicely into the routine at Drigh Road, with little to complain about, even at work, unless it was the difficulty of taking off the tail units of the Spitfires. Doing this necessitated disconnecting the control cables and padding the sharp edges of the fuselage structure with sacking. You then had to crawl into the radio compartment and work your way, head first, down the fuselage to the joint which consisted of two bulkheads bolted together with dozens of 2 B.A. bolts and nuts.

My arms ached after undoing the first half dozen bolts with Terry spanners, my legs developed cramp and the sweat dripped off my body, into the bottom of the fuselage, with monotonous rhythm. There must have been a big demand for small people during the war for this sort of job. I was glad that I had only to undo the bolts, for it would have been much more arduous to tighten them up properly.

I emerged from the radio compartment one day to be told, by somebody, to hand in my toolbox to stores and to collect my clearance chit. I was posted once more.

"Where to?" I asked,
"Chakeri," he said.
"Where's that?" I asked.
"You'll find out tomorrow, when you get there!" he rejoined, hiding his ignorance neatly. And he went on his way, seeking out the chosen, named on his list.

Feeling slightly unwanted and a little envious of the rest of our gang left to pursue their peaceful existence, I complied with the instruction and did the rounds, rushing about and queuing with dozens of others for the required signatures at the various sections. It was reassuring to find that several of my mates from Worli were included in the draft.

Chakeri was in the United Provinces, near Cawnpore, we were told and the name rang an ominous bell with me.

"Remember Cawnpore!" was a saying I recalled, but I couldn't remember what it was I should remember about Cawnpore.

The thought of going so far up-country away from the coast, at what was obviously going to be a turbulent time, did not appeal much either at first, but once I got used to the idea, I felt more excited at the prospect.

At the appointed time early next morning, we stood on the big dispersal apron with all our kit, waiting for our airlift which turned out to be the same Dakotas that brought us from Worli. They had to fly in from some other airfield, probably Mauripur on the other side of Karachi.

This Dakota squadron – one of two left in India, I believe – seemed to serve the purpose of providing an aerial bus service for the R.A.F., for they landed without fuss, taxied around the apron at a fast pace, looking like a flock of huge mouldy-coloured crows and parked neatly in line abreast, without any marshalling.

We clambered aboard and stacked our kit with increased competence at the front of the cabin. Shortly after, the steps were unhooked from the doorway and stowed. With a clatter and a shake, each engine burst into life and soon we were climbing up over the Sind desert with the hangars and buildings of Drigh Road receding behind us. They seemed to be the last outposts of civilisation on the edge of a great barren wilderness.

Inexorably, the Dakota gained height and entered into big banks of cumulus clouds, which grew thicker and more majestic the further we went. The air became more turbulent until it seemed that we were bouncing off solid cloud, or sliding down cavernous valleys with fantastic overhanging ivory towers on all sides, until we plunged with heart-stopping suddenness into a dark grey and very cold world, where even the wings dissolved into the murk.

After an interminable time we would plunge out into brilliant daylight with our shadow chasing across adjacent cloud banks, straining to keep up with us. Little could be seen of the ground during the flight, but occasionally we would cross a gap of clear air which reached down to the ground like a celestial mineshaft, at the bottom of which could be discerned the sodden land of India. Once, I looked out, just as we came out of a cloud, into an almost perfectly formed shaft, with smooth sides all the way down and, for a moment, I had a real feeling of vertigo.

We had brought no pre-packed meals with us this time and, after two or three hours of plunging, wallowing flight, we were getting tired and hungry. It was, therefore, a relief when the constant drone or roar (depending on how one's ears popped) of the engine changed note; we knew that this part of the journey was nearly over.

We landed at Palam, the international airport of New Delhi and were soon enjoying tiffin in a cool, verandah-lined dining hall. The food was strange but nice, which was just as well, as it was a case of take it or leave it.

Afterwards, we strolled back to the dispersal, where our Dakotas were parked and watched the airport movements. An Avro York G-AGOE of B.O.A.C. with the name "Medway" taxied past, resplendent in a pristine silver finish with the Speedbird motif on the side of the fuselage to the rear of the cockpit window.

To my mind, for all that the Avro York was a makeshift transport adapted from the Lancaster, it looked a real airliner with its bulky slab-sided fuselage, four engines and triple fins.

Behind the inclined rows of porthole-like windows could be seen its passengers, reclining in luxurious armchairs with big headrests and I fleetingly wondered what sort of job it was that you had to have to warrant that style of travel.

Between the showers, it was getting uncomfortably hot on the dispersal, under the midday sun. We were not sorry when the aircrew returned to the aircraft and we filed aboard. Once the doors were shut, it rapidly became unbearably hot inside the bare metal of the fuselage and we became saturated with sweat. I reached for my water bottle, only to find that the water was vile with rust. As I had resisted the temptation to drink a lot at lunch – sorry, tiffin – not knowing how long the journey might take and conscious that it was not practical to stop the plane and nip behind the nearest cumulus, I realised it was a bit late in the day to find that out!

Had I been marching across country, as in days gone by, instead of travelling by this new-fangled transport, the result would have been more serious. As it was, I sat tight and, after making a mental note to get the bottle changed, passed the time by dozing as best I could. The webbing seats became more and more uncomfortable and several chaps lay down on the metal floor and suffered there for a change.

Fortunately, this leg of the journey was shorter and we descended through the disturbed air after an hour or two, touching down on the drenched runway at 322 M.U. R.A.F. Chakeri.

I had a distinct feeling that we weren't wanted at Chakeri, for by the time we were fed and issued with bedding and billets, it was dusk and there was little else to do but turn in.

It was the same next day. Early in the morning everybody in the billet got up, washed and dressed and disappeared, except for three of our party and a couple of recumbent figures who had come off duty. The rest of our contingent were scattered among the billets of the camp, known as N4 Site, wherever there were spare beds. Ours was the cooks' billet and they did not seem very enthusiastic about our presence in it.

After an indifferent breakfast, we gathered together like sheep, lost without somebody to bark at our heels and gradually the idea percolated through to us that we should report to S.H.Q. for our arrival chits. Enquiry produced the information that S.H.Q. was somewhere to the East along a country road.

'Arriving' at any R.A.F. station usually took the form of an obstacle race when a number of people were involved. The person who started out first could be attended to first at the various ports of call. One could visit most of them in any order, but some had to be done in order of precedence. For example, Stores might insist that the Pay Accounts signature be obtained first. It could well be, however, that on confronting Pay Accounts with the chit, they would maintain that the Stores must sign first.

All the various establishments of the Station seemed to be set as far apart as possible from each other, connected by narrow roads running between corn fields and other scenes of agricultural activity. Signposts were infrequent and none of us knew our way about, so we split up and headed in various directions. Some would hit lucky and be first in a queue and others would get lost and have to retrace their steps to find themselves at the end.

If you could keep ahead of the pack by using your wits and perhaps by laying a false trail, you could be home and dry by lunchtime, but if you hit too many queues, you would finish, tired and wet, at tea-time. It rained more in the afternoon at Chakeri.

The stock-in-trade at R.A.F. Chakeri was mainly the renovation of wartime Dakotas stored in the exceptionally long hangars which stood, in two rows of four, adjacent to the airfield.

During the war years, I understood, this Maintenance Unit was the largest in India and was a major supply base for the war in Burma and South-East Asia. Now it was quite a small R.A.F. unit that shared the Station with the Royal Indian Air Force.

Because the date for Independence had been brought forward, the work of getting the Dakotas out had to be speeded up and so they sent for us!

Down at the hangars, next day, we were distributed among the different gangs working on the various Dakotas lined up for servicing. The gang that I was allocated to appeared to be a conscientious bunch of lads. Sgt. Taylor was in charge and I thought he wasn't quite sure what to do with me. His team was more or less complete and to educate me into the job would take valuable time and disrupt the organised routine required to get the aircraft out. My sole experience to date had been pulling aircraft apart, hardly a recommendation for the job of putting them together!

So I got the run-around jobs. I would fetch oil, fabric strip, dope, Bostik and anything else needed. I stuck rubber strip on to the flaps so that they wouldn't chafe the wing when 'UP', scrounged around for control locks for elevators, rudder and ailerons and, when I found them, I painted them red and attached red streamers and bungee cords with hooks. I did a good line in control locks, or so the other gangs must have thought, for they were often swiped before the paint was dry.

Working hours were nominally the same as at Drigh Road, but with no parades – 7.00 am to 1.00 pm. As Independence Day came closer, the pace of work increased and they had us back at the hangar each afternoon from 2.00 pm to 5.00 pm. There were few complaints, for the sooner the job was finished, the sooner we left Chakeri. But let it not be thought that that was all there was to it.

The usual temperature in the hangar during the afternoon was 120 degrees F. so, saturated with sweat, we worked just in shorts and sandals. The sweat would spring from one's brow in big globules and run down to the eyebrows, where it would collect until it overflowed down one's nose or cheeks. Until then, I had never realised nature's practical purpose in providing me with eyebrows.

At the same time, of course, sweat was oozing out all over the rest of your body like water wrung from a chamois leather. I developed sweat rash on my forehead and liberal applications of calamine lotion didn't improve my appearance much. However, a developing tan soon cleared it up.

When the work gang was short of components, I was sent on a bicycle to a dump of scrap Dakotas on the far side of the airfield to remove the parts needed. As I walked across the piled-up scrap, various examples of wild life could be heard scuttling away, which made me a bit nervous, so I didn't usually waste time getting what I had come for.

Some of the parts were in worse condition than the ones they were meant to replace, but I would take them back to the hangar anyway, being the best I could find, in the hope that one good part could be made up from two unserviceable parts.

Cycling back with an elevator, or some other large component, was tricky enough, but it was made even more hazardous in the late afternoon after a shower of rain, when the runway would be covered with – literally – thousands of bull-frogs of various sizes hopping about. Many of them were enormous and to have hit one would have been enough to bring me off my bike; not desiring to injure or kill one, I would walk back, but my reason for my tardy return was not really appreciated.

These bull-frogs were quite unafraid of human beings and if you stood still, they would gather round, staring at you with huge unblinking eyes. They used to come hopping into the toilets and if they saw you sitting there, they would call up their mates in honk language and approach you under the high-hung door, one by one, one hop at a time until they were squatting in a semicircle. Honking occasionally, they would watch you with fascinated concentration.

The toilets themselves were primitive in the extreme and consisted of trays below the toilet seats. The Indian coolie – an 'untouchable' – in charge of the toilets, would open a little door in the wall behind and below the seat and withdraw the tray to empty it. It was even more disconcerting than the bull-frogs if the door opened and a dusky face peered up at your posterior, as sometimes happened if he didn't know you were still there.

To get back to higher things in life; on one of my forays for spare parts, I went further afield and came upon what appeared to be one complete squadron of Liberators parked out in the surrounding countryside.

There was one transport Liberator, but the remainder appeared to be of the most recent type with nose turrets and natural metal finish with R.A.F. markings. Most still had wheel and propeller covers in place and appeared quite flyable, although one or two others had been vandalised.

The transport Liberator had an Indian family actually living in it, with washing hanging on a line strung between the propellers. Others also showed signs of habitation and I swear I saw some potted plants proliferating in the nose turret of one particular aircraft.

Having exhausted the possibilities of the scrap dumps after several trips, my usefulness appeared to be coming to an end, when nominations were called for to form a Canteen Committee. Needless to say, being the chap they could most afford to spare from work, I was duly voted onto it and given a long list of complaints about the food to air at the meeting.

Most of the complaints of the other representatives were the same as those on my list: few potatoes, small helpings, no seconds, etc., so that most of the complaints were voiced before my turn came.

I probed the matter of the potatoes however and the Sergeant cook demonstrated how every potato was hollow inside and how difficult it was to recover enough potato from what was left. It seemed a fair explanation and I said no more.

I had not mentioned at the meeting, when the matter came up about the small helpings of sweet, that each night in the cooks' billet, a tray of flan or tart was brought in and scoffed by the cooks.

There must have been some repercussions as a result of the Committee meeting and that night we three newcomers were given our marching orders. On whose authority, I did not know, but we weren't sorry to leave for a more friendly billet.

These billets on N4 site were very old, to judge by the worn tiled floor and tiny windows, from which most of the glass was missing and replaced by an open weave material, coated on both sides by a cellophane-like substance.

The roofing of the billets was quite thick and I don't know how it was made, but was probably thatch overlaid with roofing felt. It certainly kept the billets as cool as one could expect in the circumstances. There were two electric fans flicking round, day and night, in our billet and every now and then, in the evening, when the rather inadequate electric light drew all manner of flying insects inside, there would be a pinging noise as a fan blade batted an extra large hard-shelled flying beetle across the room. It was advisable, as soon as one had made one's bed, to put up one's mosquito net to keep out other fauna as well as mosquitoes.

To combat malaria, if we got bitten by a mosquito, there was always a supply of mefloquine tablets in a saucer on the table of the dining hall, of which we were supposed to take one a day. There were also salt tablets to counteract the salt we lost through sweating so much.

Drinking water was kept in baked clay pots, called chattis and the water stayed surprisingly cool due to the fact that the clay was porous, thus allowing slight evaporation.

It was said that it was from here, near Cawnpore, that General Colin Campbell set out with his troops to relieve Lucknow, during the Indian rebellion of 1857.

There was an elaborately constructed rectangular pool on the edge of the camp, which was supposed to be for elephants to bathe in, although there were then no elephants and this anomaly seemed to me to substantiate the story. Certainly, it was there long before the R.A.F. arrived in Chakeri and what would the R.A.F. have wanted with elephants?

There was little to do on the domestic site except to patronise the canteen, or buy a camera and take pictures. Further afield was the camp cinema, which tended to show a lot of Indian films and the camp swimming pool which never had its water changed while I was there, in fact, it just became greener and greener. I decided to give up swimming when I dived in one day and surfaced to see an enormous water beetle swimming elegantly past my nose.

It was, however, too late. I developed earache of the most painful kind and desperately sought the aid of the Sick Quarters. They prodded and probed for fully ten minutes, stuffing something in my ear, which made it hurt even more.

Upon returning to the billet, I lay on my charpoy for a couple of hours, suffering the worst agony I had ever known. Finally, in desperation, I decided to pull out whatever it was that was stuffed in my ear. It turned out to be nearly half a yard of bandage, soaked in calamine lotion. Nevertheless, it had done the trick, for after that the pain went away.

Back at the flights, the Dakotas that had been completed were gradually accumulating around the dispersal, ready for air testing. I perceived this fact with interest, having a fancy to go up on an air test and so put my name down for one. Nobody else could have been very keen on the idea, for I did not have long to wait. The very same day I was told to get a chute and head set and report to the pilot.

He seemed to be a good type with no swank about him and he asked me if I had flown before. I said that I had and, to my surprise and joy, he told me to sit in the co-pilot's seat and operate the cooling gill controls.

I watched, fascinated, as the pilot, with quiet professionalism, started up the engines and ran them up, occasionally taking notes on a pad.

Apparently satisfied, he then throttled back and waved the chocks away and the great tin bird taxied out towards the end of the runway. There was no hissing of brakes, only an occasional squeal, for the Dakota had hydraulic brakes by Bendix and were operated by toe pedals on the rudder controls.

I had been in the cockpit of one of the Dakotas to operate the brakes when it had been pushed out of the hangar after completion and I found these brakes to be rather tricky and awkward with a fierce action, but in practised hands (or rather, feet!) such as my pilot's, they appeared to give no trouble. A ham-footed person could easily tip the aircraft on its nose though, it seemed to me.

Taking off from the wet runway, I was worried about the bullfrogs, but I couldn't see any so I sat back, after setting the gills and concentrated on keeping my arms and legs out of the way of the duplicated controls waggling about in front of me.

There is no doubt in my mind, one of the most exhilarating sensations one can experience in a working day is to take off sitting in the nose of a Dakota.

Pushed back in one's seat by a force unseen, but manifestly unleashed by two engines, one of which could be observed straining to pull itself off the wing, one had a feeling that this was it, the die was cast and let's hope that the lads on the ground had done their job well. At that moment, I felt proud to be among their number; had I not tightened a few screws, myself, on this very aircraft?

Thundering down the runway and splashing through pools of water left by the last shower, we gently lifted off and climbed steadily into a sky laden with enormous cumulus clouds, through which we ploughed with scant respect, out into clearer air and brilliant sunshine.

Circling around the airfield, the pilot put the aircraft on a compass course, instructed me to close the gills a bit more and proceeded to make notes on his pad. This was not easy for him to do, I could see and I half anticipated his next words to me.

"Do you think you could fly this plane straight and level?"

"Yes," I said, greatly daring.

"Carry on, then," he said.

Remembering the experience with the Blackburn B-2, I gingerly took hold of the control column and placed my feet on the rudder pedals.

"You have control!" he said.

"I have control," I quavered, hoping that was the right thing to say, or should it have been "Roger!"?

As with the B-2, I found that the kite flew herself, so I held the controls lightly and let her make her own corrections.

A few moments passed and then the pilot said, "You're climbing. Keep her level." He pointed to the altimeter.

Sure enough, the larger hand was slowly going round. I eased the column forward and the hand started to go back. Pulling back on the column started her climbing again and I found it very difficult to keep the hand stationary. Also, pushing on the column to stop the aircraft climbing soon made my arms ache.

This is not as easy as I thought, I said to myself and it occurred to me that a spot of nose-down trim could be the solution.

"Do you mind if I alter the trim?" I asked.

"Go ahead," he said, still jotting down notes.

The trim worked like a charm and I found that, with an occasional touch, backwards or forwards, I could keep the hand stationary without pushing or pulling on the control column at all. It must have been hard work flying big aircraft in the days before trim tabs were invented.

"You're going off course," said the pilot, indicating the compass.

To my horror, I could see that we were nearly ten degrees off course and had visions of losing ourselves in the vastness of India, never to return to Chakeri.

I thought that I could alter the heading on the rudder alone, being a very slight turn as turns go, but the rudder pedals were extremely hard to move and although the compass did move slightly in the right direction, as soon as I took the pressure off, the compass went back again to its original position.

Obviously, the trim control was not the answer this time, so I took the bull by the horns – almost literally it seemed, as the aileron controls had some similarity with a bull's horns – and banked the aircraft over gently.

Miraculously, the compass moved round and as soon as it lined up with the two parallel bars, I levelled the aircraft up again. With satisfaction, I noted that the compass stayed in its new position.

Thus armed with the knowledge of how to keep the aircraft straight and level, I regained my confidence and concentrated on perfecting the technique, while the pilot took more notes, or sat looking out at the breathtaking view of towering sunlit monsoon clouds massed around us, as glimpses of India passed beneath us.

"Right then, turn it round and head back the way we came," said the pilot.

I looked at him, amazed at his confidence in me.

"Through 180 degrees, so that the needle lines up with the bars again", he explained gently.

I could see what he meant all right, but could I do it? That was what bothered me.

I banked the aircraft gently to port and saw the needle slowly come round, which was good enough for me, but the pilot pointed to the turn and bank indicator and said I should put on more turn.

"Keep the nose from dropping and check with your indicator," he said.

The little snippets of gen from the 'Teach Yourself to Fly' book that I had learned by practising in the old Avro Cadet at Blackburn's came back to me, including the part about keeping the nose up. Didn't the book say that elevators in a turn act partly as rudders and rudders as elevators? Ease back the control column slightly as you bank and apply opposite rudder as necessary as the turn tightened.

I decided to have a go. After all, the pilot would soon extricate me if I got in a spot. Down went the port wing and the clouds gathered speed as they passed the nose to starboard. I glanced at the turn and bank indicator, the nose was dropping slightly.

Top rudder was as difficult to get as it had been before, so I eased back the column a bit more and the nose came back up. The wing was still dropping and as I thought it had gone far enough, I eased the aileron control back until the wings stayed at the right angle.

I found that by adjusting on the control column and ailerons alone, I didn't need the rudder at all. The aircraft was tilted at an angle of 30 to 40 degrees and going round nicely. Having completed the turn, the pilot told me to keep it going back to our original heading, which I did. He then told me to do a 180 degrees turn to starboard, which I managed to perform in a similar fashion.

This time, however, I could see the wingtip and notice that the ground revolved as though the wingtip was pinned to it. I had never before realised that turns could be so satisfying to perform and I was quite sorry to have to straighten up and head back to Chakeri.

However, before we actually wended our way back, the pilot took over and proceeded to put the Dakota through turns so tight that I thought the wings would bend and I was forced down in my seat until my stomach felt as if it was being forced into my groin – not a pleasant sensation. He then throttled back and put the aircraft into a stall which seemed quite mild, with little buffeting. This was followed by a spot of cloud chasing round the sunlit white pinnacles, with the unladen aircraft being manoeuvred and rolled through 180 degrees like a fighter, performing vertical banks with the wings rippling under the stress. This rippling could be clearly seen when a wingtip pointed to the sun.

All too soon, we headed back to Chakeri and made the circuit for final approach. As we came closer to the runway reaching out to welcome us back, I noticed an Indian man crossing the end of it. He could not have heard us until we were quite close, but when he did he started to run. Realising that he did not have time to reach the other side of the runway, he turned and ran back, but it must have seemed to him that whatever he did the aircraft kept heading for him. As we floated down, he threw himself flat on the ground. He was never in any actual danger but it must have been a frightening experience for him.

I myself learned a lesson I never forgot, namely, always to check before crossing the end of a runway that no aircraft were landing or taking off, even when there was no flying. There might be an unexpected visitor, or an emergency landing on the nearest available airfield – ours! On more than one occasion in the future, such caution was justified.

After parking the Dakota back at dispersal, the pilot thanked me and suggested that perhaps it would be possible for me to help him with other test flights on a regular basis. I was all for this idea and felt that at last I had found my vocation in life, but Sergeant Taylor did not approve of the idea when it was put to him. There was enough hard graft for everybody and it would not have been fair to the others to let me go off on a cushy skive.

To emphasise the point, I was set to putting back the floor panels in the otherwise complete Dakotas which were now parked in the open.

When the sun was shining, the temperature inside the rear fuselages of the aircraft would shoot up to around 160 degrees F and I soon found that I could do the job for only a few moments before the heat became unbearable and I was forced to retreat to the open cargo doorway for a breath of comparatively cooler air.

There were several quaint contraptions standing around the dispersal which were intended to be used to overcome this very problem. In theory, they could supply cool air to the aircraft interior through canvas ducting. This air was drawn by a blower through the side of a felt-lined cylinder which revolved, like a Mississippi stern-wheeler's stern wheel in a bath of water. The whole hurdy-gurdy was driven by a primitive petrol engine and was mounted on an even more primitive trolley.

I selected the most serviceable-looking unit and dragged it up to the doors of the Dakota, pulled the ducting up inside the fuselage, leapt down to the ground again and endeavoured to start the engine. There was no petrol in the tank, naturally and as only lead-free petrol was supposed to be used, I searched around for some without success. In desperation, I drained some petrol from the Dakota and surreptitiously put it in the tank.

This was easy to do because the Dakota had little taps protruding from the underside of the wing for draining water from the fuel tanks.

I often wondered what would happen if a Dakota did a belly landing and ripped the taps off, causing petrol to escape. I knew what the answer was likely to be, but theoretically this would not happen because the Dakota belonged to the first generation of aircraft which featured retracting undercarriages.

Retracting undercarriages at that time were revolutionary and somewhat suspect, for it was not unknown for them to fail to come down again, so the aircraft designers played safe. They left half of each wheel sticking out in the slipstream, even though this tended to defeat the object of retracting them, so that if they did fail to come down, they could still be used for landing on.

Even more theoretically, by stopping the engines, the propellers could be feathered and rotated by the starter motors to an inverted 'Y' position before landing and the pilot could touch down without even scratching the paintwork.

To return to the job in hand, I succeeded in starting the single-cylinder engine and coaxed it into running continually, though somewhat erratically.

I then found that the bath held no water, due principally to the fact that there was a hole in it. Rather than go through the procedure all over again with another hurdy-gurdy, I decided to dispense with the water cooling and settle for a flow of fresh air in the aircraft.

Back on the job of screwing down the floor panels, I found that the flow of air was virtually non-existent because of the length of the duct and the many holes where it had worn, so I threw it out of the doorway, took a deep breath, ran back up the fuselage and started screwing down the floor panels again.

By taking regular breaths of fresh air at the doorway after each screw was fastened down, I found that I could just about stick the heat, at the cost of sweating so profusely that my shorts and socks were completely sodden and my shoes squelched. Finally, my socks and shorts would absorb no more and my shoes were overflowing, so that I was dripping sweat all over the floor.

It was impossible to keep a foothold on the sloping, slippery metal surface and I found myself sliding gracefully tailwards. It became necessary to regain my original position by hanging on to the frames of the fuselage and pulling myself back and then lying on the floor, securing myself with one foot against a frame and the other reaching for a toe-hold on a lashing point.

A corporal, wanting to know why a ten-minute job was taking most of the working day, came walking up the fuselage, failed to notice the tide of sweat flowing towards him and fell flat on his face before I could warn him.

Somebody else brought a special thermometer and checked the temperature as being 160 degrees F so, after that, all the other aircraft had their floor panels screwed down in the hangar, much to my relief.

Spare time was generally frittered away for lack of something to do and I and a few others, found the airfield, with firm concrete tracks to walk on, the best place to stretch our legs.

In the late afternoons, an Air India Viking, looking brand new, used to drop in and was always worth watching. It had a smooth aluminium finish, free from dents and oil stains and was a far cry from the fabric-covered Wellington that it was developed from.

It seemed to have a faster approach speed than the Dakota and, with its twin Centaurus engines driving four-bladed propellers, it had an air of business-like efficiency. At that time, of course, it was one of the latest products of the British aircraft industry and its appearance helped to dispel a feeling I had that Chakeri was very remote from civilisation.

Having seen the Ganges, which was not far away, while on the test flight, I developed an urge to go and see it at closer quarters. The older hands told us it was only a few miles away along one of the country lanes, so, one afternoon, four of us set off, feeling rather intrepid.

We followed the general directions we had been given and followed a rough country lane out of the camp area. There seemed to be no clearly defined boundary to the camp – it just trailed off into the open country – and we were soon walking between cultivated fields. The produce growing there – corn, I thought – was very tall and effectively blocked our view of the surrounding countryside.

The lane wended its way to a village which we had not been told about and we were in some doubt as to whether it was wise to carry on. However, a tall figure detached itself from the shadows and intruded into our deliberations.

"Hello", he said. "Where are you going?"

Fleetingly, I wondered if we were out of bounds, not being an avid reader of Station Routine Orders, which listed this sort of information.

"Taking a walk to the Ganges", said one of us.

"Oh, then you will be finding the river very near to here", said the tall chap. He went on: "I am the Headman of this village and I hope that you are liking your stay in India."

We assured him that we were and took a photo of him with his two sons, something he seemed keen for us to do.

His cordiality was a pleasant contrast to what I had expected and I felt myself warming to Indians generally. I remembered that, far from seeing riots or slogans written on walls such as "Jai Hind" (Leave India) which I had been conditioned to expect from reading British newspapers, I had received nothing but friendliness and goodwill during all of my short time in India.

Even in England, barbed wire had surrounded R.A.F. Stations, but here in India there was none, because none was needed it seemed. Perhaps in Delhi and Calcutta these things could be seen, but were they representative of India generally? I thought not.

We took our leave of the Headman, who told us we were always assured of a welcome at his house. He was an educated man, who spoke good English and appeared to take his position as Headman seriously.

We carried on along the lane, which in fact degenerated into a rutted track, leaving the cultivated fields behind and entering a grassy area of hillocks with a small valley down which the track wound.

To the left, in the shade of a small cliff, were some men squatting or lying down as they watched over a flock of scraggy-looking sheep and who called out to us and laughed amongst themselves. It was a reasonable assumption that they were taking the mickey out of us in Hindustani, so we replied with a few choice derogatory remarks in English, hoping that they could no more understand us, than we could understand them.

They waved back, good-naturedly enough and we responded, still calling out "Get your knees brown!", "How's your belly off for spots?" and anything else that came into our heads.

We left them behind, but were soon followed by half a dozen young boys who ran across the rough ground like mountain goats, shouting excitedly all the while. They showed no fear of us, in fact I thought they might throw a few stones to add to the excitement, but it transpired that they had spotted the camera carried by one of our party and wanted their photograph taken. Once more, our chap obliged. By now, we had rounded a corner and came into full view of the Ganges.

Due to the monsoon, it was in full spate and the huge expanse of turbulent, muddy water was awesome. The far bank was too far away to be clearly observed. Occasionally, objects resembling tree trunks floated past, out in the mainstream of the current.

One of the more knowledgeable of our party said that they might be dead bodies. He explained that the bodies of rich Hindus were burned on funeral pyres and this was very expensive because of the quantity of wood required. In some places there were no trees left for this very reason.

Poorer people had to make do with a makeshift raft to which their bodies were lashed and set afloat on the Ganges to drift with the current. Vultures would finish the job off before the raft finally disintegrated many hundreds of miles down river. On that day of fitful sunshine and lowering clouds there was a brooding atmosphere and we had no difficulty in believing him.

Certainly, the Ganges was the main sewer for Northern India and its swirling turgid waters looked most uninviting, yet the river was sacred to millions of Hindus who flocked to Benares, further downstream, in order to bathe in it. We returned to Chakeri well pleased at having broken the monotonous routine.

On another occasion, out of curiosity, I took a walk through the R.I.A.F. hangars, where Tiger Moths were being reconditioned. Stripped-down wings and fuselages lay on trestles and I was able to inspect them closely. Although not unfamiliar with the Tiger Moth from my Cosford days, I had not seen one reduced to its basic structure before and I was amazed at its simplicity. The fuselage was simply a frame of square, hollow section, steel tubes welded together, with no riveted joints such as the Hurricane had. The wings had solid wooden spars, spindled out and simple built-up main ribs, with two riblets on the top surface and one on the lower between the main ribs. Each riblet was no more than a bent strip of wood secured at one end to the top of the front spar and at the other to the leading edge member.

These aircraft were throwbacks to the earliest days of aviation and used the same methods of construction as were common in World War One, when aircraft designers had to use what materials were available, i.e. mainly wood and steel. Aluminium and its alloys, was at that time a suspect material, used only for lightly stressed parts, such as cowling panels.

The Germans used duralumin on airships and a few advanced aircraft but, generally, they too favoured wood and steel tube for airframe construction.

Fabric covering, too, was universal at that time, although pure unbleached Irish linen was hard to come by in Germany and the Germans had to find substitutes. They therefore favoured plywood-covered fuselages, which did not require scarce high-grade fabric covering.

The more I looked at these Tiger Moths, the more I felt that, given enough time and money, it was within my competence to build myself a similar sort of aeroplane.

Independence Day came closer and one would have had to be a very disinterested person not to have taken some interest in what was happening in India. All we knew was what we picked up from newspapers and the radio and official explanations were limited to a parade of the whole unit, during which the C.O. explained that we would be leaving just as soon as the aircraft were finished and he exhorted us to do our best. A tinge of bitterness seemed to enter into his talk and I got the impression that he had had enough of Chakeri and perhaps of dealing with higher authority, including possibly the embryo Indian authorities waiting in the wings for the transfer of power.

A particular mate of mine became quite a student of Indian politics and was adept at pronouncing the names of such people as Mr Rajagopalachari. His example encouraged me to take more interest in the events of the time and in the people involved in shaping the future of India as well as in Indians generally. One politician was reported as having said:

"We don't want your motor cars, your lorries, or your aircraft. What we want is bigger and better bullock carts!"

This became something of a catch-phrase down at the hangar, when we came up against a big snag on an aircraft.

The Hindu caste system was an everyday thing at Chakeri, although it was not immediately apparent unless some incident brought it to light. One chap told the bearer to sweep the billet out, although there were sweepers to do that job. For some reason it had not been done and, despite the bearer's protests, he was made to do it himself. The result was that the bearer lost caste for doing a sweeper's job – a bearer being higher up the pecking order than a sweeper. He had to undergo some ritual penance for a couple of days, in order to be purified and restored to his original caste. He also complained bitterly to the R.A.F. authorities, who gave us a stiff lecture about respecting Indian customs, however quaint they might seem to us.

It was always advisable, when walking past an Indian who was partaking of his midday snack, not to let your shadow fall on his food because the food might then become defiled and the Indian would have to throw it away. This was particularly so if a lower caste person, such as an untouchable, cast a shadow.

An A.C.2's caste could not be clearly defined, so it was as well to play safe and throw the food away anyway.

The untouchables were rock bottom in the pecking order and the only job left for them to do was to empty the bogs. You could get little response out of them if you tried to be sociable and show that you couldn't care less about caste, even if their shadow did fall on you. They would just try to avoid your attention in a shy manner. None of the bearers or the other camp workers would have anything to do with them and they lived with their families in complete isolation.

A main road ran past the N4 site, down which bullock carts would trundle, usually with the driver fast asleep. The bullocks just kept going steadily on towards their destination and some of the airmen thought it a good prank to spot a cart with a sleeping driver and turn the bullock around in the camp entrance to send it back the way it had come.

I avoided being involved in this activity as, apart from sympathy for the unfortunate drivers, I didn't feel it was an auspicious time to upset Indians.

Finally, Independence Day came and we spent it lying on our charpoys, having been given the day off, but advised not to leave the domestic site. It was a bit of an anti-climax and everything was quiet. Next day we went back to work as usual.

Now that we were on the last stage of our work, the spirits of the men rose considerably and even the most taciturn fellows became more cheerful. One fellow in our team, not noted for his jocularity, said to me one day:

"Ask Joe" (not his real name), "if his watch is really shockproof and say you don't believe him when he tells you it is."

'Anything for a laugh' was my motto, so I asked him. Sure enough, he replied that it really was shockproof.

"Go on, prove it then," I said, in feigned disbelief.

To my amazement, he took it off his wrist and threw it across the hangar floor. As might have been expected, the watch had stopped ticking when he picked it up again. Apparently, he had thrown it shortly before and the watch, by some stroke of fortune, had been undamaged.

I managed to get in one more test flight, but this time somebody else was in the co-pilot's seat, so I sat in the main compartment and took some photographs of the ground below, through the grommet hole in a window.

This particular aircraft was KN 243. Another Dakota in the line-up on the dispersal was KN 312, for the benefit of all those reading this who are interested in serial numbers.

Plate 5 Douglas Dakota KN 243

13. Leaving India

Finally the day came when all the Dakotas were completed. Many had left Chakeri and just enough remained to airlift the Unit out. Armed with our clearance chits, we set off to make the rounds of the Station for the last time. At Station Headquarters the chits had to be signed by an R.I.A.F. officer. The attitude of some of the airmen was such that they were disinclined to salute him, whereupon he refused to sign until they did so. Rather than risk delaying their departure, they saluted with a rather bad grace.

Next day, September 10th 1947, we all assembled at the dispersal and were allocated our aircraft. A large crowd of camp workers had gathered to see us off and it was rather surprising to see that none of them were looking particularly happy and some of them were even crying. An airman, allocated to the same Dakota as myself, had a parcel wrapped in newspaper pushed into his hands just as he was about to board the aircraft. It turned out to be a meal of curry and rice to sustain him during his long journey back to Blighty.

We gave a final wave to them through the open door of the Dakota, before it was finally slammed shut and took our seats with mixed feelings. Shortly after, we took off and banked round, under low scudding clouds, for our last look at Chakeri, then straightened up on course and climbed steadily away. A change in the engine note indicated that the pilot had changed from fine to cruising pitch and we settled down for the long haul to Mauripur, near Karachi.

I was beginning to dislike these long trips, it was usually chilly and it was impossible to sit comfortably in the canvas and webbing seats, but I made the best of it and tried to go to sleep. The constant roar of the engines made it easier, for it was impossible to have any sort of conversation except by shouting.

I did have a final look out at the wings bearing our heavy load so staunchly and dependably over the miles and, having seen how the wings were held on, I could not but marvel at the competence of the people who designed the Dakota. The outer wing panels were, I knew, held on by dozens of small bolts – about 5/8" diameter, as near as I can remember after sixty years. The centre section and each outer panel had flanges where they were joined and these were riveted to the Alclad skin and spanwise stringers. The flanges extended from the trailing edge across the wing, round the leading edge and back across the underside to the trailing edge again.

Each pair of mating flanges had dozens and dozens of matching holes along their lengths, rather like Meccano and were bolted together with the 5/8" diameter bolts. Because the bolts, particularly those on the underside, carried the full tensile load of holding the outer wing panels on, the load was taken directly on the threads of the bolts and through them to the root cross-sectional area, which is less, of course, than the full cross-sectional area of the bolt. The degree to which the nuts were tightened on the bolts was of great importance, as they could be over-tightened and strained quite easily. Torque spanners were virtually unheard of in those days and much reliance was placed on the fitter's skill in judging the correct degree of torque to apply to any particular size and thread of nut or bolt.

The flanges and bolts of each wing were covered with a long band, tensioned at the trailing edge and of curved section to fit snugly and keep the elements at bay. This was a typical American method of attaching wings and commonly used on such pre-war aircraft as the North American Harvard.

As I gazed out at those stout wings, the rows and rows of snap head rivets caught my attention. They seemed crude and not very aerodynamic, almost as if the aircraft was afflicted with millions of warts. It may be that they served a purpose as turbulators to break up the boundary layer and increase the efficiency of the wing. Perhaps this was the secret of the success of the Dakota.

I dozed fitfully until somebody nudged me in the ribs and shouted, "We're landing!"

I stirred and rearranged my aching bones to look through the window. It seemed to be a very bare and scrubby land beneath, not like Palam at all, which was where I thought we would land. The ground came closer as our aircraft approached the runway and just at the moment when I was sure that the runway must appear under the wing, I was amazed to see beneath us a large mud-hut village, with children and animals in walled compounds and alleyways and a few men and women walking about. None of them seemed to take the slightest notice of us as we sailed extremely low over their heads. In the next moment, the runway appeared and, a few seconds after that, we touched down.

This was Jodhpur aerodrome, as the lettering on the roof of a building proclaimed. The whole area seemed to have a reddish glow about it on account of the colour of the sandy earth. There was little or no vegetation. Gaunt hills stood above the horizon and one of them had a large building on it. We stayed here for tiffin in the Flying Club restaurant, which was quite enjoyable. After the meal we strolled back to the aircraft and waited for departure time. There was little of interest to look at. One or two Tiger Moths could be seen, but no other aircraft and the place seemed quite deserted and peaceful.

After takeoff, the terrain below became a featureless desert and I tried to doze once more. It was as well that we were on the last third of our journey, for it was becoming very irksome. The sight of the River Indus near Hyderabad reawakened our interest for we knew then that the journey was nearing its end.

An hour or so later, we landed at Mauripur, a busy aerodrome to the west of Karachi, in what was now the new country of Pakistan and we were taken in some Bedford utility coaches to our transit billets. These billets were at Squadron's Camp, presumably named after the two Dakota squadrons, Nos. 10 and 31, that had been based on that side of the aerodrome. It was also known as R.E.C. Mauripur and was a conglomeration of Nissen-type huts, bungalows and what looked like warehouses. It was the warehouses that were our billets and for the purpose were filled, tier upon tier, with bunks that resembled racking. The bottom bunks had already been claimed by previous arrivals so, rather than be jammed in one of the middle tiers, I laid claim to one of the top bunks, which I had to climb up to reach. It was very close to the roof and very hot as a consequence, but it had the saving grace of being near one of the windows which were all high up in the wall and the fresh air that it let in outweighed the other disadvantages of the bunk.

The camp was very mundane and unusually hot, possibly due to a curious feature of its construction in that every square yard of it was covered with what looked like roofing felt, even to the roads, parade ground and the rainwater gullies.

The camp rapidly filled up with airmen from all parts of India, places with strange-sounding names like Kohat, Chaklala, Rawalpindi and Ambala to mention but a few. I had not realised how large India Command had been.

Many men had come by train and the stories of what they had seen en route were enough to make one's hair curl. Some had taken photographs – although to do this had been expressly forbidden – and I remember seeing some taken at Amritsar Station, from a railway carriage, showing the sequence of events as some unfortunate Moslem was being decapitated with a kukri by a Sikh, who was nearly twice the size of his victim.

Our chaps were in carriages attached to the rear of a train taking Moslems to Pakistan and it was in the station when the Sikhs descended on it. The airmen had to sit tight, keep quiet and not interfere, while the Moslem men were butchered and the women abducted or raped or both. Finally, the train was sent on its way with the slogan "A present from India" painted on its side.

It seemed that I had been somewhat fortunate in having seen very little of what was going on in India. I did get a glimpse of one of these trains entering Karachi, while on a trip to Karachi with some pals. It looked a mess, with paint daubings and broken windows and we didn't care to investigate further, because it was obvious that feelings were running high in the city and it was wiser to keep in the background where these things were concerned.

To put matters into perspective, I believe it was true that trains going to India also suffered in the same way. Altogether I believe over 1,000,000 people were killed or went missing at this time and millions more were displaced from their homes.

All the time that we were in the R.E.C., a constant airlift was going on at Mauripur taking Hindus out and bringing Moslems in. Tales were told of pilots being entreated to cram an extra family on board, or not to leave some members of a large family behind, although the aircraft was full already. Financial inducements were commonplace.

All sorts of aircraft, many of them from airlines or charter firms, came to swell the airlift and for the unscrupulous there were rich pickings to be made. I would not, of course, suggest that all those aircraft that landed, severely overloaded, at Mauripur did it for gain. It would have been almost impossible for most pilots, in the face of heart-rending pleas, not to have packed as many people as they could aboard and get them to safety.

One Dakota landed with ninety-six people on board, having taken off with ninety-five and a York landed with a hundred and eight passengers. I was told that the York had to have its wheels replaced, because the heat from the brake drums caused so much distortion after landing that they were ruined.

Life in the transit camp was comparatively peaceful, but there was little to occupy us, apart from roll calls, as the days passed. Most of the time was spent catching up on our reading of erotic literature and dog-eared copies of the Kama Sutra and Blue Peter, amongst others, circulated round the billet. One book was distinctive in its filth content, in that all the four-letter words were printed in capitals. By flicking through the pages, it could be read in just five seconds, long enough to get the gist of the plot.

I contracted *tinea* (dhobi rash) in my groin and the infection spread inexorably despite applications of Dettol. The M.O. gave me a rollicking for not reporting sick sooner and declared that I had nearly left it too late. If he had intended to put the wind up me, he certainly succeeded. He prescribed Whitfield's Lotion, which I had to apply liberally, three times a day. The lotion had a delayed action giving me enough time, if I was quick, to get back to my bed before it started to burn. I would then writhe in agony for half an hour or so, before the effect began to wear off. It cured me in more ways than one.

After that episode, at the slightest sign of trouble, I would report sick although these occasions were very infrequent, as my health was excellent. Once, at a later date, I reported sick with a rash and after showing it to the M.O., he sighed, stood up, took off his K.D. jacket and turned round to show me an identical rash on his back. "If I can do nothing for myself, I can do nothing for you," he said, "so buzz off!" It was prickly heat.

Our camp represented a last opportunity for Indian traders and peddlers to make some rupees selling knick-knacks and souvenirs to the sahibs before they departed forever. Many and varied were the wares on offer and quite a lot were made "before your very eyes", from carvings to suitcases. It was always interesting to watch.

Two brothers did a line in brilliantly coloured silks, which were decorated in a most unusual way. They used some sort of wax, which they kneaded and softened in their hands until they could draw it out in a long thread of uniform thickness. This thread was laid on the cloth, deftly and with great artistry, to form patterns of peacocks, flowers or anything else you fancied. The pattern was then sprinkled with glitter powder, of various colours, which was pressed into the wax and the surplus carefully dusted off to be used again. The effect that this process achieved was beautiful and the brothers did a roaring trade. They claimed to be the only people in India doing this type of work and a framed page from the *Times of India*, hanging in a conspicuous position, appeared to confirm this. It was an article about their craft, which, at the time of the article's publication, was carried out in Kashmir and, according to this article, was unique.

On the airfield side of the camp, mounted on a wooden base, was the nose section of a Dakota fuselage, which was probably used for instruction at some time in the past. We took photographs of ourselves sitting in the cockpit and fooled around generally.

One day, we went by lorry to Hawkes Bay, some eight miles across the desert where the R.A.F. had a rest camp. This was a large pavilion-like building, made largely from packing cases, with a verandah facing the ocean. Apart from a few buildings for stores, etc., made from smaller packing cases, that was all there was, the Indian Ocean in front and the desert to the rear. Further down the bay was another, more substantial building, probably for officers. Apart from that, the coastline was bare and deserted.

Enormous rollers, built up by the continuous monsoon winds, crashed down onto the beach and it would have been ideal for surfing, but that was a little-known sport in those days. There was a land yacht to try our hands at, though somewhat homebuilt in appearance and utilising aircraft tailwheels. It was rather heavy, but a good effort on somebody's part.

Also, there were a couple of two-seater kayaks which were great fun, but had a tendency to sink when they were swamped by the waves. Flotation gear was provided by dozens of ping-pong balls in string bags and these were rather depleted due to the attentions of the table tennis enthusiasts.

Time continued to drag and any diversion was welcome, even a visit to the toilets, although this could be fraught with danger. They were the sort that had a constant flow of water in a channel passing through them, instead of individual flush systems and some jokers found it great fun to set alight screwed-up toilet paper and let them float downstream past all the other toilets, singeing the posteriors of the occupants therein.

Most people in my billet had yarns to tell which made mine seem quite feeble by comparison. Some had seen a lot of India as armed escorts on trains carrying military stores. A couple of chaps would be required as volunteers to escort a particular train, issued with a rifle each and some ammunition and for the next week or two they would be confined to a caboose at the rear of the train as it puffed across India. They had nothing to do except cook and eat their rations, look at the passing countryside and perhaps take a pot shot at some luckless bird.

Others told tales of wild adventures in Bombay, Calcutta, Delhi, or wherever and I began to regret that opportunities for this sort of thing had now gone, or so it seemed.

Many airmen had their names called out on parade for drafts to the Middle East, East Africa and Habbaniyah in Iraq. Some were tour expired and started for home by air. Large numbers were later shipped out on the Empire Windrush, a troopship that, many years later, was to end its days catching fire in the Mediterranean.

Some of the Chakeri lads, myself included, were posted to the Staging Post at Mauripur. At the time it was not a popular posting, as we had already seen most of what there was to see and that was very little. We were all set for pastures new.

The Staging Post billets were just down the road past the traffic island and we had to carry our kit down there on foot, which set the seal on our despondency. But life is very much what you make of it and the next couple of years were to prove some of the best of my life.

14. Sind, Sun and Sand

In the best traditions of the R.A.F. in India, Mauripur was spread over the face of the desert and, including all the various sites, extended over an area approaching 25 square miles.

The domestic site, which included the Sick Quarters, was on the east side of the Station near a traffic roundabout, from where the Military Road led to Karachi. From the roundabout, a number of other roads branched off. One went north past Squadrons Camp, another went south-west, past the power station, to various work sites and yet another went south past the cinema to Mauripur village and then went west to Hawkes Bay. A fifth road wound through the domestic site to the south-east of the Station, linking the Married Quarters, Officers' Mess and Sergeants' Mess and continued via a roundabout route to the Stores, Terminal Building, Air Traffic Control and Technical Wing site.

The Terminal Building was the only edifice of the Station to have any architectural merit, having a multitude of archways and whitewashed walls. Most other buildings were constructed from concrete blocks. The intervening terrain between the various sites was generally level, with small hillocks here and there away from the airfield area, although it was scarred in places with wadis and huge monsoon ditches, which seemed to be entirely superfluous until one considers that the wadis themselves must have been gouged out by floods and, therefore, if rain had fallen here it must have been torrential.

Sporadic clumps of cactus grew all over the surrounding desert as far as the eye could see them. Away in the distance were low foothills and beyond them, to the north-west, could be seen the blue-grey mountains of Baluchistan.

Not much of a place, you might think, but now that the monsoon was over in this part of the country, the weather became cooler week by week and I found it quite invigorating.

After the usual preliminaries of 'arriving', I was put in Tech Wing and sent to the R & I hangar. Here they did mainly Base Inspections, the Transport Command name for Minor Inspections, which occurred every one hundred flying hours.

The R & I section dealt with many aircraft, including major snags on Avro Yorks and other aircraft in transit to the Far East or to the UK and also maintained the personal aircraft of the Governor-Generals of both India and Pakistan, Lord Louis Mountbatten and Mr Mohammed Ali Jinnah respectively.

Again, I was to find that my limited experience was a drawback when it came to getting into an established team, which was overstaffed as it was and when a vacancy occurred in the Tyre Bay, I was selected to go there. It did not sound very promising and I was not overjoyed by any means, but I was to be there for the next two years and it turned out to be a very enjoyable period of my life.

Not long after I joined the Tyre Bay, an Anglo-Indian corporal was put in charge. He was Cpl. Alf 'Addie' Adams from Bangalore, who had joined the R.A.F. during the war, in India, and had served in the Burma Campaign. Now he 'lived out' in Karachi with his wife Teresa and two small boys. He was small, dark and quiet, but with a ready sense of humour and I got on with him enormously well. As it turned out, Alf and his wife and family became my life-long friends.

He had been working on an Anson XIX which had met with some major snag, during transit, of an irreparable nature and which he had to strip for shipment back to the UK. Every piece had to be listed with its part number and packed and the paperwork involved was the worst part of the job. At the end of it all, somebody must have decided that it wasn't worth shipping back and the whole aircraft was scrapped.

The Tyre Bay occupied a corner of the Ground Equipment hangar, one of several blister-type hangars joined together in two rows, with the R & I hangar set apart centrally at the east end, on a huge expanse of concrete.

Provided that aircraft wheels were available when required, nobody bothered us unduly. The other member of the Tyre Bay was Jock Bowman and the three of us enjoyed what was really a very cushy number. There were also two 'coolies' allocated to us, who did all the non-technical work such as cleaning parts and who could, nevertheless, teach me a thing or two about assembling wheels as well.

In the months ahead we were to lose these two hard-working fellows because the R & I claimed them back, their own coolies being a pretty useless lot and in their place we were given two new chaps who had to be taught the job. Luckily, they proved to be even more reliable and hard-working than their predecessors had been, a fact we did not divulge to the R & I or we might have lost them too. The R & I blokes did not get the best out of their coolies because they tended to bully them a bit, which made the conscientious ones somewhat resentful.

These new fellows were Pathanis and had a self-assured dignity that was not so apparent with the other coolies. One was called Ali and had light-coloured skin, with freckles and blue eyes and his hair was light brown. This colouring was apparently quite common among the Pathanis, because they came from the North-West Frontier, an area overrun by many invading races, both before and after Alexander the Great and who left their mark on the indigenous population as all invaders do.

One day, a few months later, Ali came to Alf and me with a problem. He was obviously worried and he told us that he wanted to go and get his wife and children from Kashmir. The district in which they lived had been overrun by Indian Forces as the result of a dispute between Pakistan and India concerning which country the State rightfully belonged to. It seemed that India claimed Kashmir because the ruler of the State – a Hindu – had opted for India, although most of the population were Moslems and preferred to be part of Pakistan. As a result, each country moved into Kashmir to grab what they could of the state and Ali's family found themselves on the wrong side of the new border.

I didn't really understand the ins and outs of the international situation, but we both had sympathy for Ali. He needed some money to carry out his plan and as it so happened that we had all had some back pay, we were in a position to lend the necessary amount, although it was doubtful that we would ever see him again.

However, he promised that he would repay us as soon he could, so with sighs of "Easy come, easy go!" we gave him the money –

about R80 or £9, which was quite a lot of money at that time – and off he set. More than two months passed and we were quite resigned to having seen the last of our money. We had a replacement coolie in the Tyre Bay and life jogged on its peaceful way. One day halfway through the morning, in walked Ali, accompanied by a North-West Frontier Policeman, one of many that guarded the Station. He greeted us and introduced the policeman, who turned out to be his brother.

He told us that he had succeeded in finding his wife and children and had brought them safely to Mauripur. He and his brother both expressed their gratitude and asked us to bear with him while he found a job so that he could repay us from his earnings. This we readily agreed to do.

Ali experienced some difficulty in getting his job back, as it happened, so I took it upon myself to go and plead with the Indian Office, as the department that dealt with the employment of local labour was still called. I extolled his merits and explained the reason why he had left his job and, rather to my surprise, they reversed their decision and took him on again. In the meantime, Ali's brother, who had only learned of Ali's troubles since their reunion and of the help we had given, had organised a collection among his comrades in the N.W.F.P. in camp at Mauripur, I believe, for in a matter of days Ali had repaid us.

As a way of showing his appreciation, Ali's brother invited Alf and me to a ramsami at the Police Camp one evening, where we were plied with food and drink. It was pretty strong drink, which was strange for Moslems, but it was probably obtained specially for us. I remember going there, but I don't remember leaving so it must have been some night!

The North-West Frontier Police camp was really a rest camp for policemen away from their arduous duties in the Frontier country and the guard patrols they undertook on the station were in return for being allowed to use the facilities at Mauripur. They certainly looked after us well. Individual policemen strolled about the domestic and work sites armed with long rifles and wearing bandoliers packed with cartridges. They seemed to have a high regard for the R.A.F. and were very friendly, although always unobtrusive.

They were generally clean-shaven, but some had trimmed moustaches and looked quite smart in their grey uniforms of baggy trousers and shirts with the tails worn outside. They wore a belt and bandolier and a turban.

One could not return to the domestic site in the middle of the night without being observed by the keen eyes of a policeman and the following conversation would generally ensue:

"Halt! Who goes there?"

"B.O.R." (British Other Rank)

"Advance B.O.R. and be recognised!"

One would approach him with respect, for the fellow would have his rifle at the ready and his finger on the trigger. Having satisfied himself that one was indeed a B.O.R., he would then say;

"Tikh hai, Sahib!"

"Thank you. Good night!"

"Good night, Sahib!"

One would then leave him to his lonely vigil with some relief, but glad that the security of one's slumbering fellow airmen was in good hands.

A curious aspect of the outlook or philosophy of the Pathanis, believed to be true by those of my fellow airmen who had been stationed in the turbulent area around Peshawar and more or less confirmed by our coolies, they were somewhat reticent about the subject, concerned the reason for their attitude to us British.

In the North-West Frontier region, warlike activities made up the Pathanis' way of life. There was always some sort of fighting going on between the British and the hillmen who, according to legend, could make rifles identical to the British Short Magazine Lee-Enfield (known as Smelly) rifle, in their mountain workshops.

The only part they could not make was the bolt, for some reason and consequently British bolts were much sought after. A British soldier or airman would therefore keep it separate from his rifle when not required and hide or secrete it on his person, so that if the rifle was stolen, the bolt would not be lost as well.

The hillmen looked upon these skirmishes as a game, rather than as a serious matter and when times were hard, or they wanted a change, they thought nothing of leaving their mountain fortress and entering into the service of the British, perhaps for years, during which time they gave their undivided loyalty, even though they might be engaged against their own brothers. When this service was finished, they would go back home and take up their old pursuits again – bothering the British! To change sides was no dishonour and all part of the game.

An example of their alertness and efficiency came a few months later, when several Sikhs infiltrated the Station for the purpose, it was said, of blowing up the power station.

What they really hoped to achieve, goodness knows but, when challenged, they kept running towards their objective. What exactly happened then I do not know for, as usual, I had missed the incident, but the N.W.F. Police were on their toes and, without further ado, took careful aim and shot them. How many were killed, I do not know. Somebody took photos of one Sikh being carried off on a stretcher and he looked a mess, although still alive at the time.

The reason for missing the incident was because I was in the model club. The Mauripur Model Club had been mentioned in the *Aeromodeller* on at least two occasions the previous year and I little thought at the time that the day would come when I would be a member too.

I went to find out about the club soon after I was posted there. It was housed in a disused billet and all of the old members had departed, but the influx of new postings included several aero-modellers and soon the club was re-established.

Peter Barnett was the Hon. Sec. elected at the inaugural meeting and he set up his office in a corner of the room with a desk, chair and cupboard.

Several models still adorned the clubroom: a Mick Farthing duration model, a large sailplane, a first class rubber-driven model of a Blohm & Voss Ha 138 and a superb $1/72^{nd}$ scale uncovered model of an SE5a fuselage complete with wire bracing, seat and fuel tank. The previous members had certainly been first-class modellers.

A club badge was designed which looked very smart. It consisted of an adaption of an R.A.F. red, white and blue roundel with the round red portion replaced by a red representation of a map of India. Above the blue circle, where an R.A.F. squadron badge would have a Crown, were the elongated letters MMC and in a scroll for the motto were the words "Sind, Sun, Sand". We had them made up as blazer badges by the camp tailor with gold wire outlines, lettering and laurel leaves.

Balsa wood was a scarce commodity, but we were fortunate in having aircraft passing through, to and from the UK and several obliging aircrews brought us materials on their return trips. Cpl. Craven built a Tiger Moth, another corporal, whose name I can't remember, bought a Mills 1.3 – the first diesel in the club – and fitted it into a club-designed control-line model. It was a very individual-looking model, with swept forward T/E and three fins on the tail, like the York. Sadly, it was not very successful, because we had to learn the finer points of control-line flying the hard way. None of us had flown a control-line model before, which didn't help matters at all.

I built a sailplane based on the Gruneau Baby, which also was not very successful, being rather heavy. The wing had an R.A.F. 32 aerofoil section which was not really suitable, aerodynamically, for model use, but one can only find out these things the hard way. It also had too large a fin area, due to a misconception I had that it was necessary, to alleviate a tendency of the model to perform spiral dives when its stability was upset in flight and it was two models and two arguments with Peter Barnett later, that I finally realised that he was right and that the large fin was in fact causing the trouble.

My next and more ambitious model was a $1/36^{th}$ scale Avro York, complete with flaps and retracting sprung undercarriage. The original power was to have been rubber, with crank drive to the propellers, but later I acquired four 'Electrotor' electric motors and fitted these for R.T.P. flying. A sophisticated control box was made for me by an electrical friend. This had stowage for rechargeable accumulators and a realistic control system for each engine. The model could be started and run up very realistically, but it would do no more than taxi round.

In the meantime, I had acquired a telescopic rod, being an aerial mast from a safety equipment emergency pack and this was used for experiments in whip control. By this means, the York finally flew, without electrical power and great delight was to be had in achieving smooth touchdowns and noting the difference in landing characteristics when flaps were used.

I learned that practice abolished any tendency to dizziness due to turning around continually, which had always seemed to be a big drawback to control line flying and if only for this reason, I would recommend whip control as a useful and inexpensive introduction to C/L flying.

By using a long light rod, as long as is comfortable to handle, with a line from the tip of the rod to the model and looped around the fuselage, virtually any small scale model can be made to perform realistically. The line should be of such a length that when the rod is held high and vertical the model is just clear of the ground. Holding it in this way, in the event of an impending crash, makes it almost impossible to damage the model. The model should have fixed tail surfaces and the C.G. at about 25% of the chord. Control is effected by the inclination of the rod and the speed at which the model is whipped around. Loops and wingovers are easily performed, but not inverted flight. However, even this is possible with the added refinement of having two lines running from a miniature control line handle secured to the tip of the rod. The lines work a bellcrank in the model, which operates the elevators as in normal control line practice. A freewheeling propeller of scale proportions and nose weight complete the model and, provided a smooth area is available to land on, many hours of enjoyment can be obtained with it.

The only disadvantage is that takeoffs from rest cannot be done as with a power model but, on the other hand, the positive advantages are: no noise, no expensive engine, no fuel and hence no oil soakage or deterioration of the finish, less danger to spectators and, not least, that it is possible to fly a true scale model without great risk of damage.

I had endeavoured to make an electric motor from an *Aeromodeller* design, but lack of the correct materials meant that it could not be completed. The freelance model for which it was made proved to be ideal for whip control however, even being timed at speeds up to eighty mph, although it was lightly constructed.

Our working hours were 0700 hrs to 1300 hrs and unless other duties intervened, such as fire picket, the rest of the day was our own. I was therefore able to concentrate on aeromodelling in a way that I had never done before and have never been able to do since.

Jet engines were the new technology in 1948 and the possibility of applying the principles to model aircraft was intriguing. Ram jets, pulse jets and turbo jets were all considered, but it was beyond our means to manufacture anything that might be successful. This did not deter one member who, although weak on theory, was keen on having a go.

The resulting engine consisted of a thin steel duct with a spray tube coiled inside and connected to a pressurised tank of paraffin. It looked remarkably like a blowlamp to me. The theory was that if exhaust gases came out of one end of a diverging tube, air would be sucked in at the other. I didn't have a lot of faith in this theory and my judgement was proved right when it sprayed a jet of liquid flame across the model club, setting on fire rubbish that littered the floor. Fortunately, we managed to put the flames out before they took hold but it was touch and go for a while.

The model club became a social centre of the camp or, at least, one of several, for there was also an Amateur Radio Club, a Concert Party and various sporting clubs, including boating, for which the enormous expanse of Keamari Harbour was available.

All long-range R.A.F. radio communication at that time was done in Morse code and one wireless operator in the radio club made his own Morse key which worked sideways on a spring leaf. It was not officially approved for use at work, but it seemed to me to be a brilliant idea because it was less tiring to use and the rhythm was constant due to the periodic time, which was adjustable, of the spring leaf. It did however make the operator anonymous, whereas using a normal key could identify an operator, rather like hand-writing.

The radio club would very often interfere with reception of Radio S.E.A.C. – later called Radio Ceylon – which broadcast programmes for British Forces. The broadcaster was a girl with a very sexy voice and she would play records that were banned on the BBC. In those days, the BBC would ban a record at the slightest hint of impropriety or sacrilegious overtones which, needless to say, made it more popular still.

Radio S.E.A.C. had no such stuffy scruples and played requests from the troops daily for such favourites as "Do it again" and "She had to go and lose it at the Astor".

It was most annoying, to those listening intently while relaxing on their charpoys, when a voice sometimes broke in, swamping the programme, saying "Testing, testing, testing! Mary had a little lamb..." and there would be a concentrated rush to the radio "shack" to tell the culprit to belt up.

Not long after the model club was reformed, there was a reallocation of billets because of the reduction in the number of airmen on the camp, which left, in some cases, only two or three airmen to a billet. The model club also had to be vacated, but a newer and brighter building was made available.

Mike Toms, who was an ACH/GD and worked for the Station Warrant Officer, managed to lay claim to a "bunk" – a small room for two occupants – and persuaded me to share it with him. He had acquired a puppy while in his previous billet, a turn of events which had not been popular with the other occupants and it had disappeared in mysterious circumstances.

The object in having the bunk was to enable him to keep a second puppy that he had acquired, called Sooty, which turned out to be quite the most intelligent dog I have ever known. He also produced another one for me, although I hadn't wanted one, which I called Duffy. As it turned out, our billet could not have been more securely guarded and even the bearer would not dare to enter uninvited in the mornings.

The pups were fed on scraps from the cookhouse, saved for us by a coolie in return for a cigarette. However, as time went on and more airmen acquired dogs, competition for the scraps grew keener and the cost in cigarettes escalated.

My dog, unfortunately, was a bitch and she came in season early in life, by which time further contractions in the size of the camp necessitated a further change of billet. It was impossible to keep her separated from the other dogs for long, as somebody invariably forgot to shut the billet door. On such an occasion, a pack of dogs would burst through the door in hot pursuit of Duffy. Chaos would reign as she took refuge on my bed and my mosquito net would collapse on top of me as I lay there, under the weight of a dozen or more dogs snarling and biting each other as they tried to get to their quarry.

I tried shutting her up in a disused wash house, but it was no use, the howling and barking that went on all night was too much for everybody to put up with.

Peter Barnett's dog was just about the only one that had no luck, because his legs were too short, so, in the seclusion of the model club, we arranged that he too had his share by standing him on a box.

Each day we would be transported to the worksite in a fleet of blue-grey Bedford utility coaches and if one or two broke down, which was quite frequently, we were taken on a Queen Mary trailer – which was enjoyable in summer but surprisingly chilly in winter, being early in the morning before the sun was up.

At this time of day, mist often shrouded the landscape and during certain times of the year, once the sun was up, there was often a mirage effect giving the impression that the Station was surrounded by water. The air at this time of day would have a wonderfully fresh, almost fragrant, sweetness of a most invigorating nature.

The work consisted mainly of stripping down York and Dakota wheels and rebuilding them. Wheels came in from the Daily Servicing Section, who had found them to be faulty in some way on aircraft passing through, or from the R & I Section, who changed the wheels, as a matter of course, on aircraft undergoing Base Inspections.

Dakota wheels were comparatively simple to work on, being easily handled. The end floats of the axles were adjusted by a threaded collar, which was locked by a grub screw engaging in a slot. The grub screw itself was secured by locking wire. The brake units, which operated hydraulically, were tested for leakage on a rig and fitted on each side of the wheel. Each unit had a backplate integral with a sleeve which was fitted by sliding it over the axle and bolting through to prevent rotation. There was a keyway in the sleeve which engaged a fixed key at the bottom of the oleo leg on the aircraft, also to prevent rotation of the brake units.

When the wheel was assembled, the gap between the brake shoes and the brake drums had to be adjusted using feeler gauges pushed through slots in the back plate. These slots were covered by pivoting spring plates. There was a ratchet sprocket which was clicked over with a screwdriver to effect this adjustment and a larger cover plate gave access to this.

It was rare to achieve precise adjustment at the various points around the brake shoes and one generally had to settle for getting them as near as possible, which could take time. The brakes were made by Bendix.

Once, I had a Dakota wheel returned for investigation, a puncture having occurred on takeoff of the aircraft it had been fitted to, which did not go down well with the aircrew, although no further mishap resulted, luckily.

Watched by the aircrew and the Chief Technical Officer, I stripped down the wheel with some trepidation and, thankfully, I discovered that the tear in the inner tube was adjacent to a gaping crack in the hub well, where the casting seemed to be exceptionally thin. It was concluded that the air pressure had caused the casting to fail, blowing the inner tube through the gap that had opened up and bursting it and so I was exonerated. It had been thought that the tyre and tube had been incorrectly assembled to the hub, but there were no creases in the tube and french chalk had been applied inside the tyre. Nevertheless, the episode was a salutary reminder of the responsibilities of the job.

The number of landings done by each tyre was noted on its log card, the average number being 50 to 60 before the tyre had to be changed, usually because the tread was worn-down to the breaker strip. The breaker strip was a white band embedded in the casing, to indicate the maximum permissible wear and it was particularly useful on smooth tyres without tread patterns, such as were found on Anson wheels.

When each wheel was reassembled, the final touch was to paint two small rectangles diametrically opposed on one side of the wheel, overlapping the joint of the tyre and the hub, known as creep marks, which were to indicate if the tyre had crept around the hub while in use. If this happened, there was a danger that the valve stem might be torn from the inner tube. White paint was used.

Each tyre had its own three-figure number prefixed MAU, stencilled also in white paint, on the tyre wall.

Chocks & Driptrays ~ 143

York wheels were identical to Lancaster and Lancastrian wheels and, as far as I know, Lincoln wheels. They were of a different pattern to those used on Lancasters during the war, which had bigger section tyres and smaller hubs of quite a different appearance.

The York tyres came in two makes, Dunlop and Goodyear and either make was used, depending on availability. Dunlop tyres had square block treads in staggered rows around the tyre, whereas Goodyear tyres had a staggered diamond pattern.

The Goodyear tyres seemed to last longer, a fault of the Dunlops being that occasionally a square block would be ripped right off and, at their very best, they feathered along the edges of the blocks and wore away rather more rapidly. An average number of landings in the life of the Dunlop tyre would be 50, whereas Goodyear tyres could achieve up to 70.

We had equipment for vulcanising patches onto the tyres when they were damaged on the tread but these proved to be very unsuccessful, which was a pity as the scrap rate could have been reduced considerably.

York tyres were very difficult to remove from the hubs and usually resulted in them being scrapped. The only means we had for removing them were eight huge tyre levers which had to be driven in with a sledge-hammer to prise a bead off its seat. One then worked around the bead with a pair of smaller levers, trying to force the remainder of the bead away, usually without success. The technique usually followed at this stage was to run soapy water, or, in extreme cases, petrol, around the rim and retire to the 'duftah', or office, for a cup of char and a smoke. A quarter of an hour later, a loud clanging of falling tyre levers would announce that the application had done its work and we would then turn the wheel over with the assistance of a number of coolies and proceed to do the same on the other side.

York wheels were particularly heavy and their inertia when touching down on a runway must have accounted for most of the tyre wear. The tyre alone was too heavy for one man to lift upright and, with the inner tube inside, it required up to four or five men to lift it off the ground and place it down around the hub. The detachable rim would then be fitted and held in place with a large locking ring, after which the axle and brake units would be fitted.

The differences between the York and the Dakota undercarriages interested me. The axles of the Dakota were rigidly clamped to the bottom of the oleo legs, whereas the York axles were merely secured by pivot pins.

Because of this arrangement, York wheels had a tendency to lean to one side or the other, particularly when taxiing, giving a drunken effect to the aircraft. This puzzled me, as it seemed that the oleo legs must have bent to be able to accommodate this, because they were rigidly braced at the top ends. Lancaster and Lincoln undercarriages also had this feature and were, as far as I know, identical.

Another feature which must have been hard on the tyres was that the oleo legs were vertical only when the York had its tailwheel on the ground. This meant that unless the landing was a perfect three-pointer, the wheels would move slightly forward as the oleos took the landing shock, causing a large rearward load on the unsupported bottom ends of the legs. Certainly, I always found that landings in a Lancaster, or its derivatives, were rather bone-shaking events, in the years to come.

This effect would have been even more pronounced on the Dakota, because the single forked radius rod on each side of the aircraft would have been connected to the bottom ends of the sliding portions of the legs, but for the insertion of two curious little linkages which connected the legs to the fork. These gave a compensating backward movement to the wheel as the oleo legs compressed when landing. It was little details like this which gave the Dakota its air of being a quality product, in contrast with the York which was strictly utilitarian, although an impressive and effective aircraft.

For example, the brakes on the York were extremely simple, though efficient. They were operated pneumatically by inflation of a circular, or ring-like bag, rather like an inner tube but of flat section, which caused pressure to be exerted radially on the brake shoes, pushing them into contact with the brake drums.

The brake shoes were very short and were laid end to end around the full circumference of the unit. They were located by only two prongs on each shoe which passed, one each side of the airbag, through the inner drum of the unit and were secured by a leaf spring. There was no adjustment such as the Dakota had and when the shoes were worn down they were replaced.

The brake drums, which were also replaceable, had small cooling fins turned on the periphery, while vanes on the revolving hubs directed air through the gap between drum and hub.

One morning, we went to fit the axle to a York wheel, which had been left leaning against a wall overnight and, as we began to move the wheel, a silver krait popped its head out between the vanes and hissed at us. It then retreated to the interior of the hub. Being an extremely poisonous snake, it gave us a nasty shock and we let go of the wheel which fell back against the wall. No amount of poking with a long rod could dislodge the snake from its hiding place and we finally resorted to squirting petrol at it. The krait did not take kindly to this and again poked its head out, hissing defiantly. Another application of petrol and a further poke with the rod finally did the trick and it slithered down the wheel on to the floor where it thrashed about like a whiplash, apparently very annoyed.

In a flash, we leapt onto the benches nearby, out of harm's way and proceeded to hurl spanners and anything else that came to hand, at it. By sheer luck, somebody hit it on the head with a spanner and stunned it, after which it was quickly despatched with a sledge-hammer, to our great relief.

15. Mystery and Suspense

I have never been a superstitious person, or one given to thinking much about religion, but in India or Pakistan these things were never very far beneath the surface of life. One had time, however, to think about and discuss such matters at Mauripur and, although I never saw the Indian Rope Trick, I did hear and see enough to shake my complacent disbelief.

One chap, an Anglo-Indian airman, was persuaded to do some conjuring tricks in the Tyre Bay office one day, during the mid-morning break. So many airmen crowded into our little 'duftah' that there was practically no room to move and any sleight-of-hand movement would have been easily detected, I am sure. He did mainly card tricks which were uncannily clever and I was extremely impressed. Obviously, tricks were not magic, but I could not see how some of them could be logically explained away, even though I knew that this was the essence of a good conjuring trick.

One day, an itinerant conjuror came to the domestic site, a basket slung from his shoulders and with a mongoose on a lead, offering to put on a display of baffling 'magic' for the price of a few annas from each of his audience. A group of us readily agreed and we all squatted around a board that he had laid on the dusty ground. He was an old but sprightly man who had entertained several generations of British troops in this manner, to judge from his knowledge of English jargon, including the anglicised Hindustani that we commonly used. He kept up a constant patter as he went through his routine, which was as entertaining as the tricks themselves.

He did many excellent tricks that did indeed baffle us, but the one I remember best was a very intricate one with coloured balls and cups. He appeared sometimes to fumble, so that we could catch him out when he asked us what colour ball was under a particular cup, but we were wrong every time.

In the basket, he carried a cobra, which he proceeded to charm after the tricks were completed. The snake was a long time in appearing and we suggested that perhaps it had died.

"No, no!" said the fellow, "Lazy bastry just sleeping" and gave him a prod. "He come thora peachy."

Eventually, the cobra rose out of the basket and swayed around to the unmelodious sound of the flute. We found this to be rather unexciting and somebody suggested that the mongoose should have a fight with the cobra. At this, the old man raised his hands in feigned horror.

"How would I get another cobra, Sahibs?" he remonstrated. "They cost many rupees."

As the mongoose had so far taken no part in the proceedings and it was difficult to see what other useful purpose it served, the wily snake charmer had us where he wanted us.

"How much do you want for the mongoose to fight the cobra?" we asked him.

"No, Sahibs, it would cost too much," he parried.

"How much?"

"Twenty-five rupees it will cost me to buy another cobra!"

This was going to cost us five rupees each and there was much pocket searching and some borrowing, before we finally handed him twenty-five rupees.

Still muttering to himself with anguish, he tipped his faithful cobra out of the basket on to the ground, which made it rather naggy. It lay coiled on the ground with its head raised, hood extended and its fangs visible; it looked extremely dangerous.

The mongoose, which until then had appeared to be quite uninterested in anything, had the appearance of a large grey-brown weasel and looked no match for the cobra. He soon perked up, though, when the lead was removed from his neck and we all stepped back a pace, not knowing what might happen next.

The mongoose advanced towards the snake, with caution, in a circular path. The cobra twisted around to keep facing its adversary and started to lunge at the mongoose, which stopped just out of range. Its eyes glittering, the mongoose watched the snake intently. Then, in a flash, it sprang at the cobra and gripped it below and behind its head. There was a terrific flurry and then it was over, before we quite realised what had happened. It had taken no more than five seconds for the mongoose to do its job.

This concluded the performance. The snake charmer, now minus a snake, quickly put the mongoose back on the lead, picked up the dead cobra and bid us farewell. He was no doubt well pleased with his half-hour's work, having scooped up more money that most bearers earned in a fortnight.

Back at the billet, I was telling the bearer about some of the snake charmer's tricks and discussing with him whether or not magical powers really existed. The bearer agreed that most tricks were just that and no more, but he insisted that real magical powers did exist. In the face of my scepticism he became hesitantly confidential, offering to show me an example.

He produced a length of string and a stick about two feet long. I was bidden to tie each end of the string to his wrists and so tightly did he insist that it should be done that I was worried about stopping his blood circulation. His arms, body and the string thus formed an unbroken loop.

While he squatted down, I was instructed to put the stick through the loop so that one end touched the ground and to press down as hard as I could on the other end. Thus, there was no way that he could get free without breaking either the stick or the string. He commenced to agitate the string until I could hardly see it except as a blur. When he stopped, the string no longer passed around the stick, but hung freely from his wrists and he was able to stand up and move away while I was still pressing the stick to the ground.

He would never repeat his display of magic again and I think that in some way he felt guilty, or frightened, to have given away a secret ability entrusted to him.

I suppose there must be a reason of some sort for how he did it, but I found it quite inexplicable. There is a similar sort of trick where two people are looped together with string between their wrists and it is quite easy for them to get free from each other when the secret is known, but none of the principles were applied in this instance, as far as I could see.

In my last year at Mauripur, I frequently visited Karachi and once saw a celebrated fakir give an exhibition of magic in Bunder

Road, a main road in the city. Most of his routine was unexceptional but cleverly done and well received by his audience who crowded around his pitch and obstructed the traffic. The police made no attempt to move him on, it was not a wise thing to upset a fakir of his reputation. The highlight of the performance was a display of levitation. One of his several assistants lay on a low trestle table, which closer inspection revealed was in several separate sections and the fakir put him into a hypnotic trance.

One by one, the inner trestle sections were removed, leaving each end trestle to support the head and feet of the assistant, the rest of his body being completely rigid and straight over the intervening gap. A member of the audience was invited to stick a pin into the assistant to prove that he was, indeed, in a trance.

Tall freestanding frames were then placed around the assistant and a long, continuous sheet was draped over them to form a screen, the top of which was above eye level. The attention of the eagle-eyed crowd was drawn to the fact that no other person was inside the screen, which was then closed up and the sheet adjusted to completely shut off the assistant from the view of the crowd.

After a prolonged incantation and blowing of trumpets to heighten the excitement, the inert body of the assistant gradually appeared above the screen, apparently floating about within its confines. He did not rise high enough to clear the screen and the logical conclusion was that he was supported by a second person who had popped up out of a manhole in the road. Unfortunately for that theory, there was no manhole and it was unlikely that a second person could have been concealed in the folds of the sheet before it was spread. The crowd, pressing in on all sides, would surely have detected such a deception. There were people in an adjacent building looking down who could see inside the screen, but if they saw how the illusion was done, they kept the secret well as they clapped and cheered with the crowd.

After a few moments, the assistant disappeared below the screen and to the sound of further trumpeting the sheet was dropped, to reveal the assistant again lying on the two sections of the table. The remaining sections were replaced beneath the assistant, who was then reawakened. This concluded the performance; the crowd contributed generously and dispersed, well pleased.

I, too, left the scene, sceptical but not completely certain that it was just an illusion. Things do happen which cannot be explained away and the truth of this fact was brought home to me in no uncertain fashion several years later when I was back in England.

It seems appropriate to relate the story in this chapter rather than in the chronologically correct chapter, not least because I don't propose to mention the name of the place where the incident occurred. The present-day owners of nearby properties may not be happy to know that they have a neighbourhood ghost, for I assure you that the story is true.

I had been visiting my girlfriend and was dressed in my 'civvy' outfit. Walking back to the R.A.F. station, about two miles away, my mood was quite cheerful as I padded along silently in my 'brothel creepers', as crepe-soled shoes were called by my fellow airmen. The road, illuminated by streetlights, was otherwise deserted at that late hour. After leaving the streetlights behind, the road sloped down for several hundred yards to a bridge over a stream and continued up a hill on the far side. The streetlights were behind me, but I could see quite clearly, although there was no visible moon, when I spotted a chap further ahead who was walking in the same direction.

As we proceeded down the bank, I gradually caught up with him and conjectured as to who it might be. He, too, made no sound as he walked along. I was on the other side of the road when I drew level with him and could clearly see his face as I endeavoured to identity him. He had on a dark coat or mackintosh, but no hat and was about 5'-10" tall. I did not recognise him and he appeared not to notice me but continued to look ahead as he strode along.

I was about to speak to him, expecting that he would be somewhat startled to find that he had company. Before I could utter the first word of greeting, I found that I had difficulty in keeping my eyes focussed on his face, as parts of it kept disappearing like a jigsaw picture being taken apart, place by piece.

In a matter of seconds he had completely disappeared, a fact that I had some trouble in grasping, but I was in no doubt that the sensation I felt very strongly indicated that my hair was standing on end. The sensation was similar to that experienced when pulling a nylon shirt off over my head, but was far stronger.

I was filled with extreme fear, felt very cold and instinctively started running down the road and across the bridge, as fast as my legs would carry me.

There were actually two bridges, for the stream was divided at the point where it passed under the road and it was not until I had crossed the second bridge and was running up the hill that I began to feel safe. During the remainder of the walk back to my billet, I mulled over the details of my experience and came to the conclusion that I should say nothing to my oppos. I would not have been believed, I was sure and there was no point in making a fool of myself.

16. Personalities and Politicians

Group Captain Grice's Air Force
Is the best in Pakistan,
But with a couple of Daks,
We'd better make tracks,
And get out while we can!

The above song, sung to the tune of 'Eleven more months and ten more days', was one of the items in a camp concert party show, that went down very well with the airmen and also with Liaquat Ali Khan, who was the Prime Minister of Pakistan and who came as the guest of the Staging Post.

He was, at a later date, assassinated, but for that evening the cares of state were left behind and he appeared to enjoy himself enormously. He laughed heartily and appeared very much at ease in our company. He was a short, jovial type of person, wore a well-tailored suit and spoke good English. He was believed to favour a European style of living and his wife, the Begum Ali Khan, was a leading figure in the campaign for women's emancipation in Pakistan.

Most Moslem women in Pakistan were kept very much in the background and, if they went out into the streets, had to wear a burqa, a grey-coloured garment that enveloped them completely, except for a grid pattern of square holes for them to see and breathe through. The Begum Ali Khan fought long and hard against this demeaning and unhygienic practice. Her face was invariably uncovered in public and, being of striking appearance, she undoubtedly upset the entrenched male Moslem hierarchy.

The Governor-General of Pakistan, Mohammed Ali Jinnah, was a different sort of person entirely, although his sister was also progressive. He wore a particular style of hat, known as the Jinnah hat, which started a fashion in Pakistan and a long multi-buttoned coat which must have been a bit hot to wear. He was known as the 'Quaid-i-Azam' and appeared to the public as a tall, austere figure who rarely smiled, a surprising contrast to the exuberant Liaquat Ali Khan. His personal aircraft, a Dakota, had a similar emblem to Mountbatten's aircraft and R.A.F. markings. Later, the servicing was taken over by and the markings changed to those of, the Pakistan Air Force. However, before we relinquished the aircraft, it was used as a backdrop for a photograph of the Staging Post personnel.

One afternoon, we were called from our billets to a special parade to be informed that Jinnah had died and that we were to be on the funeral parade. We had an hour to get ready, which was a bit of a shock for very few of us had unblemished khaki drill. We had three changes which were used in rapid rotation and even the flying dhobi could not remove all the oil stains. It was fortunate that some of us had clean jobs and there was frenzied borrowing and trying for size. Fortunately also, all the K.D. had individual dhobi marks applied by our bearers, so there were no ownership problems afterwards. Nevertheless, we were far from pristine.

We were taken into Karachi by bus and slotted into the procession at the assembly area. The cortege was drawn by men of the Pakistan Navy, followed by a troop of the Governor-General's bodyguard on magnificent horses. There was a body of R.A.F. airmen seconded to the Pakistan Air Force looking rather smarter than we were, but then, their K.D. was still new and their knees hardly brown.

The Staging Post personnel were near the end of the procession, which was quite long and well organised considering that there was not much time in which to do it, for, in the sub-continent, funerals were carried out in almost indecent haste. Jinnah did, however, lie in state for a while, for people to pay their last respects.

I assume that Jinnah was cremated where he lay, but I did not see this because the parade was dismissed before we reached the ornate canopy under which he lay. I had a quick look at the place and spent the remainder of the evening with friends in Karachi.

In retrospect, there were two incidents that stick in my memory. One was the balcony, crowded with spectators, that collapsed onto the pavement below, also crowded with people. It seemed wrong to keep marching by, but there was nothing we could do that was not being done by others. The other incident was to see a battalion of

Punjabi troops marching away after the parade. They had an air about them, which you wouldn't find in the Pakistan Air Force, of smartness, discipline, fitness, pride in themselves and cheerfulness.

They had formerly been a part of the Indian Army and most wore campaign ribbons. They impressed me very much and I understood a little of what it meant to the British in Burma and in other parts of the world, to have men like these, fighting alongside, to rely on. These men were the other side of the coin to the politicians who tried to make capital out of British misfortunes during the war.

Gandhi, I suppose, was one of those, but I have to admit that he was respected, as far as I could tell, by Indians of all castes and religions. When he was assassinated, the papers in Karachi, including the English language paper *Dawn*, reported his death in banner headlines with black borders around their front pages. There was no other Hindu who could command such respect in Moslem Pakistan. There was a fear at the time that he had been murdered by a Moslem, which could possibly have caused a bigger outbreak of violence than had already occurred at the Partition. As it turned out, a fanatical Hindu was responsible and the sadness of the Pakistanis was tinged with some relief.

We did not see a lot of Mountbatten, except when he passed through on his way to and from Britain. One such occasion was for the wedding of Princess Elizabeth and Prince Philip. His personal York, MW 102, was normally based at Palam, near Delhi and a small R.A.F. detachment serviced it but, in preparation for its long journey to Britain, it was sent down to Mauripur for a Base Inspection. When it arrived at the R & I hangar, the first person aboard was the Flight Sergeant, whose job it was to remove the small chromium-plated electric fan that sat on a table and was one of the few concessions to luxury in the aircraft. It was an 'attractive item' and was placed under lock and key for the duration of the servicing.

The carpet and interior furnishings were all in the standard R.A.F. VIP decor of blue-grey and the five or six seats appeared to be of a standard pattern, albeit very comfortable. I know they were comfortable because we had a similar one in our tyre bay office.

The seats were draped and brown paper laid on the carpet, to protect it from the oily shoes of the airmen coming and going. Quite a lot of interior panelling had to be removed, so that rivets in the fuselage could be renewed. Apparently, the snap heads of the rivets had a nasty habit of popping off, which was generally believed to be caused by the metal polish that the coolies used to polish the aircraft. The coolies found it easiest to clean the sides of the fuselage which were, consequently, the shiniest areas of the aircraft. They were also the areas where most of the rivets were missing. The replacement rivets were anodised purple and green depending on the composition and strength and stood out from the polished heads of the other rivets.

Plate 6 Avro York MW 102

I had assembled and signed for the two particular wheels, taken from our built-up stock, that were fitted to MW 102 later. I was quite relieved to see, on a newsreel, that the old crate had landed safely at Heathrow and considered that the day off that we had on the Wedding Day was well earned.

After Mountbatten had relinquished his position as Governor-General of India, R.A.F. Palam closed down and the personnel came back to Mauripur with many varied tales to tell. I was told that whenever Mountbatten returned from a flight somewhere, he would call at the hangar with his two daughters to thank the ground crew for a safe journey.

During 1948 the Staging Post was to be inspected by the A.O.C., whose HQ was at Habbaniyah in Iraq. His area of command extended over many thousands of miles and took in the various staging posts between the Canal Zone and India, such as Sharjah and Bahrain. Our C.O., Group Captain Grice, held a parade of the Staging Post personnel on a piece of open ground between the Sick Quarters and some of the billets. He eyed us in a good-humoured fashion as we airmen, drawn up in three ranks, wondered what was in store for us, in view of our scruffy turnout.

Clasping his left arm with his right hand across his chest in his characteristic stance, he spoke:

"Well, chaps, we've had a pretty easy time up to now and, as you know, the Air Officer Commanding is coming to inspect us. We have three weeks to tidy ourselves up and put on a good show and I mean a really good show, for the A.O.C. You will all report to the stores and draw a new kit of K.D., shoes, socks and field service cap. The K.D. will be tailored to fit by the dhurzi-wallah and, afterwards, given the full treatment by the flying dhobi, that is, starched and pressed and kept in that condition for the big day.

"We will have two rehearsal parades to brush up our drill, for which your ordinary K.D. will suffice and I expect you to put all your efforts into getting it right, so that no extra parades are necessary. I expect the worksites and billets to be on top line and also the various recreational places on the camp, the Radio hut, the Model Club and so on.

"After the A.O.C. goes back to Habbaniyah, satisfied with our turnout, we can slide back into our usual sloppy ways."

And so it was done. We put our backs into improving our drill and Groupie Grice declared himself satisfied if we could maintain our standard on the day. We lined up at the stores, where the staff had their busiest day for some time, collected our kit and instructed our bearers about the standards of bull required for the visiting Burra Sahib.

At the Tyre Bay, the office was cleared of old fag packets and accumulations of sand and everything painted that didn't move and also some that did, such as the two-wheeled trailer on which York wheels were mounted upright for transport down to the Daily Servicing Section.

In the model club, the floor, normally covered to a depth of an inch or more with the debris of intensive model building, was swept for the first time since we moved in and dried spilt dope and paint chipped off the tables. The models were tastefully arranged around the clubroom; Peter Barnett's D.H.2 and my Bristol Fighter were each attached by strong 40 lb. aircraft thread to a tip of one of the two-bladed punkah fans. The speed of the fan was electrically controlled and, at the slowest setting, the two models were pulled around at a reasonable scale speed.

The billets and our kit were always kept clean and tidy by the sweepers and the bearers respectively, so there was not a lot left for us to do as the open ground for the parade was levelled, watered and rolled by a team of coolies.

The A.O.C. turned out to be Air Vice Marshal J. N. Boothman who, as a Flight Lieutenant back in 1931, had won the Schneider Trophy Race for Britain in a Supermarine S6B at 340.08 m.p.h. For the occasion of his visit to Mauripur, he piloted a Devon from Habbaniyah, accompanied only by his wife and his Aide-de-Camp. Far from the vision we had of him descending on us like a ton of bricks, it seemed that it was more of an opportunity for him and his wife to get away from his H.Q. for a brief holiday by the sea.

Certainly, the inspection went off well and he appeared to be very pleased with what he saw. As we were supposed to gaze intently straight ahead as he passed by, I didn't get a very good look at him, but he seemed to be a gentlemanly type. He stopped to speak to those airmen with medal ribbons and seemed to be very interested in their replies. The canned music for the march past threw us out of step when the needle jumped a groove and, in spite of the watering and rolling, our shoes were soon covered in dust. However, he told us that he was impressed with our turnout and he considered that we were doing a good job in difficult circumstances. For the rest of the day he toured the worksites and domestic sites. The Tyre Bay and the rest of the R & I passed muster to everybody's satisfaction and after the A.O.C. had left to tour the domestic sites, we retired to the duftah to relax with a cigarette.

A member of the model club had been detailed to stand by for the inspection and later we heard his account of the interest the A.O.C. had shown in our efforts. Apparently, he had been particularly pleased to see the models of the D.H.2 and the Bristol Fighter, as these were aircraft he had flown in the First World War and he had even stood on a chair to get a closer look as they flew round.

A week later, the A.O.C., his wife and the A.D.C., returned to Habbaniyah. Group Captain Grice gave us his congratulations and, sure enough, we slipped back into our old sloppy ways.

17. Mad dogs and Englishmen

There was a sailing club of which some of the Staging Post personnel were members but, like most activities, it cost money to join and enjoy the benefits, such as they were. Personally and possibly with a touch of sour grapes, I felt it was a boring pastime, tacking up and down Keamari Harbour.

When the sailing urge overcame us, a day on a bunder boat fitted the bill nicely. To hire one, complete with crew, was not expensive if the cost was shared among half a dozen of us. The object was mainly to go deep-sea fishing and, if lucky, have our catch cooked on board.

Bunder boats, which were sailing boats with lateen sails that plied the harbour, could carry three or four dozen people when used as a ferry across the calm waters of Keamari Harbour to Manora, the Royal Pakistan Navy base situated at the end of a long isthmus that enclosed the south-west side of the harbour. In the open sea they would have been swamped with such a complement, for they heeled over in the wind. It was necessary for a plank to be secured so as to project over the side about eight or nine feet, with one or two people sitting on it, to balance the craft.

One day a group of us hired a boat, with the intention of visiting Oyster Island, which was just outside the harbour. We first had to call at the village on the isthmus for the cooking equipment. While we waited for the crew, we passed the time throwing annas into the water for young boys to dive for them from the masts of other boats. Some were so young that they could hardly walk but, after they had finally climbed a mast and hurled themselves off like chubby dolls, we were relieved to see that they could swim like fishes.

Returning across the harbour, we passed an old steamer having her bunkers refilled with coal. To me it was an extraordinary sight, for it was being done solely by women enveloped in grimy saris. Scaffolding had been built with poles and ropes up the side of the steamer, from the lighter alongside. It had landings, alternating with each other on each side, at six feet spacings, so that a landing on one side was about three feet higher than the other. On each landing were two women who lifted sacks of coal up from the lighter to the next landing and so on up the side of the ship to the deck, where it was tipped into the bunkers. It must have been incredibly hard work dressed like that in the heat of the day.

Once out at sea, I felt like Sinbad the sailor in our craft, particularly when we passed large, sea-going, dhows, some drawn up on the beach for careening and some at anchor. It was a scene that portrayed a type of commerce, which had flourished unchanged for centuries and, together with camel trains and camel carts, operated as a counterpart to modern commerce with steamships, railways and lorries.

Landing at Oyster Island, there was nothing much to see, for it was just a large rock sticking out of the sea. The receding tide had left pools in which various fish had become trapped. One pool held an expiring sea snake about six feet long with vicious-looking teeth, which we felt was best left to its fate, but we threw a few fish back into the sea. It would have been unsporting to have cooked them and, in any case, they didn't look very appetising.

The fishing was a failure, the tackle being rudimentary to say the least, but fortunately the crew must have anticipated our lack of expertise, for they produced some fish already cut and cleaned, for which I was quite thankful, being a bit squeamish! Apart from the stove nearly setting the boat on fire when a gust of wind blew up, the fish was cooked to perfection and, washed down with beer, made an enjoyable meal.

When we set sail back to harbour, I volunteered to walk the plank and sit on the end, dangling my feet in the water. I was not prepared for a school of porpoises to decide to accompany us part of the way. The first I knew about it was when a porpoise leapt out of the water, knocking my feet and nearly tipping me off the plank. My shout of alarm was met with gales of laughter from my oppos and anxious instructions from the bunder boat skipper – he with the Jinnah hat – to stay where I was as the wind was freshening. So I stayed and managed to enjoy the sight of the marvellous creatures leaping joyfully under my perch, until they turned away with a final leap of farewell.

One of the reasons why we did not catch any fish was because, around that time, they actually were scarce. The local fishermen had complained that something unusually large was driving them away, according to the papers. It sounded rather a tall story, but it was true. The fishermen finally managed to catch the culprit, by some wonderful means for it was as big as one of their boats. It turned out to be a whale-shark about eight feet wide and thirty feet long, with a mouth three feet wide. It was put on show at Baba Island, with a rope fence around it and was quite a tourist attraction, being a very fearsome-looking creature.

Swimming was usually done at Hawkes Bay for ten months of the year. For two months it was banned because of a yearly influx of jellyfish, including Portuguese Men of War. I had the idea that swimming across the mouth of the harbour would be all right and so it proved to be for several weeks.

The favourite plan was to dive off the Oil Jetty at Keamari and swim about a mile across to Manora. More often than not I cheated, for on those occasions a passing bunder boat on a ferry run would throw me a rope, which I hung on to and it pulled me through the water until my arms ached and I had to let go, with a final wave to the crew.

One day, I carelessly dived off the jetty into a mass of floating jelly rather like frogspawn, which gave me rather a shock although it was, luckily, not of the stinging variety. I surfaced to find a large bubble floating past, about six feet away and almost ran across the jelly in my haste to get out of the water.

Occasionally, packs of pariah dogs (known as piards), nasty-looking beasts with dingy yellow fur, would roam through the camp to scavenge. A well-aimed stone would usually send them off as they seemed fairly timid, but one day a large pack of about fifteen dogs proved to be more persistent than usual. Accompanied by Sooty, who thought it was great fun, I chased them through the billet lines and out into the open space beyond. Once away from the camp, the demeanour of the dogs changed and, as we stopped, they turned around and encircled Sooty and myself, snarling and yelping as they perceived an opportunity for a good meal. Back to back, Sooty and I faced them as they advanced and hurriedly I picked up some stones which, fortunately, were plentiful and proceeded to throw them to good effect.

Gradually, we managed to edge back towards the camp as, with aching arms, I kept up a fusillade to deter them from getting closer. I had no doubt that if I had stopped for an instant, they would have overwhelmed us. Finally, we regained the safety of the camp area and returned to the billet, exhausted and thankful to have escaped the consequences of such a stupid caper.

The responsibility of keeping two bitches, the other being Sooty who had been bequeathed to me by Mike Toms on his return to the U.K., gave me some anxious moments. There were an increasing number of dogs on the camp and it was decreed that they had to be registered and to have collars with name tags, otherwise they were liable to be shot. I had to replace the collars and tags several times. Duffy carried her first-born into the billet and dropped it on my stomach as I lay on my charpoy, being her way of informing me that her time had come.

I had organised a wooden box with a sandfly net over it on the verandah and I put a spare blanket in it. Unfortunately, the blanket became blood stained when the other puppies were born and I disposed of it, for which I was fined R9 and confined to barracks for ten days. Jankers, as it was called, was not an arduous punishment at Mauripur, but it curtailed my social life for a while.

There were enough takers for the pups who had soon made their presence known by barking and yapping at all hours and the other occupants of the billet were very forbearing when their beauty sleep was disturbed.

When the Berlin Airlift started, work in the Tyre Bay was much reduced and I filled in the time by volunteering to pack parachutes over in the Safety Equipment Section. These parachutes were never issued because Transport Command never supplied them for passengers and the aircrew, in consequence, did not feel it was right that they alone should have them. Every month, the parachutes were opened, inspected and repacked which created a lot of extra work for the section. I quite enjoyed the work, particularly as nobody was likely to risk his neck by actually jumping with one.

One day my other dog, Sooty, decided to follow me to work. She eyed the airmen leaving the cookhouse but failed to spot me because I hid myself in a group of oppos until I was on the bus. Realising that I had escaped and that all the airmen had left, she dashed round to where the transport was parked. The buses were all leaving but she jumped on to the Queen Mary which had the tailboard lowered. Too late, she found nobody on board but, before she could get off, the Queen Mary moved off after the buses.

When my bus stopped at the Terminal Building, the Queen Mary came in sight travelling at about twenty miles an hour, with Sooty's head sticking out through the side girders. She must have seen the bus and decided that I was on it, for she leapt out on to the road, rolled over several times, picked herself up and chased after the bus.

"Wait for Sooty!" I begged the driver.

"No dogs allowed on the bus," he replied.

"Let her on, you mean sod!" chorused his passengers, who had been watching. With bad grace, he complied, the door was opened and Sooty bounded up the steps and worked her way along the bus, inspecting each airman until she found me and covered me with dog hairs and great licks of affection.

Arriving at the work site, I was in a quandary to know what to do with her, but she lay quietly in the office and kept a beady eye on me though the open door.

During the morning, the C.O. sent for me so I gave Sooty the slip and went over to the office block, only to find that she was following me. No threats or orders would make her go back, but she kept her distance about 20 yards behind.

I tapped on the door of the C.O., Flight Lieutenant Cogger, who bade me enter and closed it carefully behind me.

"Leave it open, Newton, it's getting a bit hot now," he said. Reluctantly, I opened it again and stood to attention in front of his desk. "Now, Newton, I understand you've been helping out in the Safety Equipment Section."

"Yes, sir." Out of the corner of my eye I could see Sooty peering into the office.

"Have you done any work on dinghies and Mae Wests?"

"A bit, sir." I could see Sooty creeping across the floor to the desk. The C.O. did not see her and continued:

"How do you feel about transferring to the Daily Servicing Section? We're short of a Safety Equipment worker at the present time."

"Would I have to sign for the equipment, sir?" I queried. Sooty was now sitting under the table, looking bored.

"Of course, Newton!"

"Well, sir, I don't feel that I am suitably qualified on Safety Equipment to take the responsibility for aircraft flying to Negombo and Sharjah." Sooty was investigating one of the C.O.'s bare knees.

"Nonsense, Newton, there's nothing to it!"

With horror, I watched Sooty reach out her tongue and lick the C.O.'s knee.

The C.O. shot six feet into the air, it seemed to me. When he came down again, he peered under the table and saw Sooty, who remained sitting quietly there.

"Is this your dog, Newton?" he barked.

"Yes, sir," said I, meekly.

"Well, get it out of here. You know dogs are not allowed on the work site."

And that was all he said about the incident. He was disappointed that I did not want to transfer to the D.S.S. but did not press me further. He probably found it difficult to concentrate on the matter after a shock like that.

On my resumed forays into Karachi, I invariably cut it fine when catching the last bus back. On several occasions I missed it and had to walk back some twelve miles. Once, there was a curfew in force and I had to walk fast to leave the city behind me before it came into effect. It was a long and lonely walk back to camp, but I never met with any trouble.

Next day, I would be worn out and, on one particular day, Addie Adams suggested that I should have a kip on the floor, under the office table. He would wake me up if anybody came into the hangar. Using a pile of fresh cleaning rags as a pillow, I lay on the hard concrete floor and went out like a light.

I awoke to hear footsteps approaching the office doorway and as it was too late to scramble out from under the table, which was under the window next to the open door, I stayed where I was. A pair of legs came in and stood not twelve inches from my nose, which tickled ominously.

I held my breath and kept perfectly still, for I knew it was an officer by the way the khaki stockings were neatly pulled up and the fact that his shoes, unsullied by oil, gleamed even in the darkness of the office.

Minutes seemed to pass before he turned and left. I stayed where I was until I was certain he had gone and then got up, cautiously made my exit and rejoined my workmates. They had been caught out by the sudden approach of Flight Lieutenant Cogger and could do no more than watch with bated breath for his reappearance, when they were able to draw his attention away from the office.

The second time I felt the need for a kip, I decided to slope off back to the billet several miles away, as there was no work to do at the time. I had gone a couple of miles when a CPU vehicle pulled up beside me. A voice I recognised only too well said,

"Going to the Sick Quarters, Newton?" It was Flight Lieutenant Cogger.

"Yes, sir," said I. There was not much else I could say, because I remembered that it was Thursday, the day one could go to the Sick Quarters to have one's jabs brought up to date.

"After you, Newton!" said he as he ushered me into the Sick Quarters, when we had arrived. "Wait for me and I'll drive you back to the work site."

The medical orderly looked at my pay book, whistled and said: "Full house for you, chum!"

In those days, disposable syringes had not been heard of. The orderly would pick one of several needles lying in a tray of disinfectant, push it on the syringe and fill the syringe from a phial. As the needle had been used many times, it was blunt and had to be stabbed, or even thrown like a dart into the recipient's arm or buttock. Strong men, who were next in the queue, were known to faint at the sight.

After being pumped full of dead germs and aching in my posterior and both arms, I was duly driven back to work. I could swear there was an amused gleam in Flight Lieutenant Cogger's eyes.

On yet another occasion, I was walking to work along the same route for some quite legitimate reason. It was a deserted road, hot and dusty and I had several miles to go when the bonnet of a Humber Super Snipe with a little flag on it, glided to a stop beside me.

"Pull your socks up, airman!" said an authoritative voice. I did so with alacrity, for the words were uttered by a chap with scrambled egg on his peaked cap, who was driving.

"Where are you going?"

"Tech Site, sir," I said,

"Well, don't just stand there, jump in!"

I did so and off we went. It turned out to be Air Marshal Sir Richard Atcherley, who was the Officer Commanding of the Royal Pakistan Air Force at the time.

"How do you like Pakistan?" he asked.

"I like it very much, sir," I replied.

"Humph!" he said, almost in disbelief. I had the impression that he wasn't enjoying being in Pakistan as much as I was, but in his position he could have had problems I knew nothing about and I felt that perhaps there were some advantages in being just an ordinary airman.

"Remember, laddie," he said as he dropped me off at the turning to the Tech Site, "that while you are in Pakistan you are representing the Royal Air Force and you never know who is observing you, so keep up a smart appearance at all times!"

With this mild admonishment, he returned my smart salute with a wave and a smile and drove off.

An oppo of mine, Pepperal, was obsessed with the idea of building a patio-type garden for our new canteen, with a flight of steps illuminated with a light at either side. By diligent persuasion, he managed to enlist my support and we spent several weeks on the project.

He had organised the use of a truck and a team of coolies and we scoured the desert for suitable stones. The coolies were paid, in theory, to work for a whole day of each day of the week, but they normally finished work when we did, at one o'clock.

They were not very happy to be called upon to work for no extra pay in the heat of the early afternoon, but with a bit of persuasion, which included the use of some choice Anglo-Saxon expressions and, when they had earned them, an issue all round of Mars bars – bought with our own money – they were soon working cheerfully enough. I remember one of the coolies had twelve fingers and twelve toes, so he was told to get two fingers out!

They turned out to be quite a cheery bunch once they had got used to the idea of working with two mad Englishmen, who knew enough of the current hit song "Humari jan hai Sunday ke Sunday" (literally "I live from Sunday to Sunday") to join in the chorus.

We sweated to get the project finished for the Station dance, to which all the girls we knew were invited. It turned out to be a disaster and the last dance to be held while I was there, for the first bus to take the girls home crashed into a fruit and vegetable stall, demolishing it. The bus did not stop and the following buses received a fusillade of projectiles which broke some windows. The girls refused to come again, not unnaturally.

18. Pakistan Zindabad!

Many people have the impression that the British were hated by the population of what was India and some have insisted to me that this was the case although they have never been there. They forget that the politicians and the media do not necessarily represent the feelings of ordinary people, either in India or anywhere else and I think the following personal account may put a different complexion on the matter.

A bearer from the next billet who knew me came to me one day to ask a question. He had had an argument with some fellow bearers about whether or not Britain would come back and take over again if India and Pakistan did not get on and perhaps went to war with each other, which in fact they subsequently did.

He maintained that Britain would do so if it became necessary, with which his friends did not agree. He came to me to seek support for his argument, but would accept what I said. It was with a heavy heart that I told him that, as far as I knew, Britain had left for ever and India and Pakistan had to sort any trouble out by themselves. Crestfallen, he accepted what I told him.

My heart was heavy because I realised for the first time that British rule had meant peace and stability for millions of Indians. It was right that British rule should end and India, as it was, should get its independence like Australia, Canada, etc, but we, the British, had abandoned them in petulant impatience because people at home did not understand and did not care about India, our responsibility. As a result, more than a quarter of a million people died, some of whose bodies I had seen myself.

I saw only one riot and that was in Karachi in 1949, my last year in Pakistan. I was heading back to Saddar to catch a bus and had to cross Bunder Road, a wide main thoroughfare which was packed with people. They were chanting "Pakistan Zindabad" (Long live Pakistan) and looked rather annoyed, to say the least.

I edged my way through the crowd, trying to look inconspicuous, but was unable to move very far before I came face to face with a very tall, bearded, Pakistani. At that moment, there was the sound of rifle fire further up the road. The Pakistani looked down at me and said, in good English, "Are you British?"

"Yes," I said, trying to put on a brave face. "What is going on?"

"Some Indian High Commission people have hoisted the Indian Flag outside a building where they live and the crowd don't like it and are trying to take it down."

"What about the shooting?" I asked.

"That is the police," he replied. "They are trying to stop us. Do you agree that it is wrong for the Indians to insult us in this way?"

"Oh yes! They shouldn't do that!" I said, playing safe.

"Where are you going?" he asked.

"Saddar, to catch my bus."

"You will never get to Saddar that way," he said. "Follow me!"

He turned and, in a loud voice, shouted to the curious throng who had gathered around.

"Make way for the Sahib! Make way for the Sahib!"

I could have sunk through the ground, but realised that I might as well act the part so, holding my head high, I followed him. Escorted by half a dozen hefty-looking chaps, who seemed to have appointed themselves as my bodyguard, we made our way across the road as the crowd fell back to form an unobstructed path for us.

I was led up a side road and I half expected to be mugged, but there they gave me directions for an alternative route to Saddar. After they had all shaken hands with me, they returned to Bunder Road.

On an earlier occasion, it had been raining heavily, being the monsoon time. I had been caught unexpectedly, for it hadn't rained in Karachi for several years and was sheltering in a cafe doorway. I was accosted by a well-dressed chap in his late twenties who, having ascertained that I was British, proceeded to condemn Britain for exploiting India. I defended Britain's actions as best I could, pointing out that India and Pakistan had had their freedom, what more did they want?

He replied that Britain had got out after bleeding the country white (sic), to which I replied that Pakistan's economy was strong and she had not devalued her currency as Britain had had to devalue the pound!

It transpired in further conversation that he was a schoolteacher who was going to a job in East Africa and I remarked that, as an educated man who could afford to travel, he hadn't done too badly under British Rule. I pointed to the fine buildings of the High Court of Sind and the Civil Hospital, the wide road with trams running up and down, all built by the British that Pakistan had inherited.

"The British looked down on Indians and belittled us in their books!" he rejoined.

"Do you mean people like Kipling?" I asked.

"Yes, yes, Kipling! He wrote 'Gunga Din' in which he belittled the Indian water carrier, Gunga Din!"

I replied, "You would have found that the last line states, 'You're a better man than I am, Gunga Din', if you had taken the trouble to read it in full!"

My impatience with his attitude finally caused him to turn and go and I decided to risk being soaked by walking to the bus stop. As I hesitated before taking the plunge, the cafe proprietor tapped me on the shoulder.

"Have a cup of char, Sahib!"

"No thanks, I only have enough money with me for the bus," I replied. This was quite true, for my pay seemed to go nowhere after paying for the bearer, flying dhobi, cigarettes, beer and the other essentials of life.

"No, No, Sahib, you don't understand. This is on the house!"

My amazement at his generosity must have shown, for he said, "I want you to know that we don't all think like that fellow!"

Grateful to be able to retreat from the rain, I followed him into the cafe. He pulled out a chair for me to sit on, instructed a waiter to bring me a cup of tea and excused himself. Shortly after, the waiter returned with a packet of twenty Players which he put on the table.

"No, no, thank you," I protested.

"It is from those fellows over there, Sahib. They have bought them for you," and he indicated a bunch of customers sitting around a far table, who looked none too prosperous to me.

Feeling rather embarrassed, I called to them, "Thank you very much!" They seemed pleased with my acceptance of their gift, as they laughed and waved before returning to their general conversation. I was unsure how to respond to their generosity, but it was apparent that I was to be left in peace with my cup of tea and cigarettes, to unwind after the argument.

I looked around the cafe, which was neither posh nor dingy and not in an area where most Europeans went. It had three columns set in one wall and on each column was a full-length picture. One was of King Edward VII, another of King George V and the third of King George VI. Each monarch was dressed in full Coronation regalia.

The proprietor came back and asked if the tea was satisfactory, which it was of course. I told him that I was surprised that the pictures were still there two years after Independence.

"They were good men and we respect them. Why should we remove them?"

With a feeling that I had rather put my foot in it, I changed the subject, thanked him for his hospitality and, as soon as the rain had eased off, said a few words of valediction to the group at the table and left.

On yet another occasion, I went to the Oil Jetty at Keamari for my customary swim, to find the way to it barred by a picket of about twenty rather ugly-looking men who stopped me and brusquely demanded to know who I was and what I was doing there. An explanation, in rather sketchy Urdu, seemed to satisfy them. Their attitude changed and they offered to keep an eye on my clothes while I swam, an offer I felt it was expedient to accept. They explained that the picket was there to stop any crew members from leaving a South African tanker which was tied up to the jetty. It was apparent that they did not take kindly to the colour bar in South Africa.

I changed behind a shack and left my clothes where they could be seen by the pickets. Some of the crew were leaning over the taffrail, looking pretty morose and a grin from me met with no response so, without further ado, I dived into the water and swam about for twenty minutes or so. The water, incidentally, was tidal and very clean.

My swim over, I climbed back on to the jetty and retrieved my clothes. Everything was as it had been left and, after dressing, I thanked the pickets who were now much friendlier. They all insisted on shaking hands, possibly for the benefit of the South Africans, but Pakistanis were always ready to shake hands in any case, after which I wended my way back to Karachi.

From the foregoing accounts, it can be seen that the personnel of the Staging Post were not restricted as to where they went, out of duty hours, which was in sharp contrast to life in the Canal Zone in Egypt, as I was to find out.

An American ship, the U.S.S. Toledo, on a courtesy visit to Karachi, invited the Staging Post on board for a day. My impression of the Americans was that they were very outgoing and very hospitable, but unable to adapt to their surroundings. They never left the ship, except in large groups and were fleeced in the bars, cafes and restaurants and wherever else they spent their money.

Most of the crew were young conscripts whose main ambition was to get back "Stateside" and the thought of being in a place like Karachi for two and a half years appalled them. The ship was well endowed with things like an armour-plated projection room for the open-air cinema screen which was hung up on the after deck, ice cream machines and record players, but there was no beer—all U.S. Navy ships were dry.

This was in sharp contrast to a courtesy visit by two Royal Navy ships. The crews were the guests of the Royal Pakistan Navy, who took them everywhere and by all accounts they had a whale of a time.

When returning to Mauripur after a sojourn in Karachi, I could return, by the R.A.F. 'liberty' bus, from the Union Jack Club last thing at night or, if earlier, the civilian bus by catching it in Bunder Road. If I chose to return on the civilian bus, there was a cigarette seller by the bus stop who always had a packet of my favourite cigarettes put by for me.

He was a refugee from Cawnpore and had been a civil servant. Now all he had was a large tray, containing his wares, which he sold on the pavement to support his wife and several children. We became very friendly and, when I showed up one day, he sent one of the boys into a nearby cafe to borrow a chair which he asked me to sit on. I felt a bit of a Charlie but didn't like to hurt his feelings, so I sat on the chair, which blocked half the pavement, while I waited for the bus. Every now and then, he would introduce me to a friend who was passing by and there was much hand shaking.

Thereafter, I was always provided with a chair and it was amazing how soon one got used to the situation.

We had been warned, from the day we arrived in India, to guard against 'loose wallahs' (thieves) by always keeping our kit under lock and key. This was impossible to do, as our bearer had charge of all our kit and, as it turned out, was totally unnecessary. I would like to place on record the fact that I never had anything stolen while in India or Pakistan, which is more than I can say about any other period of my R.A.F. service.

One day, I was particularly hard up for money to buy cigarettes and my dejection must have been apparent to the bearer.

"What's the matter, Sahib?" he queried.

"I'm skint, bearer."

"Oh, no, Sahib, you have money!"

"I'm not kidding, I haven't got a bean!"

"Oh, yes, you have, Sahib!"

"If I had any money, I wouldn't be gasping for a fag, would I?"

"I show you, Sahib!"

"Please do, bearer!"

Whereupon he went to my bedside locker, took out an old cocoa tin I hadn't noticed before and handed it to me.

"You see, Sahib, you have money!"

I opened the tin and, with disbelieving eyes, I saw that it was full to the top with half annas and pice pieces, which were copper coins like washers and each worth very little. However, when all the coins were added up, there was enough to buy a packet of twenty Players and I was quite humbled by the honesty of the bearer, to whom the coins were more valuable and who could have appropriated them without my having ever known. Needless to say, he was rewarded on the following payday, although he insisted it was not necessary.

Two of the best examples of honesty occurred in Karachi. On the first occasion, I was on a tram on which, oddly enough, the conductor would not allow standing passengers. I gained a seat only because various passengers squeezed up to make a space on the bench-type seat that spanned the width of the tramcar and insisted that I sit myself down before the conductor told me to get off. I did so, gratefully, although it was a bit of a squeeze.

Arriving at my destination, I arose and was about to step off the tram, when my fellow passengers called me back and pointed to a roll of rupee notes which had fallen out of my trouser pocket. There was about R 80, consisting mainly of back pay, which was a large sum for me to lose. I retrieved the money with mumbled thanks—(I seemed to be always thanking people in Karachi).

The other occurrence was on my last night out in Karachi. I had gone to buy more beer to replenish the stocks at a farewell party my friends in Karachi had thrown for me. I could well afford to do so for once, as my newly acquired wallet bulged with R 100 which was my pay to last me until I got back to the UK.

It was not until I was due to leave the party to return to Mauripur that I discovered that my wallet was missing. A hurried search failed to uncover it and I left on the plane to Habbaniyah next morning without it.

The ship which brought us home from the Middle East was waiting for the tide to take us over the Mersey Bar, when a pilot boat brought our mail from England. In my mail was a small parcel from my mother. Enclosed in it was my wallet, which still contained the money. There was also a letter from the Senior Administrative Officer at Mauripur, explaining that the wallet had been picked up in a street in Karachi and handed to a Royal Pakistan Air Force Officer, who forwarded it to the Staging Post and who, in turn, sent it to my home address.

It was an incredibly lucky turn of events, but characteristic, I knew, of the honesty of the average Pakistani.

19. Ships that Pass in the Night

To return to the main theme of aircraft; many different aircraft staged through Mauripur to and from, the Far East in addition to the aircraft of Transport Command, for which the servicing was our primary concern.

A typical example was a Lincoln (RE 414) named 'Mercury II' which I was to meet up with again back in the UK. Another Lincoln was 'Crusader' (RF 498 coded DF-P) in natural metal finish.

Plate 7 Avro Lincoln RF 498 'Crusader

We also had a visit from 9 Squadron on an affiliation exercise with the Royal Pakistan Air Force. It was a detachment of six Lincoln aircraft, complete with ground crew who were soon joining in our social life. The Flight Sergeant in charge of the ground crew, one night down at the Union Jack Club, took exception to my use of the Urdu words "tikh hai" (OK) in conversation. He thought I was putting on a bit of swank and offered to smash my teeth in – he'd had a few – and had to be restrained from doing just that. I had, in fact, used the word unconsciously as it was part of the Staging Post slang. The Flight Sergeant was an old India hand and I suppose he had a point after all. I hastily apologised but he was set on beating me to a pulp – and he would have done it, too, if his oppos had not held on to him.

Next day, I had a telephone call to go and see him down at the flight line. Quaking in my boots and with unsympathetic jokes and laughter from my mates, I went.

Recovered from his libations, the Flight Sergeant turned out to be an extremely nice chap. He apologised sincerely for his behaviour and was very concerned that I should have no hard feelings about the incident. With relief, I said it was nothing and we shook hands on it.

Lockheed Venturas came through occasionally, FP 592 being one I photographed on a visit to the Daily Servicing Section. Working, as I did, at the Tech Site half a mile away, I did not see all the aircraft that passed through, but I often used to visit the Section in the afternoon, if a particularly interesting type was to be seen.

Such an aircraft was a Viking (VL 248) of the King's Flight, in natural highly-polished metal finish.

Another was the first Hastings (TG 503) to pass through on a proving flight. Everybody on the unit seemed to be taking a look, for this was the type of aircraft that would replace the York. One of the Staging Post ground crew servicing the aircraft opened the flight deck door, entered and promptly disappeared through an open hatch in the floor, breaking both his ankles when he fell some 15 feet and landed on the concrete below.

Several Bristol Mk 10 Beaufighters with long-range tanks staged through to Malaya, RD 817 being one. Later, Bristol Brigands also staged through to replace the Beaufighters for use in the Malayan emergency.

Other Air Forces used the facilities at Mauripur. The U.S.A.F. frequently had Dakotas and Skymasters make an overnight stop en route to Japan or Europe. One Skymaster was numbered 49048.

On one occasion, a U.S.A.F. Dakota, more correctly known as a C47 Skytrain, had wheel trouble. I happened to be in sole charge of the Tyre Bay that day, not that the responsibility weighed heavily on me. The two crew members, pilot and navigator, still dressed in their flying overalls and baseball caps, hitched a lift to the Tech Site and came into the Tyre Bay.

Plate 8 Handley-Page Hastings TG 503

"Hiya, Bud, we've had a spot of trouble with our airplane. Could you sell us a good wheel?"

I laughed. "My feet wouldn't touch the ground if I sold you a wheel!"

"Huh? I don't get yah, Bud. We're stuck on the ground if you don't!"

"I mean, I'd be in the slammer so fast," I explained.

"Oh, sure, we understand. Perhaps you could lend one to Uncle Sam?"

I thought this one over. We had more Dakota wheels than we were ever likely to need in six months, as we now had only one Station Dakota, KN 543, an olive green well-worn work horse, the other natural-finish Dakota having left for other skies; for Dakotas in transit, replacement wheels were rarely needed. One exception was KN 691 coded 'T'.

"When will you be back?" I asked.

"Waal, it could be two months, ah guess, but you can be sure we'll be back."

"All right," I said, "I'll let you have a wheel, but you'll have to sign for it."

What good that would be, I didn't know, but it seemed to put an official stamp on the arrangement. After all, handing over Air Force property to any passing Tom, Dick or Harry could have consequences detrimental to one's career prospects!

So, I extracted all the details I could: number, rank, name, etc., wrote them on the log card, obtained a signature and gave them instructions on how to get to the Palace Hotel in Karachi, where they had decided to stay.

That was that for about twelve weeks. The wheel was not missed and I had quite forgotten about it when, one morning, a fifteen cwt. truck rolled up to the hangar, with the two Americans in it and a brand spanking new, unused, Dakota wheel in the back.

"Here you are, Bud, told you we'd be back!" one said. "Thanks for helping us out."

They unloaded the wheel, thrust a packet of 200 Lucky Strike cigarettes at me, leaped back into the truck and were gone.

A French-built Junkers 52/3M turned up one day, which I lost no time in going to see. It had a silver finish with Red Cross markings, matt black anti-dazzle finish between the central engine and the windscreen and a blue, white and red rudder.

It really seemed an incredible aircraft to me, like a flying Nissen hut with no finesse at all, but having the air of a Teutonic juggernaut. I had been accustomed, in my younger days, to seeing newsreels and magazines that showed paratroops jumping out of these machines before the war and for many years after and its association with violent events in Spain, Poland, Holland, Crete, etc., gave me a twinge of fearful revulsion.

A French mechanic was nonchalantly sitting on the nose, working on the carburettor of the centre engine. With horrified disbelief, I noticed that he was smoking a cigarette and hastily removed myself from the area until he had finished, after which I asked in schoolboy French if I could look inside the fuselage.

Permission given, I climbed aboard and looked around with curiosity. The internal structure was very basic and ruggedly functional, with absolutely no concession to comfort, not even having seats in the main cabin.

There were a few tubular poles lashed to the structure, which appeared to be components of a framework for supporting stretchers. The only other things in the cabin were a crate of wine, a pile of well-thumbed French girlie magazines and a spare wheel. Being a Red Cross aircraft, no supplies to prosecute the war going on in French Indo-China (Vietnam, Cambodia etc.) could be carried.

However, French troops did pass through Mauripur, mainly Foreign Legion troops who stayed overnight in the Transit billets. They were dour, taciturn men, mainly German, who seemed to lack the cheerful banter to be found with British servicemen. Perhaps I would not have been so cheerful either, if I had been going with them, for of those who survived the vicious fighting, many would fly out of the battle zone, badly wounded, in one of the Red Cross Junkers.

Plate 9 Junkers 52/3M

We were fortunate in our peaceful exile, for although the war had been over for three years there was still bloodshed in many parts of the world: Greece, Palestine, Malaya, French Indo-China and, rather nearer, Kashmir,

Even in Karachi there was occasional bloodshed. One day, the Sikhs, who had been troublesome to us when they attempted to blow up our power station, were rounded up secretly and taken outside the city to be put on a train to India, together with their families. A mob found out about the arrangements and followed on foot or by any transport they could find and massacred the Sikhs on the railway station platform.

The whole affair was kept remarkably quiet. The first I knew of it was when I was sitting in the Civil Hospital garden waiting for my date and recovering from the shock of a coconut just missing me and nearly killing me as it fell out of a palm tree, when a lorry quietly entered the grounds. It was piled high with bodies covered in muslin, except for the legs sticking out grotesquely, which had been brought there to be unceremoniously disposed of.

Death did intrude into our lives unfortunately, although not the death of any of the Staging Post personnel. We had a British Army Warrant Officer in the Sick Quarters who seemed to be recovering nicely from some illness, but he had a relapse and died. I was detailed for the funeral party to go to the British Military Cemetery. The funeral party was issued with rifles, for the first time since Drigh Road days and given some quick drill practice.

Arriving early at the cemetery, we had time to wander around and read the tombstones, many of which were quite ornate. It was a large cemetery and had been in use for a century or more, judging by the inscriptions. I had never realised, when I used to read of John Company, the East India Company, the Indian Mutiny and so on in my boy's adventure story books, how many thousands of young British lads had lived the great adventure and paid for it by dying of wounds and pestilence. This was just one of hundreds of cemeteries scattered throughout the sub-continent. A typical inscription might read:

"Subaltern A. J. Carruthers M.C. 1st Baluch Scouts 1875-1894. Died from wounds and disease while on active service during 2nd Afridi Uprising."

Chocks & Driptrays ~ 181

Some strange units, places and events were mentioned, but the names were uncompromisingly British and the causes of death depressingly repetitive: cholera, typhoid, typhus, smallpox and wounds.

Another unfortunate death was that of Capt. Stack, the son of Neville Stack, the pioneer aviator. He was involved in an accident outside the Officers' Mess and his father attended the funeral.

To return to a more cheerful subject, the Daily Servicing Section worked in shifts and aircraft came and went 24 hours a day. One York MW 238 in transit became unserviceable and had to be taxied up to the R & I hangar to have a major snag fixed and subsequently had to be flight-tested.

Being one of the few opportunities there were for a local flight, I applied to go on it. Aircrew always liked to have a member of the ground crew along on test flights, it seemed to give them more confidence in the quality of the work carried out. Unfortunately for their confidence, I had not done any work on this aircraft and the general feeling of the R & I chaps seemed to be that I was a fool to risk my neck when it was not necessary.

I sat in solitary comfort in the main forward cabin, in line with the undercarriage so that I could see the punishment the tyres took when landing. The noise from the engines, at full throttle, penetrated the cabin, apparently unimpeded by the interior panelling and I was not sorry the trip would last only half an hour.

By the time we had taken off, the sun had already set, due to the flight having been delayed because of various other snags that also required attention. It was therefore quite an interesting experience, as the aircraft climbed, to see the sun reappear over the horizon and then slowly set again, after which there was not much to see apart from the lights of Karachi.

Every now and then, a red-hot spark would be ejected from the engine exhausts and disappear over the wing, but everything seemed to be working well, including the undercarriage and flaps which were raised and lowered several times.

When we finally landed, it was too dark to see the touchdown clearly and although it was a good landing, there was quite a jolt and a loud squeal from the tyres. I have always felt that a means of spinning the wheels before landing would prevent a lot of tyre wear and that such an invention would be worth a lot of money.

Soon afterwards, the York took off again on its belated flight to Negombo in Ceylon, the next staging post on the route to the Far East.

Another York MW 233, coded TB-Q, on another occasion took off to fly the same route. For some reason, the coolant of the port outer engine was lost, causing the engine to overheat and seize. The pilot feathered the propeller and diverted to Santa Cruz airport near Bombay. Unfortunately, the aircraft swung off the runway after landing, ran across the grass and into a hillock, which collapsed the undercarriage and bent the fuselage. A number of the R & I personnel were flown down to Santa Cruz to dismantle the aircraft. I was not one of them, to my disappointment, but the incident was a reminder of the responsibilities of our jobs.

When I was posted and likely to have to leave at short notice, the thought of leaving Sooty and Duffy to pine and starve, for there was no possibility of taking them with me, forced me to make a difficult decision. I had seen other dogs, similarly left behind, increasingly neglected as their new owners were also posted and I felt that I could not leave them to an unknown fate. I had been lucky to place the pups with people I thought would take care of them, but to find homes for two grown bitches was impossible. With a heavy heart, the pain of which I still feel, for they were the most affectionate and intelligent of dogs, I had them put to sleep. As it turned out, my action was sadly premature, as I did not leave Mauripur until another six months had passed.

The chaps in the Safety Equipment Section had thought up a new type of equipment pack for use in Air-Sea Rescue. It consisted of a parachute, two canisters of emergency supplies and a dinghy, all connected in that order by webbing and was intended to be dropped from a search aircraft to survivors who had ditched in the ocean.

Permission was given for a trial drop, using the resident Dakota KN 543, to be carried out over the airfield. The equipment pack was laid on a tabletop, which protruded through the opening in the fuselage formed by the removal of the passenger door. The pack was dropped by the simple method of lifting the inner end of the tabletop, so that the pack slid out of the aircraft. An attached line opened the parachute when the pack was clear of the aircraft and a further lanyard from the parachute to the dinghy operated the CO_2 system that inflated it.

The idea was that the dinghy would land in the water near the survivors, who would swim to it and climb in. All the supplies they needed, tinned water, 'K' rations, Horlicks tablets, pep pills marked "Only to be taken when all hope has been abandoned", radio and aerial complete with box kite, compass, cigarettes and many other things were in the containers. These would be floating nearby, to be pulled into the dinghy by the webbing when required.

I was detailed to accompany 'Moggie' Morgan in a jeep to retrieve the equipment when it landed and also I took along my folding Brownie camera to record the drop.

The pack was successfully and accurately released from the Dakota, but when the parachute opened, the webbing between the two containers parted. The dinghy, which had inflated, then acted as a parachute and deposited one container heavily on the perimeter track, exactly on target. The parachute itself, relieved of part of its load, drifted off with the freshening breeze into the desert, taking the other container with it.

Leaving the dinghy and its pack in the charge of some ground crew who were observing the drop, Moggie Morgan and I shot off into the desert in hot pursuit of the parachute. I had to hang on with both hands as the jeep careered over the rough ground, swerving now and then to avoid a cactus or an outcrop of rock. So intent were we to keep our eyes on the parachute, rapidly disappearing into the distance, that we failed to notice the wadi ahead of us. We hurtled straight over the edge and dropped heavily about four feet into the sandy bed, with a loud protest from the jeep.

A quick examination failed to find any damage to the jeep or to ourselves and, after heaving and rocking back and forth a few times, we extracted the vehicle and set off down the wadi, as there was no way of getting out up the sheer sides. We travelled about a mile before finding a spot where we could climb out and head back to the airfield.

We had to return the jeep, but managed to obtain a fifteen cwt. truck and set off once again in the general direction of the parachute which, by now, was nowhere to be seen. The Dakota, having landed in the meantime, took off again to try and spot it, but the wind was getting stronger and the ground was obscured by a sandstorm.

We were several miles out into the desert when the sandstorm struck us and we had to stop. The Dakota passed over us once in the murk but we did not see it again.

We pointed the vehicle into the wind and huddled behind the windscreen – the vehicle had no side screens – to sit out the sandstorm. The sand stung and penetrated everywhere. We had to keep our eyes shut and our hands over our noses for some two hours, until the storm blew itself out.

We then cleaned out the radiator as best we could and also brushed away accumulations of sand from around the engine, which appeared to be otherwise unaffected. It started without trouble and we headed back to the airfield.

A further expedition, by the M.T. Section next day, finally retrieved the parachute and canister.

20. Lighter Moments

Sixteen annas one rupee,
Seventeen annas one buckshee,
Hey, Deolali Sahib! Hey Deolali Sahib,
Seven long years you seduced my daughter,
Now you are bound for the Blighty water,
May the boat that takes you home
Go niche rokna pani, Sahib."

The above was one of the favourite songs of the R.A.F. in India, which reflected the impression we liked to give of ourselves, in our conversation and activities, of being dissolute and half-mad.

For example, one Sergeant bought a complete set of fishing tackle and headed off into the desert. He passed an airman who greeted him and said, "Going fishing?" in a joking fashion.

"Why not?" said the Sergeant. "You have to find something to do in this place, or you would go round the twist!"

He carried on into the desert and was not seen for the rest of the day.

One Christmas, there were three Irish chaps in detention at the Guardroom which was in the charge of a corporal. On some pretext, they called him over to the iron-barred door of the cell in which they were incarcerated and as he stood there, they reached through the bars and grabbed his arm which they proceeded to twist until he yelled with agony and begged to be released.

"We'll let you go if you promise to unlock the cell," they said, giving his arm another twist. They, naturally enough, extracted the promise and the corporal, having given his word of honour, unlocked the cell door and let them out!

The three Irish chaps immediately locked the corporal in his own cell, ignoring his protests, put the key back on its hook, went to their billets to change into civilian clothes and caught the bus into Karachi for a night on the tiles.

They ended up in an exclusive restaurant where they tucked into a good meal, washed down with plenty of beer. They were enjoying themselves very much, until the table next to them was taken by a party that included the officer who had given them the detention sentence. Fortunately for them, he was well oiled and merely said:

"Evening, chaps, enjoying yourselves?"

"Yes, Sorr, thank you, Sorr, Merry Christmas, Sorr!" they stammered back and settled down to finish their meal, before making their way back to Mauripur.

In the meantime, the officer had had time to reflect on where he had last seen those faces. The truth dawned on him at last and he left the party to return to Mauripur as quickly as he could.

Back at Mauripur, the Irish chaps returned to the Guardroom, unlocked the cell, bundled the corporal out, locked the door and threw him the key. Being Christmas, nobody had been near the Guardroom, to the great relief of the corporal who sat at his desk and carried on reading his book as if nothing had happened.

Shortly after, the officer arrived, wild-eyed and excited.

"Corporal, where are the men on detention?" he demanded to know.

"They're in the cell, Sir," was the reply.

"They can't be! I've just seen them in Karachi!" he almost squeaked.

He went over to the cell and peered in at the recumbent forms of the airmen.

"I saw you in a restaurant in Karachi this evening," he shouted through the bars. The figures stirred, rubbed their eyes and sat up.

"Us, Sorr? No Sorr, how could we be? We're locked up!"

The officer, his certainty ebbing away, turned to the corporal.

"Is it true, have these men been here all evening?"

"Of course, Sir, I have the key here," was the nervous reply.

Dumbfounded, the officer shook his head in disbelief, turned and left the Guardroom, muttering under his breath:

"I could have sworn...!"

As officers and airmen became tour-expired and returned to the UK, fresh chaps were posted in to replace them. One of them was a sergeant, fresh out from England, who felt it was his duty to stalk the airmen's domestic site warning the airmen, who invariably wore just a pair of shorts, that they were improperly dressed and should be wearing bush hat, sunglasses, tunic and shoes, in which he, himself was invariably dressed. He was very emphatic about the dangers of sunstroke and was obviously taking no chances himself, for apart from his knees and hands which were bright red, he was lily-white. We were as brown as berries from long exposure to the sun and intended to remain brown, so kept out of his way as much as possible. After a week of his self-imposed duty he was laid low with sunstroke and we were left in peace.

Another chap was a new Administrative Officer who was appalled at our slovenliness and who instituted a regime of weekly billet inspections.

On the verandah of one of the billets there was a table, on which was a parrot in a cage. The parrot belonged to one of the airmen, but was a great pet of the whole billet. During the day, the cage was covered with a cloth to keep him quiet when the night shift was sleeping, for he was a great talker.

When the inspection regime started, airmen passing the cage would lift the cloth, hiss three words at the parrot and cover the cage again. This went on during the week before the day of the first inspection.

On the big day, the officer, followed by his retinue, toured the domestic site, billet by billet, with the Station Warrant Officer taking copious notes. Eventually they came to the billet with the parrot and the officer stalked onto the verandah and paused by the table.

"What is this doing here?" he demanded, striking the cage with his stick and knocking the cloth off.

The startled parrot squawked in anger and, in a loud clear voice, said:

"F--- off, Kelly!" This was followed by a long string of unprintable and derogatory epithets, the choicest in his repertoire, as he settled back on his perch, his feathers ruffled.

The feathers of the officer were, figuratively speaking, also ruffled considerably, as he realised by the parrot speaking his name that the episode had been engineered deliberately by the billet.

Nevertheless, there was not a lot that he could do about that, or to stop the story going around the Station. Possibly it reached the ears of Group Captain Grice too, for the officer was soon posted away and once again we were left in peace.

A day rarely passed without some incident to chuckle over. One airman bought a pair of pigskin shoes, of which he was very proud and wore them to a binge organised to celebrate the imminent departure to the UK of an oppo.

Unfortunately, he left them under the bed instead of putting them in his locker, as he usually did on returning to his billet. The chap in the next bed, feeling the need for an urgent leak in the night, grabbed one of the shoes and used it as a receptacle.

To say that the owner was peeved when he found it filled to the brim next morning, would be an understatement. Unfortunately, the urine had stained the shoe and no amount of washing could restore its original colour. He had no option, other than throwing them away, but to do the same to the other shoe, after which they matched perfectly.

Another chap was greatly enamoured of a Parsee girl that worked in S.H.Q. and became engaged. He must have informed his father of his impending nuptials for the father sent a telegram to the C.O. insisting that the R.A.F. should get him out of Pakistan.

Upon receipt of the telegram, two Service Policemen were dispatched poste haste to the Parsee Fire Temple and arrived just as the airman was about to enter for the ceremony. Grabbing him by each arm, they bundled him into a Police truck and returned to Mauripur. The airman's feet scarcely touched the ground as he was put aboard a plane bound for the Middle East. He was not pleased at all, as he forcefully told me, when I met him again at El Hamra in the Canal Zone.

I must say, however, that several chaps did get married to local girls, without parental objections and the R.A.F. gave them the usual considerations as married men. When they were tour expired, their wives returned with them to the UK.

21. Per Ardua Ad Asbestos

Modelling proceeded apace in the Club building and after being offered the use of a Frog 1.75 petrol engine and a beautiful pair of Riderwheels by Peter Barnett, I embarked on the construction of a high wing monoplane to my own design of 54" wingspan, which was based on the Hillson Praga in general layout.

The ignition circuit took a bit of understanding, but I finally got the engine running beautifully. The high tension wire to the sparking plug was merely wound around the plug, as there was no clip and one day the spark jumped from the wire directly to the cylinder head and due to an excess of fuel on the outside of the cylinder, the engine caught fire. Luckily it was put out without damage to the model.

With this incident in mind and the fact that the ignition system consumed pencell batteries faster than I could afford to buy them, the engine was changed for a Frog 100, which also belonged to Peter. The model would glide beautifully from a hand launch and the landings with the well-sprung undercarriage were a delight to behold. I had great hopes for the model, which was named 'Dumbo'.

A very small compass from a Safety Equipment survival pack was fitted in the Dumbo's cockpit and also a small pack of Horlicks tablets, for if the model performed as I expected, they could have been very useful in the desert if I had lost my way while retrieving it. What use they would have been if I didn't find the model, hadn't really occurred to me.

About this time, the Club received an invitation from the Aero Modellers Society of Karachi to their 'First Model Aircraft Flying Competition' which was to be held at Clifton near Karachi on the 30th of January 1949 and for which the Club members worked feverishly to prepare an excellent line-up of models.

The organisers of the meeting obviously hadn't expected the crowd of several hundred spectators that turned up at the Clifton Ground and it proved difficult to clear the area for unobstructed takeoffs. As soon as a model was released, the crowd would surge forward to have a better view.

'Dumbo' required a longer run to get airborne than I had expected and, in doing so, it veered off to the left. With a sinking feeling in my stomach, I watched it disappear into the advancing throng through a gap which opened up almost magically. The sound of the engine indicated that it was continuing to run strongly. With relief, I saw that it had passed safely through the crowd and was climbing away. My relief was short-lived however as it banked round, showing signs of spiral instability, dropped its nose slightly and zoomed over the crowd, before climbing back to its original height.

Again it banked round and gathered speed to repeat the manoeuvre, to "Oohs" and "Aahs" from the crowd who seemed to quite enjoy being dive-bombed. Twice more it repeated the manoeuvre and to my consternation, the runs across the crowd became lower and lower until people were having to duck to avoid being hit. On the final run, there would be no escape and I was extremely worried, but the flight was terminated when Dumbo flew into a bicycle that a spectator held up to protect himself. He apologised profusely, but I was only glad that nobody had been hurt. Apart from a broken propeller, the model was scarcely damaged and I counted myself fortunate.

I have always considered that the characteristics of an aeromodeller that should set him apart from any other model maker, are that he is prepared to take the risk of damaging his model in order to see it fly and if it is lost or destroyed, he accepts the fact with cheerful stoicism. It is not the end of the world to him if somebody accidentally steps on his model, whereas an accidental scratch on any other type of model usually drives the maker to a fury worthy of a prima donna.

That is not to say that an aeromodeller should risk his model to the danger of others and the event I have related was a major lesson to me on the necessity to fly safely.

Fortunately, the Club's reputation was retrieved by the models of the other members, which put up excellent performances in the various classes. There was a large sailplane, a half size Eros, a Mick

Farthing lightweight rubber duration model, a Frog 45 and several others that I can't recall.

The flying meeting was judged to be a great success and a good example of how aeromodelling can foster good international relations, not that we thought of it in that light as we felt quite at home in our environment.

I had left Mauripur by the date of the next meeting, but the Club, after passing through a stagnant period, was revived mainly by chaps seconded to the Royal Pakistan Air Force who participated in the 1950 and 1951 Pakistan Concours and Flying Competitions and gained trophies.

This information was sent to me in a letter from Sgt. J McCafferty, who took over as Secretary of the reformed club which was relocated at Squadrons Camp.

Several models survived, including the half size Eros, Peter Barnett's Hawker Cygnet, a Flying Flea and a twice size Frog 45 which flew successfully, powered by an ED III and were taken over by the reformed club who put them to good use.

22. Final Year at Mauripur

Now that the time was approaching for my repatriation to the UK, I did not want to leave Mauripur. It came as a shock, therefore, when, with some six months of my tour still left, I was posted to the Middle East. Fortunately, there were more passengers for the aircraft than there were seats and I was left behind because my name was at the bottom of the list. I quickly made friends with the clerk in Air Movements and arranged to have my name at the bottom of each weekly list thereafter.

This ploy worked like a charm and I remained at Mauripur until I was tour-expired.

At the time, the Berlin airlift was still going strong and very few Yorks were staging through. Nevertheless, a number of other interesting aircraft were seen.

One was a Hawker Fury, flown by Neville Duke, which was demonstrated to the R.P.A.F. The demonstration must have been successful, for it resulted in the sale of quite a number of Furies to equip the RPAF squadrons. From my own point of view it was a superb demonstration with high-speed runs, upward rolls, eight point rolls and a slow speed fly-past with undercarriage and flaps down. I had never seen such high-speed precision flying before and I was amazed that the wings stayed on.

We also saw a demonstration of the rival contender, a De Havilland Vampire, flown by Geoffrey de Havilland. If the demonstration was unsuccessful in obtaining sales, it was not the flying programme that was to blame. If anything, the speed of the Vampire was greater, but it appeared to be just as manoeuvrable as the Fury. It was the first jet I had seen going through its paces and it made a lasting impression on me.

Yet another demonstration aircraft was the Bristol Freighter G-AIFF. It too was very impressive, in its portly way, with slow and fast runs, first with two engines and then with one, which was powerful enough to allow a steep climbing turn at the end of the final run. This particular aircraft stayed for a week or so and I set out with my trusty folding Brownie to photograph it. I had some difficulty in persuading a Pakistani sergeant to allow me near it, mainly because it was being used in trials to transport a large field gun, presumably to Kashmir for that was where the action was. It would have been very difficult to get such a gun there by any other means because of the mountainous terrain.

Plate 10 Bristol Freighter G-AIFF

The two NWF Policemen guarding it had no such reservations and insisted on standing smartly to attention in front of the aircraft, to be photographed as well.

Because Pakistan had not devalued her rupee and the exchange rate was now R 9 to the pound, our pay fell sharply as a consequence, in spite of the local overseas allowance. There was, therefore, no lack of volunteers for a spot of work on the side when Sidney Cotton, an Australian millionaire and the inventor of the Sidcot suit, came to Mauripur to set up a gunrunning operation to the State of Hyderabad.

He had obtained some sort of arrangement with the Nizam of Hyderabad to fly arms and ammunition into the State. Hyderabad was being invaded by India, who objected to having an independent state within its border and the Nizam, who was reputed to be the richest man in the world, wasn't going to give in without a fight.

The whole affair was highly hush-hush and carried out with the connivance of the Pakistan Government. Although I saw the Lancastrians, which were the aircraft used, taking off each evening, I only found out what was happening when I asked where some of the chaps were, who could normally be found lying on their charpoys in the afternoon.

They were working on the Lancastrians at dispersal on the far side of the airfield and received a rate of pay that was almost unbelievable in comparison with our normal pay.

The Lancastrians were flown by freelance aircrew and BOAC aircrew on leave. They would depart from Mauripur in the evening, loaded up with boxes of rifles and ammunition and fly a course parallel to the Indian coast, gaining height all the while. When they came level with Hyderabad, they would turn off to port and cross the coast with engines throttled back in a fast glide, losing height until they reached their destination.

This went on for several weeks until the whole affair was blown wide open when a Lancastrian crashed on take-off, killing the BOAC crew and scattering the cargo along the runway.

Sidney Cotton was asked, I believe, by the Pakistan Government to use his aircraft to fly supplies to Kashmir, but he refused because the money offered was not sufficient. Whatever the situation was, he fell out with the Pakistan Government who then impounded his aircraft, which languished in dispersals around the airfield. I don't know the eventual fate of the Lancastrians, but Sidney Cotton himself was indicted on charges of gunrunning, in the High Court in London and went to prison.

To complete the picture of life at Mauripur, I should perhaps mention the animal life of the area, not because I made any great study of it, but for the way it intruded into our lives.

Bread was scarce, for a time, in the cookhouse and we had to make do with ships biscuits. These were all right until we found there were weevils in them. We learned to tap a biscuit on the table to dislodge the minute creatures from the holes in the biscuit. How many more were inside the biscuits themselves we didn't know, but we ate them anyway.

Apart from silver kraits, which were commonly found in a dump of old aircraft parts – you could hear them slithering away as you walked over the wings and tailplanes – there were chameleons and other lizards, chipmunks (one of which I had as a pet until he was accidentally killed) and two sizes of ants, to name a few.

The ants were fascinating to watch. They lived in a nest underground with access down a small hole. If a small pebble was placed over the hole, they would all gather round and heave it out of the way. From the hole, paths radiated in every direction with branches off to cover the whole area within a hundred yards radius. They were like miniature arterial roads swept clean of any obstacles with two streams of traffic. Closer inspection showed that the homeward bound ants were all carrying booty of some sort. Between the radiating paths could be found individual ants acting as scouts. If they found an interesting object, like a piece of something edible I had laid on the ground, they would nip over to the nearest road, fetch a stream of ants that were heading out and organise its collection.

The ants did not usually intrude into the campsite except when they grew wings and swarmed. They then became an absolute menace as they found their way into beds, clothing, food and anywhere else your imagination can visualise. One extra large ant crawled up inside Mike Toms' pyjama trousers and bit him in a very tender spot.

It was at night that they swarmed and the best defence against them in the billet was to douse the lights and hang a lighted bulb on a flex outside the window, with a full bucket of water underneath. Next morning the bucket would be full of dead ants. Fortunately, the swarming only occurred for a week or so each year,

On the way to Hawkes Bay one day, I saw, from the back of a lorry, an enormous lizard-like creature plodding slowly along. It was all of ten feet long and of a colour that so closely matched the desert that it was difficult to see, in fact, when I tried to draw it to the attention of the other chaps, they could not see it at all.

We once had a swarm of locusts, but that was enough for me. One afternoon a black cloud, rather like a thundercloud, appeared from the west and all aircraft were grounded. The cloud came closer and I quite expected a storm. Instead of rain, it was locusts that were falling on the ground. Millions of them lay on the ground, knocked from the sky by each other, or by flying into walls and other obstacles, but this was nothing to the countless billions, darkening the sky and obliterating the sun, that continued to fly relentlessly onwards to the east.

The cloud of locusts must have been over a thousand feet high at the very least and the noise of their wings beating was eerie. It took three quarters of an hour for the last of the stragglers to pass over and every square foot of ground was littered with dead and dying locusts, all of which were at least four inches long, with four powerful wings that made them look even larger.

Perhaps the most frightening thing about them was the purposeful, almost single-minded, way in which they forged on to their destination, the sheer numbers apparently undepleted by their prodigious losses en route.

Apart from the use of a few lorries, obviously ex-service, to be seen in Karachi, most transportation of goods was by camel trains or camel carts. Camel trains regularly passed through Mauripur en route to Baluchistan, Afghanistan and points west. Camel carts were very common in Karachi and could get up a fair turn of speed, although the cart was liable to shed its load as it swayed from side to side on account of the camel's gait. They also carried people and could be hired for picnic parties to the seaside. I rode on one once, but fell off when it started to sway and had to run as fast as I could to get back on.

I did not like camels, they would as soon bite you as look at you. One day, the civilian bus I was on drew level with a camel cart at the traffic lights. The bus windows had no glass and the camel put his head through a window and endeavoured to bite the passengers. Luckily for me, I was at the back of the bus. I have rarely seen such a panic, as people climbed over each other to get out of the way.

The civilian buses, too, had their idiosyncrasies. I noticed, as I travelled in one particular bus, that every time we passed a stall, it would collapse, precipitating the fruit, goods, or whatever, into the road. When we passed a rickshaw, the occupants would suddenly disappear below the window. Curiosity about this phenomenon made me get up from my seat, cross to the other side and look out of the window. I saw, protruding from the back wheels, a long bar which was probably the half shaft. As I looked, it scythed down yet another stall and I yelled "Roko!" to the conductor, who seemed reluctant to stop the bus because we hadn't reached the bus stop. It was only after bellowing in his ear and pointing to the back of the bus, that he realised the seriousness of the situation and spoke to the driver. I left the bus and continued on foot, as the perplexed crew got out and examined the offending half-shaft.

The civilian buses were ancient, bone-shaking, vehicles with wooden seats and normally made their stately way along the rutted and cracked concrete Military Road at about fifteen miles per hour.

One particular day, the bus had left Karachi and had travelled about three miles when there was a sharp crack and the bus accelerated to its maximum speed of about forty miles an hour. The springs were virtually solid and the passengers were bounced around on the wooden seats until they could stand no more and clamoured for the driver to slow down. He took no notice and kept his foot hard down all the way to Mauripur where he pulled up with a screech of brakes at the RPAF Guardroom. Much agitated conversation took place and a RPAF truck with several Service policemen shot off back the way we had come. Enquiring of my fellow passengers, mainly Pakistanis, what all the fuss was about, they pointed to a neat hole in the projecting roof above the seat of the driver. Somebody had apparently taken a shot at him.

Back on the camp, we often went about the billets with bare feet, which toughened the soles wonderfully. I was dissuaded from doing this for a time when we found a scorpion, about half a mile from the camp, while flying models one Sunday morning, out on the flat area near the salt works.

It was of a sandy colour and not easily seen. We gathered round in curiosity, for they were not very common within the area of the Station. We wondered if it was true that if a scorpion was ringed with flames it would sting itself to death. Model diesel fuel, being the nearest thing to the proverbial petrol, was poured in a circle around it and set on fire. I can state categorically that the scorpion did no such thing but merely settled in the sand until the flames died down. Nobody liked to kill it, not even with shoes on and as it was nearly tiffin time we beat a hasty retreat.

In the last year, after eighteen months of active aeromodelling, I felt a bit jaded by it and commenced a social whirl, which went on until I finally left. I was invariably called 'Blondie' Newton after the strip cartoon character and the bearer used to call me Brandy Sahib which lent a rakish air and fitted in with my new lifestyle!

Evenings were spent with friends, civilian and Service, at the Union Jack Club for swimming and drinking, at the Locomotive Institute for dancing to *Pat Blake and his Hotshots* and watching the Golden Gloves Boxing tournaments and the Napier Fleet Club for tombola. There was also the Paradise Cinema which showed British and American films and a host of other cinemas showed Indian films, made mainly near Bombay, which were very innocent in nature – for a bedroom scene, a clip showing ocean waves rolling into the shore would be substituted – but they were quite enjoyable when one could understand some of the words.

Our pay was eventually increased and included 12 months back pay. Having lived so long on a pittance, it was riches indeed. I bought a suit and a sports jacket and trousers, hand-tailored by Liaquat Ali Khan's tailor, which were not cheap but were ready in two days, also a watch, cigarette case and lighter and still had money to spare after sending £100 home.

A good Pakistani friend, Kassim Afghan, (his surname was pronounced 'Afwan'), knowing of my windfall, offered to invest R 100 for me, repayable in one month, with interest also of R 100. Never having been careful with money, I eagerly pushed the money into his hands and waited patiently for the dividend.

One day, he asked me if I would like to see my investment working for me. Full of curiosity, for I had never asked how the money had been used, I accepted and he led me down to one of the many bazaars in Karachi.

Around us, on every hand, were stalls and barrows loaded with goods of all descriptions: fruit, jalebis fried while you waited, plastic mouth organs, cigarettes, cloth, sweets, to name just a few and also, dates. There were several barrows selling dates only and these, more than any others, were doing a roaring trade with people queuing up to buy.

The great demand for dates puzzled me and I asked Kassim why it was so. He explained that it was the month of Ramadan, when all devout Moslems fasted during the hours of daylight. After the sun had set they could eat, but they first broke their fast by eating dates. I was marvelling at the ease with which the customers were parted from their money when Kassim said:

"That's your barrow over there!"

I looked over and saw a barrow piled high with dates and a chap in a turban taking money as fast as he could while his customers served themselves. Each customer bought only a few, but the pile of dates was fast disappearing.

Watching the scene unobtrusively in the gathering darkness, away from the hissing carbide lamps of the dozens of stalls, I felt, for perhaps the only time in my life, the excitement of astute investment and the promise of 'high finance'.

True to his word, at the end of the month, Kassim returned my R 100, together with the R 100 interest. I demonstrated my incapacity to be a successful financier, by blowing the interest on the hire of a fifty-seat launch to take the nurses of the Civil Hospital on a picnic to Standspit. At any rate, it paid for a day out to remember!

I had many interesting conversations with Kassim. He worked in the High Court of Sind and could speak English well. He was a Moslem, but not fanatical and he explained several things to me.

The tradition of having more than one wife, he said, started during the Crusades when, if a Moslem warrior was killed in battle, his best friend took the warrior's widow and children into his household and took on the responsibility for their welfare. In return he received conjugal rights. There was no welfare state then and they would otherwise have starved.

He was scornful of the hierarchy of the established religions and extolled the virtues of the 'holy man' who needed no fine apparel or pomp and ceremony, but who travelled about the country dispensing teaching, wisdom and advice. When he arrived at a village, he sat under a tree and everything he needed was provided for him—food, water, clothes, a bed and anything else he asked for.

I saw a holy man once in Karachi. I knew it was he, by reputation, because all he was dressed in was a pair of sandals. All his worldly goods were tied in a bundle to a stick carried over his shoulder. People made way for him and treated him with due respect. I felt there was a lesson to be learned there in tolerance.

Kassim had never been close to an aircraft, so one day I invited him up to the Station to look at one after I finished work. He arrived promptly and waited in the billet while I had a shower and changed.

I had managed to arrange transport to and from the Daily Servicing Section and I was able to show him round a Dakota that was there, which seemed to interest him greatly. What appeared to impress him even more were our living conditions. "You British do live hard!" he remarked. I believe he used to think we lived in luxury!

In return, he invited me to a 'real' curry and rice meal, at a restaurant he knew. It was wonderful, but I needed several glasses of water with it!

I remember one particular day we were walking along the road when we passed a beggar. Kassim gave him some money and I asked why he had done so, for there were so many beggars he would soon give all his money away.

He replied, "They are our brothers. It is our duty to look after them!"

I felt ashamed and never passed a beggar again without giving something, however small.

On one occasion, I was crossing Bunder Road and had to negotiate six lanes of traffic, which included a tramway in each direction. I was nearly at the other side when I heard a cry of:

"Sah'b, Sah'b!"

I looked behind me and witnessed an appalling sight. A young beggar, virtually still a child, was crossing the road after me, dodging all the traffic. What appalled me was the fact that he was deformed, with his feet twisted around to face the other way and he was crossing the road on his hands and knees, to which wooden blocks were attached.

I was badly shaken by this and scolded him for taking such risks, but he was so cheerful for having succeeded in his effort to catch up with me, that I no choice but to give him what I could.

After thirteen months, the Berlin Airlift had come to an end and the Yorks started staging through again. They had suffered considerable wear and tear during that period of concentrated usage and it showed. When the floor panels were taken up for some reason on one York, there were still traces of coal and flour dust.

During my time at Mauripur, I had been given trade tests on Dakotas and Yorks and had reached the heady rank of LAC. I was now twenty years of age and thought myself to be a real old sweat.

Finally, the day came when I was told to get packed and ready to go, for there would be no dodging the draft this time. The mouchi-wallah (shoemaker) made me a leather suitcase, for such was his versatility, with my address beautifully painted on it in Gothic lettering by the camp engraver.

My preparations completed, I journeyed to Karachi for the last time to say goodbye to my friends who, as I have previously related, had organised a farewell party, unbeknown to me, which took place at a flat, the balcony of which overlooked Saddar. In the moonlight, the vibrant city had never looked more entrancing and I strongly felt the poignancy of the occasion.

Early next morning, I and about twenty other tour-expired air-men, climbed aboard a venerable Dakota and settled down, as best we could, on the uncomfortable seats, for the long journey ahead.

23. Homeward Bound

The Dakota climbed away from Mauripur and headed out across the sea, with the propellers in coarse pitch for the long haul of over 700 miles to Sharjah.

Soon we were flying parallel to the Makran coast. The Makranis were largely of African extraction and were often seen in Karachi, being easily distinguished by their frizzy hair. They were descended from, or may have actually been, slaves, who had escaped from slavery in Arabia to the comparative freedom of British India.

Somewhere along this coast was Jawani airfield, where a detachment from Mauripur was stationed. The tour of duty at Jawani was for a maximum of six months, short enough to prevent airmen from going round the bend. There was nothing to do there, apart from attending to the occasional aircraft which called in to have a snag fixed or to be refuelled. Nevertheless, there was never a shortage of volunteers – I was not one of them! – and they seemed to revel in eccentric behaviour. Because I was never there – I didn't go to Quetta either, (where there was a rest camp available to us by courtesy of the Pakistan Army), because I was officially on the postings list – I cannot vouch for the following story which I was told by an old Jawani hand, but it is worth telling anyway.

After the war, a number of Spitfires were at Jawani in various stages of decrepitude and the order was given to dispose of them. The airmen who were there at the time occupied themselves by getting the engines working and taxiing the Spitfires to a cliff overlooking the sea. Near the edge of the cliff they were stopped, the control surfaces were locked, the airmen climbed out on to the wing and pushed open the throttle before jumping smartly off. The aircraft would then accelerate quickly down a track and over the edge of the cliff, making a short and final flight before crashing spectacularly into the sea.

The coastline moved steadily past the windows, as we droned along. In the distance, huge barren mountain ranges could be seen and the whole area looked most inhospitable. It was somewhere along this route that the Handley Page 42E 'Hannibal' disappeared without trace. 'Hengist', converted to an Eastern version, was burnt out at Karachi and another HP42 had a narrow squeak near Sharjah.

Around lunchtime, the note of the engines changed, indicating our arrival at Sharjah. We touched down on what looked like virgin desert, rather similar to Southport beach and taxied towards a small group of buildings dominated by a substantial fort.

We trooped into the cookhouse and enjoyed a better lunch than I expected in that God-forsaken hole. It was getting rather hot, although it was December. We were dressed in our best blue for our journey home and we found it very sticky after wearing K.D.

The Straits of Hormuz could be seen, shimmering in the distance and to the left was a town about five miles away, built of what looked like light-coloured stone and unchanged for hundreds of years. There was no vegetation at all that I could see, not even cactus.

Talking to one of the airmen stationed there, I asked about the fort and he told me that it came in quite useful when marauding tribesmen came down from the hills looking for loot. At such times, everything transportable on a horse was taken into the fort and the chaps barricaded themselves in until the tribesmen had gone away again.

When it was time to take off again, the air was hot and lifeless. The Dakota seemed to take a long time to get airborne, even allowing for the fact that it was heavily loaded with petrol and it took three long bounces before the lift of the wing finally overcame gravity and raised us off the boundless desert. We headed out over the Persian Gulf, as the engines strained to gain altitude and we again settled down for the even longer journey of 900 miles to Habbaniyah.

We skirted the coast of Iran where more barren ranges of mountains could be seen and passed an occasional tanker, but there was nothing to hold our attention. As the hours passed, the sun declined and finally set and it became very chilly next to the windows as the airstream blew fitfully through the holes. One by one, the passengers lay on the floor to stretch out, using their side packs as pillows as they tried to sleep.

We were airborne for nine hours, the longest flight that I can remember and I felt we must surely run short of fuel. The lights of Basra were left behind and the desert below was black and featureless for nearly three hundred miles until the lights of Baghdad appeared to starboard.

Shortly afterwards, the Dakota landed at Habbaniyah where we were to stop overnight. In the dark, not a lot could be seen of the place, but it appeared to be a large, well established Station with substantial buildings and well-made roads and pathways. The ground was sandy, but there was a profusion of palm trees and vegetation between the buildings and lining the roads.

Blankets were issued and we were taken to the transit billets which were a big improvement on those at Mauripur. There were mattresses on proper beds, so it was no wonder that people passing through Mauripur complained about our string charpoys and the dhurris. I had slept on them for two and a half years and was to find I could not get comfortable on a mattress!

After a hearty tea-cum-supper, it was too late to enjoy the facilities of Habbaniyah, but we were not sorry to go to bed. Early next morning, after a good breakfast, we collected our kit and were taken to our aircraft, which turned out to be a Hastings.

The policy of Transport Command at that time was to have all the passenger seats facing the rear in all their aircraft and the Hastings was the first I had seen with this arrangement. The seats were very comfortable but had the disadvantage, due to the angle of the fuselage when on the ground, that one tended to slide out of the seat. The acceleration of the aircraft as it took off, accentuated the effect and the lap strap dug into one's stomach. However, once the aircraft was in level flight, one could settle back in luxury.

After leaving Habbaniyah, the aircraft set course across a desert which was as desolate as any I had seen. Low, regular hillocks of sand stretched as far as the eye could see, with nothing to break the monotony and I began to appreciate the achievements of the first aviators to fly this route, carrying mail in Vickers Vimys between Egypt and Iraq after World War I.

I found most long-distance flights to be extremely monotonous and perhaps the pilot felt so, too, for he engaged the automatic pilot and came into the gangway to fill his mug with cocoa from the urn with the rest of the aircrew. The aircraft lurched, causing some cocoa to be spilt and the pilot had to return quickly to his seat to check that 'George' was still working correctly.

It was a flight of some 750 miles of boredom, relieved only by a good view of the Dead Sea as the pilot lost altitude and circled round it for our benefit, before continuing on the last stage of our journey to Fayid in the Canal Zone.

Fayid was a busy airfield set in yet more desert, of which a large area of this part of the world seemed to consist, close to the Great Bitter Lake which formed part of the Suez Canal. After a smooth landing, we left the aircraft and were loaded, together with our kit, on to three-ton lorries.

The trucks set off south, down the road to El Hamra transit camp. On the way we passed a large number of Army camps, each with its own regimental or unit badge and name on a board, spaced at intervals along the Military Road. Everything seemed to be rather basic and there were a lot of tents. The air blowing past us was quite warm, but noticeably different from Karachi air and had an invigorating keenness, it seemed to me.

El Hamra transit camp looked very like a P.O.W. camp, surrounded by barbed wire fencing and the occasional searchlight tower could be seen. My first sight of the place did nothing for my spirits. There were permanent buildings for offices, the cookhouse and so on, but the main accommodation was tented. The ridge-type tents were erected over shallow brick-built pits with steps out and the ablutions were pretty basic too.

We had a nondescript meal, allegedly our lunch, drew some blankets and returned to our allotted tents until teatime,

We were to be at El Hamra for ten days, although we were not told this and each day expected to be called out on parade for a flight to the UK.

We soon found that we were required to guard the camp during our stay. Every three days we were on guard duty from 2000 hours to 0800 hours next morning in 2-hour shifts, with 4 hours off in between. One day I was detailed for the 2400 to 0200 and 0600 to 0800 hours guard duties. The last guard duty was on the main gate and I had strict instructions not to let anybody without a pass into the camp. It was remarkably cold and I found it necessary to wear my greatcoat which had not seen light of day for nearly three years.

Armed with a rifle and five rounds of ammo, I felt a real prat standing there at ease. It got more interesting when the Egyptian cookhouse staff began to turn up for work. None of them had passes, they claimed that these were in the pockets of their overalls, which were hanging up in the cookhouse. Obeying my instructions to the letter, I refused to let them in. Time passed and the muttering queue of Egyptians grew longer. At about a quarter to eight, the Orderly Officer turned up, looking hot and bothered.

"What are all these men waiting for?" he demanded.

"They don't have their passes with them, sir and I wouldn't let them in without passes, as I was instructed," I replied.

"For Pete's sake, let them in!"

I lowered my rifle and motioned them to go into the camp, which they did, still muttering. Shortly after, the guard was dismissed and I collected my irons from the tent and went to the cookhouse to find a long queue impatiently waiting for their breakfast.

"What's the hold-up? Why are we waiting?" I heard one chap say.

"I heard that some prat on the gate wouldn't let the cookhouse staff into the camp!" His oppo replied.

A number of opinions were expressed, couched in down-to-earth R.A.F. terminology, concerning the intelligence and appropriate chastisement of the person responsible.

I assumed an air of blameless disinterest and hoped that nobody would recognise me as the culprit and, thankfully, the incident passed off without further repercussions.

Once, we went to speedway racing at a well-built track near Fayid. We travelled there by lorry, escorted by a chap with a rifle. Apparently, the Egyptians were not very friendly and attacks on the troops away from camps were fairly common.

Another diversion at the end of a long, boring, day was to go to the Naafi or the Lady Lampson Club. The Lady Lampson Club was an institution famed throughout the R.A.F. It was run by an autocratic lady of indeterminate age, who, many airmen assumed, was Lady Lampson herself. This was not the case and the Club was so named in memory of Lady Lampson, I believe, who was a dear friend of hers.

Decorum was rigorously enforced in the club, which was housed in a large tent. Its main stock-in-trade was the sale of char and wads, for which one queued up to buy the appropriate tickets which were immediately collected by the lady who supervised the dispensing of the refreshments. She never smiled or joked with the airmen and would tell anybody guilty of exuberant laughter to leave immediately. We would sit glumly stirring the sugar in our tea, eat our not inexpensive cakes and talk in subdued tones while the lady watched us with eagle eyes.

It was much the same in the Salvation Army and YMCA tents. The Naafi was no better, but it did sell beer which I couldn't afford anyway. I was existing on some spare cash, changed into dinars and piastres, which was all I had left after losing my wallet.

We were not sorry when our names were called out one morning and we were told to prepare to move out. Our destination was Port Said where we would embark on a troopship for the UK. It was disappointing not to be flying home in comparative luxury, but at least we would be going in the right direction.

Early next morning we piled onto the lorries and trundled off back up the Military Road, passing all the military camps again and the signposts pointing to various airfields such as Shallufa, Kabrit, Kasfarit, Fayid, Deversoir and Abu Sueir – names I knew well from chaps who had been there.

Eventually, we arrived at Ismailia, a town that looked rather down at heel and was to look worse in years to come, especially in the Arab/Israeli wars and we were set down at the railway station.

The scruffy looking engine of our train had an Egyptian crew and pulled a string of equally scruffy carriages with wooden seats. We were besieged by small boys trying to sell us all the usual rubbish, but without much success and we quickly retreated aboard the train which eventually moved out of the station.

The railway line ran parallel to the quaintly named Sweet Water Canal for several miles. It was reputed to be so polluted that if you fell in it, you were required to report sick and be jabbed against just about every known disease. I could well believe this, for, at every settlement along the route, people were bathing and doing the family wash in the murky water.

The journey to Port Said took about 2 hours. We were taken to the dockside where we boarded a lighter that conveyed us to a small troopship moored in the harbour. The name on the bows read 'Empire Pride'. The usual preliminaries took place and again we found ourselves packed in with the Army on a ship, run this time by the Bibby Line.

Shortly after, the Empire Pride weighed anchor and we moved out past the long breakwater into the Med. Life was much as it had been on the Arundel Castle, but the discipline was noticeably more relaxed. There was less room to move about, but there was a recreational saloon with a piano available in the evenings.

After a day or so, the speed of the vessel dropped considerably and opinions were expressed that we might have to row home. Fortunately the sea was like a millpond. On the fourth day afloat, land appeared, covered with buildings and with a big stone breakwater, which we passed to enter an interesting harbour, which we immediately recognised as being Grand Harbour, Valetta.

We had arrived at Malta, where we were to stay for Christmas Day and Boxing Day while repairs to the ship's engines were carried out. The weather had changed and low scudding clouds gave a strange atmosphere to the place as church bells rang out.

We were allowed ashore on Christmas afternoon and explored Valetta, gravitating naturally to Straight Street – the Gut – which was a long, sloping, narrow street lined with bars and dance halls. At the doorways of some of the smaller establishments, girls would call out "Come on in, Raff", but we made for the larger hostelries like the *New Life* and the *Egyptian Queen*, in one of which a fight broke out.

One of those that came off worst was an R.A.F. chap I didn't know, but my mate and I dived into the fracas, extracted him and cleaned the blood off his face with handkerchiefs dipped in our beer. Two very large Maltese policemen came up the wide steps and crossed the floor to speak to the manager. He talked angrily to the policemen and pointed at us.

"Come on," said my oppo. "Let's get out quick!"

Dragging our casualty with us, we ran down the steps into the street, with the two policemen in hot pursuit. Fortunately, they were too large to run fast. We dodged round a corner and my oppo grabbed my arm.

"In here!" he shouted and we dived through a doorway and found ourselves in a small crowded bar. Working our way through the throng as inconspicuously as possible, we grabbed some seats on the far side. Nobody followed us in and we ordered more beer.

It was a very small room with a bar down one side and benches around the other three. In a corner was a washbasin, which served as a urinal and which had an inadequate curtain in front of it to provide a modicum of privacy. I noticed that some old dears were sitting on the adjacent bench and every time the facility was used, they would turn their heads to peer with interest through the gap between the curtain and the wall and whisper comments in Maltese.

A huge R.N. matelot, who was well away, decided to stand in the middle of the floor and entertain the customers with his repertoire of filthy songs, most of which I had never heard before. The customers had, though and joined in the choruses with gusto. As we now felt quite secure, we stayed to enjoy the performance until he finally flaked out and his mates took him back to his ship.

On Boxing Day, the powers that were decided that a route march would keep us out of mischief and a lighter took us to a landing stage. We set off along a road out of Valetta into what passed for countryside, small sparsely grassed fields with stone walls and ended up at the Marsa Club. A bottle of beer all round made the march worthwhile and we returned to the ship in a more cheerful mood.

The afternoon was spent sightseeing and watching two poor squaddies marching up and down with unbelievable precision outside the Army H.Q.

We saw a cruiser, HMS Kenya, leave port, with the crew lining the decks, which looked very impressive.

On returning, we had to take a gondola-like boat out to the ship and I nearly fell into the harbour as I stepped down on to the narrow, covered, front end of the boat. Luckily, the boatman grabbed me with a practised hand.

During the night, the repairs must have been completed, for we awoke next day to find ourselves at sea again. From the position of the sun, I was startled to observe that we were heading back east. As I have observed before, we were never told anything.

A day or two later, we entered a battered looking harbour with masts of sunken ships sticking out of the water. It was Tobruk, where we were to pick up more Army chaps, who were transferred across in a crowded lighter. It was not difficult to imagine, from the damage around us, what it must have been like during the war. It was a barren and inhospitable place.

Out at sea, I was glad to perceive that the ship was heading west again. The troops we had picked up were from Mauritius and seemed to be quiet chaps, quite sociable but speaking little English.

Next day, the ship approached land again and entered Tripoli harbour, which had fewer signs of war damage. Palm trees and quite elegant whitewashed buildings, could be seen on land.

The ship stopped for a short while to drop off some other troops and finally sailed out to begin the long run home. Now that boredom was setting in, it was almost a pleasure to be detailed to hump fresh supplies of potatoes, in sacks, from the bowels of the ship in No. 4 hold, to the galley at the forward end. Because the ship's engine room was in the way, it was not possible to move them along the lowest deck and then up to the galley and we had to hump them up flights of steps to the aft well deck and then up more steps to the promenade deck, down another flight of steps to the forward well deck and finally down another couple of flights to the galley. I certainly earned my meals that day.

In the meantime, the wind had increased to gale force and the ship began to roll alarmingly. Several times, I was sure we would capsize. The piano in the recreational saloon came adrift from its moorings and rolled on its castors from one side of the saloon to the other, crashing into the walls and destroying half the furniture.

The troops had to remain up above during the day and the time was spent dashing across the sloping well deck from one side to the other to avoid the spray, which would have otherwise drenched us.

For New Year's Eve we had planned to finish off a crate of beer on the aft well deck, as the recreational saloon was a shambles and the piano pulverised, but the bad weather continued and it turned very cold, so we slung our hammocks and turned in early.

After passing the Straits of Gibraltar, the weather improved and the Atlantic Ocean was pleasantly calm. Nothing else of note occurred except that, as we moved north, it became even colder.

Finally, after receiving our mail off Anglesey, which was the first really green countryside I had seen for 2½ years, we docked beside the Princess Landing Stage at Liverpool on January 4th 1950, where I was greeted by my mother with an big maternal embrace. I was rather relieved to observe that I was only one of many to have an emotional homecoming.

24. A Lancaster of my Own

Back in Leeds, I found the cold weather as unbearable as the old dragons, sitting at rows of card tables in the Food Office, who issued me with my ration coupons.

It seemed to me that conditions in Britain had not improved since the war. Even bread and potatoes were now on ration and the Black Market flourished. I renewed my aeromodelling friendships, built a Southerner Mite and fitted it with a new Mills .75 – the first engine I had owned.

On its first outing it performed very well, but I was so cold that I turned blue and had to go home. Most days I stayed in bed until midday, which gave me a chance to recover from the excesses of the previous year.

Having six weeks disembarkation leave at that time of year did not give much scope for me to enjoy myself. Dances and the pictures were expensive and did not fill the day. I tried for a couple of temporary jobs but the cold weather defeated me. I made the best of it, however and eventually I was notified that I was posted to the Technical College at R.A.F. Lindholme, near Doncaster, which would enable me to travel home each weekend.

I reported to R.A.F. Lindholme and found myself in Flying Wing which had three Lancasters and two Mk XVIe Spitfires. These were used for fighter affiliation and other exercises, for the benefit of officers attending the Technical College. I knew little of the activities of the College as I was soon fully immersed in my own duties as a rigger (as airframe mechanics were invariably called, engine mechanics were called fitters) on one of the Lancasters. I have no record of its serial number, but I think it was in the PA series. It was finished matt black on the under surfaces and matt grey on the upper surfaces of its wings, tail and fuselage and was in very good condition.

It was quite a thrill to have my own aircraft to look after, but I quickly learned to treat this reality with the same matter-of-fact nonchalance as the other riggers. I studied the aircraft handbook and soon became familiar with the various systems, pressures, lubrication points and other details of the airframe.

Generally, snags were few, but I remember one in particular which gave me some trouble to rectify.

My Lanc had landed and was taxiing over the grass to the hard standing by the hangar and at first glance it looked remarkably like an elephant. As it rocked over the uneven ground, I saw what looked like an elephant's trunk hanging down from the underside of the wing centre section. It was a convoluted rubber hose which discharged jettisoned fuel and was normally stowed in the wing and retained there by a hinged panel secured by a pin. The pin was withdrawn by the jettison control through a Bowden cable, to release the panel and allow the hose to drop down and trail in the slipstream. It was a very simple arrangement and the trouble proved to be the pin not being fully engaged, because the cable was not quite long enough, causing it to slip out.

Being the rigger, I had several opportunities to fly in the Lanc and, as it had dual controls, was allowed on a couple of occasions to sit in the flight engineer's seat and fly the plane for short periods.

The controls appeared to be heavier than those of the Dakota, which was to be expected, being a larger aircraft with four engines instead of two, but not excessively so. It seemed to require time to overcome the inertia of the big wing with its engines, in order to bank. Once the bank was begun it was comparatively easy to increase it or to hold it. The ailerons were not visible from the flight deck, being obscured by the well-rounded leading edge, which was so blunt that it didn't seem possible for the wing to produce lift.

Each of the fixed side windows had a blister into which one could put one's head and see vertically downwards. It was a novel sensation to know that the slipstream was tearing past and not to actually feel it. The astrodome gave the same sensation and I wondered what would happen if the Perspex broke under the strain, for I did not have a lot of faith in the strength of that material.

The worst jobs as a rigger were to clean out and replenish the Elsan toilet, which passengers seemed to require to use with annoying frequency, or to clean the flight deck windows, which were difficult to reach all over particularly on a cold or windy day. Nevertheless, I enjoyed the outdoor life.

Fire picket came with monotonous frequency. Being in a technical trade, I was sometimes picked to stand by the booster pump engine, to start it when required. The engine was lovingly cared for by an AMWD civilian (Works and Bricks, we called them) and he would stand by with anxious suspicion while my mate and I tinkered with the priming taps. A feed pipe supplied petrol through the taps to little cups, one for each cylinder. When each cup was full, the turning of another tap would allow it to flow into the cylinder.

It was a two-man job to swing it over compression and, if not enough effort was put into it, the engine would kick back with painful results. Having got it cranking, the ignition would be switched on, usually by the AMWD chap and hopefully the thing would fire and pick up. The engine drove a pump that boosted the pressure in the Station water mains which supplied the various fire hydrants.

On a still evening, it was a joy to have the whole aerodrome in which to fly the Southerner Mite and I could increase the engine run to extend the flight time quite safely, or so I thought. One evening, it caught an unexpected thermal and drifted downwind as it circled in the glide. It crossed the airfield boundary and was last seen descending well inside a large marshy area adjacent to the airfield.

Whole bomber aircraft were reputed to have disappeared into this marsh during the war, when they failed to make it back to the runway, so I didn't hold out much hope for the Southerner Mite. I made an attempt to find it by working my way between the more treacherous areas of ground, but gave up when it began to get dark.

A week or two later, there was a notice on the Station Orders notice board stating that a model aircraft had been found and could be claimed from the Station Dental Officer.

I attended the Dental Centre at the first opportunity, described the model and was presented with the Southerner Mite which had been recovered intact.

On expressing amazement that anybody could have found it in a marsh such as that, the D.O. explained that he had been given a flip in the Tiger Moth belonging to the Communication Flight, a lodger unit in the next hangar to the Flying Wing and had spotted it while coming in to land.

He had been sufficiently keen to retrieve it, for him to ask the pilot to go round again so that he could pinpoint its position. The Tiger Moth was flown directly over the model to land on the airfield in line with a landmark on the far side. The D.O. immediately got out of the Tiger Moth and walked back, checking his direction by keeping the plane between him and the landmark. He soon came upon the model which had not gone as far into the marsh as I had thought. I was extremely grateful for the trouble he had taken, for, although the model could have been replaced, I could not have afforded another engine at that time.

The Flying Wing billet was in Trenchard Block, one of several well-built two-storied pre-war barrack blocks spaced on two sides of the parade ground, or square as it was more often called. The Waafs occupied another block which had frequent attention from the AMWD people for blocked drains. On such occasions, being upstream, we had to refrain from running water or flushing toilets until they were cleared, which caused considerable profane jocularity in our billet.

I decided to apply for a Fitter IIA course, being the only way to further promotion and increased pay. Rather to my surprise, the application was successful, although Chiefy scratched his head and jokingly asked if it was because the company wasn't good enough for me!

I left on April 27th, my 21st birthday, for St Athan in South Wales, in a blinding snowstorm.

I arrived at Gileston railway station, about a mile down the road from St Athan, late in the day and feeling rather tired. The sight of another large camp with rows of wooden barrack huts and bodies being marched about, did nothing to make me feel more cheerful. But this was the way I had to tread to achieve any advancement.

Together with other new arrivals, who included a few old oppos from Mauripur, I was put in Pool Flight for the first week. Apart from a couple of days occupied with delivering coal to the married quarters, we were, as senior airmen, left pretty much to ourselves and passed the time in the inevitable card school.

R.A.F. St Athan consisted of East Camp and West Camp and was, if anything, bigger than Cosford. East Camp straddled the road to Gileston and I never really saw the full extent of it. West Camp was the home of 32 M.U., whose stock-in-trade at this time was the refurbishment of Meteors.

All the entrants for the Fitter IIA course were made up of L.A.C.s like myself with several years experience and we were treated with due deference rather than as trainees. We still had to march smartly to and from, work but were required, very often, to take charge of a column of less senior trainees going back to their billets on the other side of the road. Often other entries were tacked on behind by permanent staff N.C.O.s to save them (the N.C.O.s) a double journey. By the time the traffic had been halted by a Service Policeman (S.P.) to let the column march across the road, one found that instead of the thirty or so bodies one started with, another five hundred or more were following on, all automatically obeying one's commands without question until they were dismissed. It was difficult not to enjoy the brief feeling of authority as one bellowed:

"Entries, Hallttt! – Waitt forritt! – Dissss-misss!"

Why they took any notice of me, an ordinary LAC, instead of just disintegrating into a rabble and pushing off to their billets, I never really understood.

The course was similar to the Mechanics course at Cosford, but the various subjects were dealt with in greater detail. Most of the instruction was based on the Gloster Meteor Mk IV, but general workshop practice was expanded to include materials to British Standards, properties of metals and their use in airframe repairs.

The hydraulic system of the Meteor and other types of aircraft, including testing and servicing, took up several weeks; the use of high pressure charging apparatus, remote controls, pneumatics and levered suspensions of undercarriages took up several more.

Summer was approaching and the urge to do some model building and flying caused me to seek out the Station Model Club, for which an empty barrack hut served as the clubroom.

Due to a determination to work hard and pass the course, I only managed to build a KeilKraft Cadet, which was small enough to fly on the cricket ground. The cricket ground was used more by the modelling fraternity than for cricket and flying was only discouraged on one particular Sunday when a friendly match was played between the Station XI and the West Indies Test XI. The West Indies lost that day.

One chap in the club used to build power duration pylon models of his own design, that were invariably good enough to fly away on the first flight, usually in the direction of the Bristol Channel. Suggestions that he should fit a dethermaliser fell on deaf ears and he seemed to be quite happy to buy a new engine and build a new model for the following week, just to lose that as well.

It was during this period that an Avro Tudor II crashed at Llandow, an airfield just up the road, with great loss of life, which shocked the Station considerably.

Most days the Bristol Brabazon could be seen in the distance, on test over the Severn Estuary. It looked very large but also gave the impression of being very slow. Its contra-rotating propellers could be clearly seen flickering as the blades passed each other.

Meteors on test from the MU were often seen coming into land and I was surprised by the power that the engines seemed to be producing, to judge by the shrill crescendo and the shimmering efflux from the Derwents, when a Meteor was on final approach in what seemed to be a very nose-up attitude.

At this time, the sailing ships Pamir and Passat were docked at Penarth near Cardiff and when the Pamir was moved to Barry Docks, I decided to go and see her. She was carrying grain, which had been condemned and there was some uncertainty about the ship's future.

She had the beautiful lines of a clipper but looked very dingy and uncared for. There was a mass of rigging and it was a mystery to me how the crew could tell one rope from another, not that any of the crew was aboard, for the ship was quite deserted and this added to the air of desolation. The Pamir was lost in the South Atlantic with all hands in 1956.

We were given some leave part way through the course and I think it was about this time that there was a parliamentary election campaign. Winston Churchill came to Leeds to give a speech in the Town Hall. I went along out of curiosity, but the Town Hall was packed and I joined several hundred others at the foot of the steps to listen to the speech being relayed through loudspeakers. Churchill must have been told that there was a large crowd outside for he came out to the top of the steps and gave another speech completely without notes. His eloquence betrayed no sign of his advancing years and Tory ladies were fainting with adoration at the sight of him. He failed to get back into power then, but he did succeed at the next election shortly afterwards.

The leave over, the Fitter IIA course recommenced with further instruction in metal repairs, advanced riveting and heat treatment of ferrous and non-ferrous metals. The use of salt baths for heat treatment and the mysteries of various anti-corrosive treatments were explained to us at 32 M.U. by the staff, who seemed to be very conversant with and enthusiastic about, their work.

The hangars on the East Camp side of the airfield held some rare and interesting aircraft. One hangar was full of Westland Welkins, similar in layout to the Whirlwind, but much larger. They were all in very good condition and were finished in a high altitude colour scheme. They had never been issued to the squadrons and, after undergoing attention from trainees, would never fly again. They had been developed as a stratospheric fighter to intercept German high altitude reconnaissance flights and for this purpose they had pressurised cockpits, the technicalities of which also formed part of our studies.

Another hangar contained Bristol Buckinghams and Buckmasters which were variants of the Bristol Brigand, of which there were also one or two examples. They were of very solid-looking construction and were used to practise planned servicing, a system that seemed rather pointless to me. Later experience did not dispel the belief I formed that it could be positively dangerous.

The final part of the course covered some of the more fragmented aspects of the trade such as tube rolling, crack-testing, hulls and floats, adhesives and sealants, Air Publications and other relevant paperwork.

During the course, each week, we had a talk in the lecture hall from a visiting personality or dignitary. They were usually quite interesting, but the one I remember best was from a Nigerian Chief. He was dressed in his Chief's robes and was an impressive figure with a jovial personality. He spoke good English and gave a very interesting lecture about Nigeria, with questions and answers afterwards. He invited us all to visit him if we ever went to Nigeria.

One of the questions asked was how he could be happy about being ruled by Britain. The answer he gave was that Nigeria was virtually ruling itself anyway and he was happy for the country to be in association with Britain. When he finally left the stage, he received the loudest and longest applause I had heard for any speaker.

Social life was rather restricted and I only visited Cardiff and Barry Island a few times. The local pub in Gileston was quite lively and had a lady who played the accordion. At chucking-out time she would insist that we should stand up and sing, to her accompaniment, the Welsh National Anthem – Cymru, Cymru – followed by God Save the King, which had the desired effect of reminding us that we were guests in another country.

The course having finally come to its end, we sat our trade tests and, for those that passed, each emerged as an L.A.C. Fitter IIA. The trade was in Group 1 and carried the top rate of pay. According to one of our civilian instructors, we could expect to be promoted to Corporal within two years and his forecast proved to be absolutely correct.

With a great sense of relief and satisfaction, I went on leave for two weeks, before returning to my old unit at Lindholme.

I returned to Lindholme to find that life was going on much as before. My bed was still unoccupied, in the billet which still housed my old oppos and I soon settled in as I was regaled with tales of the happenings of the past six months.

Down at the hangar, Chiefy welcomed me by asking how I had enjoyed my holiday in South Wales. I asked about my Lancaster, as there were only two on the flight line and neither of them was it. Chiefy said it was in the next hangar, so I asked what it was doing there. He suggested I went and looked at it and found out for myself. Full of misgivings, I went to see my Lancaster collecting dust, with chocks, wheelcovers and driptrays in position and I walked around it, inside and out, checking for obvious signs of damage. There appeared to be none, so I climbed up into each wheelbay and inspected the structure for signs of a hard landing. There were none.

Baffled, I returned to Chiefy's office.

"What did you find, then?" Chiefy asked.

"It looks OK to me," I said.

He retorted. "You've just been on an expensive course and call yourself a Fitter IIA! You'd better go and have another look".

He was putting me to the test and I decided to keep looking until I found something.

The inspection was repeated and every square inch closely examined. This time I opened the escape hatch above the fuselage centre section, climbed out, walked down the fuselage to the tail unit and examined its top and inner surfaces thoroughly. There was nothing untoward. I retraced my steps back up the fuselage, stepped down on to the port wing and walked out to the tip, carefully scrutinising the skin from leading edge to trailing edge. To check the latter, including the ailerons, incurred the danger of sliding off the wing, but I persevered. Still nothing was found. I climbed over the fuselage on to the starboard wing and started to inspect that, too.

Working my way out along the centre section, I suddenly noticed a small ripple in the skin over the front main spar. After inspecting the remainder of the wing, which appeared to be all right, I returned to the ripple and examined it more closely. It was thick skinning at that point and the rivets appeared to be sound.

It became apparent to me that the member to which the skin was attached was also buckled and could only have been caused by an immense bending load on the wing. Replacing the hatch, I left the Lancaster, returned to Chiefy's office and told him what I had found. He nodded assent and told me that on some previous flight, the pilot had done an extremely tight turn and had overstressed the aircraft. I would never have thought that anybody could bend a Lancaster wing.

25. Two-Six on the Bamboo Bombers

Shortly after my return to Lindholme, our Lancasters were replaced by shiny new Lincolns. They appeared shiny because, although the colour scheme was the same, the black finish was gloss synthetic paint. Rather late in the day, some boffin had discovered that gloss paint showed up in the glare of a searchlight, or on a light night, less than a matt finish. Due to the curvature of the surfaces, most of the reflected light was directed away from observers on the ground, whereas a matt finish would show a dull silhouette of the whole aircraft.

A week or two later, Flying Wing was posted to R.A.F. Debden in North Essex, which had been a Battle of Britain fighter Station. The ground crews flew down in the Lincolns, huddled in the darkness of the fuselage. All of the airmen were invited, in turn, to climb over the mainspar and watch proceedings for a few minutes on the flight deck.

After landing at Debden, a lorry conveyed us and our kit to our new billet. "What's it like here?" we asked a passing airman as the tailboard was lowered.

"Cushy!" he replied and with this cheering news we soon felt at home as we settled in.

Our first – temporary – billet was a large old Nissen hut, with two coke stoves and an earth floor, which had been occupied by the Americans during the war. You could tell the Yanks had been here by the large painting, on the wall of a disused cookhouse, of the Eighth Air Force emblem, similar to that at Burtonwood.

The weather turned very cold and everybody tried to have their beds near a stove. If one was near a stove, one sweated, if further away, one froze. However, before several weeks had passed, we moved to a pre-war centrally-heated barrack block, similar to the one we had at Lindholme.

The Station was similar to Lindholme, but there were plenty of trees which made it seem more homely. Several of the billets and the Naafi/cookhouse block had new brickwork where bomb damage had been repaired. Down at our hangar, we examined with interest the several holes in the hangar doors caused by cannon fire.

In the adjacent Empire Radio School hangar stood a forlorn, dust-covered Lincoln with an aluminium finish. It was 'Mercury II', last seen at Mauripur and, although she had obviously seen better days, the School personnel were very proud of her.

The Wing was expanded into two flights, 'A' and 'B'. 'A' Flight, known as Heavy Flight by everybody, had three Lincolns and two Mk XVIe Spitfires. 'B' Flight, known as Light Flight, had three Oxfords, two Ansons and a Tiger Moth. As the only airframe fitter other than the N.C.O.s, I tended to be transferred from one Flight to the other, according to the work load, which gave me plenty of variety.

In the evenings, I recommenced modelling activities by building a 64 inch wing span "Mercury Monocoupe" kit, bought for £3/3/-, which was quickly completed and finished in Squadron markings with 'N' as the individual letter. It was kept in the crew room, so that I could fly it as soon as work had finished and before darkness set in.

One day it was missing and nobody seemed to know where it was. I toured the offices, stores and workshops built along each side of the hangar and drew a blank. Feeling frustrated and annoyed, I crossed the hangar back to the crew room and came across it standing under the wing of an Oxford. Like all the other aircraft in the hangar, it was parked with little yellow-painted chocks and a neat drip tray, which my oppos had obviously made for a joke. I went along with the joke by continuing to park it so each night, until eventually a hut was made available for a newly-formed Model Club.

The Tiger Moth seemed almost like a model aeroplane compared with other aircraft. Apart from a square section tubular steel fuselage, it was very similar in construction and appearance to the wood and wire creations of the First World War.

It was the only aeroplane in R.A.F. service, at that time, which still had a tailskid. The tailskid provided the sole means of braking the aircraft after landing, which was usually on grass. To avoid wearing it away when on tarmac, or when moving it in and out of the hangar, two chaps would lift the tail up by the ends of the tailplane struts, until the aircraft was nearly balanced on its wheels and walk it along. One chap could manage on his own on smooth, level ground, but if he tripped or lost his balance, the result could be rather painful and didn't do any good to the Tiger either.

I flew in the Tiger whenever I could and was usually allowed to take the controls which were light and responsive. It was necessary to trim the elevator, with the quaint spring-loaded adjustment, to prevent my arms aching from pushing on the stick to keep the aircraft from climbing. The spring was not very strong but it helped a bit. During one of these flights, sitting in the rear cockpit, the pilot asked if I was properly strapped in.

"Yes," I replied, with careless nonchalance, whereupon the pilot proceeded to loop the aircraft several times and followed this by doing stall turns and spins through several revolutions to both left and right, until I was dizzy. After the last spin, he straightened up the aircraft, regained height, dived and zoomed up again into what I thought would be another loop, but this time he levelled off at the top so that the Tiger was flying inverted.

Immediately, my weight went on to my Sutton harness shoulder straps, as my parachute pack came out of the seat and my feet left the floor of the cockpit. To my consternation, I could feel the straps begin to slide off my shoulders as the gap between me and the seat increased to more than two inches.

Holding desperately on to the seat, a quick glance showed that the straps of my borrowed parachute, which had not been adjusted because its owner objected to having to readjust them upon its return and which was worn merely to comply with regulations, were also slipping off my shoulders under the pull of the Sutton harness. I was restrained from leaving the cockpit only by two lap straps, lying across the 'V' formed by my body and my thighs, as my knees hit the bottom of the control panel.

Below, above my head, I could see the village of Newport and the A11 which formed the High Street, with traffic passing through and people walking about. It occurred to me that I could be right down there amongst them, sooner than I expected.

To my great relief, just as I began to think I ought to say something to the pilot before it was too late, he did a half roll and headed back to Debden. I said nothing about the incident, but made sure, in the future, that Sutton harnesses were always tightened down well for both pilots and passengers when I strapped them in the Tiger Moth. They often complained of the tightness, but they little knew that I spoke from experience when I told them, "Better safe than sorry!"

On another occasion, when out flying the Monocoupe on the airfield, I misjudged the strength of the wind and the model ended up in some tall trees. I could not see it anywhere and after searching for some time I abandoned it to its fate. The Monocoupe's absence from the hangar was soon noticed by Sergeant Maynard, who was an excellent pilot and very keen to accumulate flying hours, so that he could qualify for a job with BOAC when he left the R.A.F.

"Get the Tiger out," he said, when he had heard my tale of woe and he went off to get authorisation for a flight.

We were soon off the ground and making steeply banked turns over the trees in question. The Monocoupe was quickly spotted nestling in the high branches of a tree near the airfield boundary and bounded by several equally tall trees. Sgt. Maynard sideslipped down and landed lightly on the grass. He taxied over to the trees, cut the engine, turned to me and said:

"Well, we've found it! All we have to do now is get it down!"

The problem was immediately solved by the hasty arrival of the airfield fire tender. The firemen had watched us sideslip and disappear below the crest of the hill on which the airfield was situated. When we did not reappear, they immediately assumed that we had crashed and seemed to be quite disappointed when they found us safe and sound.

"Got a ladder with you?" called Sgt. Maynard.

"Yes," said the fire crew N.C.O., looking puzzled.

"Could you get it out and put it against that tree?"

"Well, yes, I suppose so."

The N.C.O. looked even more puzzled. Sgt. Maynard quickly explained the situation and the firemen looked more cheerful, for their job could be quite boring and a diversion like this was welcomed.

Before I could release my harness and climb out of the cockpit, a chap was up the ladder and he soon reached the Monocoupe. To shouted instructions, he detached the wings and threw them down, but carefully carried the fuselage down the ladder to the ground. The Monocoupe was taken back to the hangar on the fire tender, I swung the prop of the Tiger Moth, climbed back in the cockpit and we flew back across the airfield at a maximum altitude of five feet.

Flight Lieutenant Jarvis was the Commanding Officer of 'B' Flight and was the exemplification of an officer and a gentleman in the best sense of the words. It was also true of most of the officers I came in contact with, I am happy to record.

I had built a rather rough biplane control line model, loosely based on the Hawker Fury I and was flying it in the lee of a hangar one windy evening. I was having some difficulty keeping control of it and noticed, out of the corner of my eye, that Flt. Lieutenant Jarvis was watching with interest.

"May I have a shot at flying it, Newton?" he asked.

"Well, Sir," I replied, "I'd rather that you didn't, just now. It's rather tricky in the wind."

"Dash it all, Newton, I am a pilot!" he said with obvious disappointment. But I was adamant and after a while he departed. I still feel badly about the incident, for the model was of no great value.

Sadly, I never had a chance to redeem myself for having rebuffed him, by letting him have a go in calmer conditions. A week or two later he was practising formation flying for Battle of Britain Day, in one of the Ansons, when there was a mid-air collision with the other Anson, flown by a pilot attending the College. Both pilots were killed.

An incident occurred to one of the Ansons, a few days before, that might have prevented the accident. The Anson's engines were to be run up to check that a mag drop had been fixed and the rule was that there had to be a fire extinguisher ready for use near the aircraft.

The only CO_2 extinguisher that was available had been commandeered by 'A' Flight, so that a Lincoln could be started. Cheetah engines never caught fire in my experience, so I gave the fitter in the cockpit the sign to start the port engine. It started to turn, fired and spat back through the carburettor before stopping again. It had been overprimed and, with horror, I saw that the petrol dripping from the air intake was alight.

The nearest available fire extinguisher was in the hangar and was of the foam type. I raced across to pick it up and ran back, rather more slowly for it was both heavy and awkward to carry, to the Anson where liquid flame was dripping down to a spreading pool of petrol, also well alight. Shaking the inverted extinguisher, I prayed that it would work and, fortunately, as it seemed to me at the time, it did, to good effect. A thorough application of foam was required to completely dowse the flames.

No damage had been done, except that the cowlings needed respraying, but the engine had to be thoroughly washed and cleaned. Another thirty seconds and the fire would have taken hold. At the very least, the aircraft would have been unserviceable for some time and unavailable for formation flying. The accident could not have then happened. The two Ansons were numbered VS 598 and VS 603 to the best of my memory, as I did not keep any records of serial numbers, to my later regret and most of the ones quoted in this book are gleaned from old photographs.

The three Lincoln B 2s, with Packard Merlin engines, had the grey and glossy black finish previously described and two that I remember were numbered RF 443 and RF 302(TDE-G) in small red characters. They did not have the huge white serial numbers that were in vogue at that time and which most Lincolns carried.

The two Mk XVIe Spitfires of 'A' (Heavy) Flight were similar to Mark IXs except for the clipped wings, teardrop cockpit hoods on the cut-down rear fuselages and Packard Merlin engines. They were numbered RW 386 and TE 189. A third Spitfire that the unit also had for a time was TE 208 coded S - B (the original unit code TDE was later changed to S). The finish was aluminium synthetic dope overall including the spinners.

The Oxfords, Ansons and Tiger Moth all had the Flying Training Command colour scheme of aluminium finish with trainer yellow bands on wings and fuselage.

Oxford LB 458 was coded TDE-K and the other two had serial numbers SL 328 and HN 204. The Tiger Moth was T7997 coded TDE-M.

Individual aircraft were never, for some reason, referred to by the ground crew as 'B for Baker' but always as '208', to give a Spitfire as an example.

Plate 11 Vickers Supermarine Spitfire Mk XVI TE 208

For one particular Battle of Britain Day, a control line model flying display was organised in an empty hangar. At the side of the control line circle the Monocoupe stood on a table, newly fitted with a single channel radio control system built by Johnny Dumble (one couldn't buy ready-packaged sets in those days). Some ten feet away, the transmitter stood on another table so that it could be operated to demonstrate the system to the public.

The transmitter was contained in a large wooden box, with a webbing strap to carry it. It was too heavy to hold on account of the large batteries. When in use, it normally stood on the ground and control of the model was effected by a hand-held micro switch connected to the transmitter by a length of flexible cable. A large plug-in dipole aerial was used, each leg being about six feet long. With a test voltmeter plugged into the side of the Monocoupe's fuselage to show the voltage drop, the whole system looked quite impressive, even if all it did was move a rudder the size of a trim tab and it was reliable.

Johnny had built it from *Aeromodeller* plans from scratch and although when he started he knew little about radio, being an engine mechanic, by the time he had finished he was an expert in my eyes. To me it was a magical box of tricks and the only part that

I understood was the rubber driven escapement which gave right rudder when the micro switch button was pressed and held. To obtain left rudder, the button was pressed, released, pressed again and held. The rudder centralised when the button was released.

At this time, the Officer Commanding Flying Wing was Squadron Leader Laurie Ellis, a Canadian, a keen aeromodeller and the designer of the 'Vultan' and the 'Javalan' A.P.S. models loosely based on the Vulcan and Javelin respectively. He was keen to have a model flying display and instructed me to concentrate on that when the Day came.

Chiefy had ideas on things for me to do, other than "playing with toy aeroplanes" and sent me off with the Lincolns to the far side of the airfield.

In the meantime, the weather 'clamped'. The cloud base was about 200 feet and there was no chance of it lifting for the full-sized flying display to go ahead.

The lack of any activity in the control line circle soon came to the attention of the OC and, as the waiting spectators were getting restive, I was soon transported back to the hangar with urgent orders to get circulating.

Luckily, Johnny Dumble had organised my models even to the point of fitting his Amco 3.5 into my Junior Musketeer to give it some badly needed poke. Rather too much poke as it turned out, for in the gloom of the hangar it was only visible when it passed the windows. I took it as near to the roof trusses as I dared, several times, but no low beat-ups could be risked, for, at the speed it was travelling, it could have killed somebody if the lines had parted.

The next item in our rather limited programme was to fly two models in the circle. I flew the Fury type biplane powered by an Elfin 1.49 which played up by alternately tightening and running free for a while. The biplane could do no more than take off, climb about ten feet, do a powered descent to a rather nice three-pointer landing, taxi round until the engine freed off and then repeat the performance.

However, the crowd seemed to think that it was all part of the act. Johnny circulated the Junior Musketeer with cool competence and there were loud "Oohs" and "Aahs" every time there was a near miss, as the Musketeer hurtled past the Fury. This display went off better than I had dared to hope and we gave repeat performances all afternoon.

The Monocoupe, in the care of a pressed volunteer from the Flight, was, in the meantime, earning money for the R.A.F. Benevolent Fund, as the public queued to pay their sixpences to experience the novelty of pressing the micro switch and making the rudder waggle.

Wednesday afternoons were always given over to sports on R.A.F. Stations and aeromodelling was officially recognised as a sport.

It was not necessarily recognised by those N.C.O.s and Physical Training instructors, who were ever eager to pressgang an unwilling airman into becoming a section team member for cross-country running, rugby football, or some other pointlessly energetic activity.

Since our rather lame effort for the Battle of Britain Day, we aeromodellers nevertheless found that the effort was appreciated and, with the full backing of Sqdn. Ldr. Ellis, that henceforth we could pursue our particular interest undisturbed.

We were encouraged to represent the Station at the Technical Training Command Championships and R.A.F. United Kingdom Championships of the R.A.F.M.A.A. and Chiefy had to give up in despair when I told him I would be away for four days – two days flying and two days travelling – to attend one of these meetings.

The selected club members, and I was fortunate to be usually included, travelled to R.A.F. Stations at Newton, Horsham St. Faith, Conningsby, Spitalgate and Cosford, mainly in somebody's car. I invariably had a great time, meeting well-known names in the aeromodelling world and old friends (which included some ex-Mauripur chaps), even if my models did not come up to expectations.

I soon found that I was very far from being an expert, faced with competition from people like Ian Dowsett, Sgt. Doug McHard, Sqdn. Ldr. Verney and many others.

I was flying a new model at Horsham St Faith one hot humid day, in the control line stunt event. There was occasional thunder in the distance but the airfield itself was bathed in sunshine. I found that every time the model flew higher than about ten feet an electric shock went up my arm. The judges waited impatiently for me to start my routine which proved to be impossible. When the engine finally cut out and the model landed again, my explanation was greeted with scepticism until somebody else tried to fly the model and suffered the same effect.

I applied to go on an Aircrew Selection Board for training as a pilot, to which the C.O. agreed. He had me flown down to R.A.F. Hornchurch in an Oxford, which was a very nice gesture of confidence in me. Unfortunately, although I passed all the tests, I muffed the final interview by being pig-headed. The interviewing officer asked if I was prepared to accept aircrew training other than as a pilot. The question caught me unawares and I replied that I only wanted to be a pilot. It was a classic example of how one stupid remark can affect one's whole life, for I was turned down. However, I could console myself with the fact that my job involved flying which gave a lot of satisfaction. It was possible to re-apply in four years' time, but I never did.

Part of my satisfaction stemmed from working on the Flights, where I was able to work on my own initiative. For other airframe fitters down at the R & I hangar, life was more like being in a factory. The R & I (Repair and Inspection) section carried out minor and major inspections on Technical Training Command aircraft, including our own. Our aircraft invariably had more snags when they returned to the Flights than they had before and Chiefy thought it would be a good idea to send me down with them to ensure that the job was done properly.

The first 'kite' I went down with was an Oxford and it was to be serviced under a Planned Servicing scheme, which was carried out on a timed work basis.

I was given a certain time to carry out a glued joint inspection on the port wing, for which a large number of panels, each held on with a dozen or more screws, had to be removed from the underside. I diligently started to remove the panels with an Archimedean screwdriver, which made my arms ache, poked at the glue blobs to check that the glue had not gone soft and ensured that the joints were still sound in the interior structure.

I was man 'A' on the servicing team and man 'B' was doing the starboard wing. The job was half done when the R& I sergeant came up to me and said:

"What are you playing about at? You should be finished by now!"

"It's taken me until now to get this far and I haven't stopped yet," I replied.

"Well, you've run out of time anyway," he continued. "Man 'B' has finished and is in the crew-room until his next job is due."

"I can't help that," I retorted. "I'm doing the job properly," and 1 carried on. The sergeant returned to his little mobile hut, defeated, to re-adjust his schedules which had been badly dislocated. When I finally finished, I clocked off, went to the crew-room and dropped into an old armchair beside man 'B', worn out with the exertion.

"How did you manage to do that job in the time?" I asked him.

"Simple," he replied. "I only took half the panels off!"

I mulled this information over in my mind. If this was how the chaps had to work, no wonder there were unrectified snags. It seemed to be a hare-brained scheme to me. If two chaps each had work to do in the cockpit, for example a rigger and an instrument mechanic, one had to wait in the crew-room until a certain time, when the other had to leave the cockpit even if the job was not finished. A lot of the servicing time seemed to be spent in the crew-room although it may have been true in theory that a quicker turn round could be achieved this way. It never seemed to be the case in practice.

Not being a permanent member of the R & I staff, I was not in awe of the system and carried on doing the job properly in my own way, no doubt creating chaos with the schedules, until the job was done.

The next time, I was sent down to work on one of the Spitfires. One inspection item was to remove the upper fuel tank so that the engine bearer attachments and bracing struts could be examined. I was assisted by another airman from 'A' Flight, who accidentally dropped a spanner down the gap between the lower fuel tank and the inside of the fuselage.

It became apparent that there was no way of retrieving the spanner except by removing the struts and taking out the lower fuel tank as well.

We took some of the load off the bearers by supporting the engine with an adjustable trestle and proceeded to remove the tank.

The sergeant saw what we were doing and came dashing up.

"What do you think you are doing? Your schedule doesn't require you to take the bottom tank out."

I explained the situation and, after uttering a few choice words, he let us get on with the job. We eased the tank out, laid it on a wing mat and surveyed the dark pit thus exposed. The spanner could not be seen.

"Well, you dropped the spanner," I said to my assistant. "You can dive in and get it. I'll hold your legs."

He lowered himself, head first, into the fuselage as I held on to his legs. His muffled voice came up from the Spitfire's nether regions.

"Hey, look at this. The main spar is all covered with some white stuff".

I pulled him back out, together with the spanner and peered down at the main spar but could see nothing.

"I'll hold your legs!" he grinned, which made me suspect a practical joke. "Pukka gen, it's covered in white stuff."

So he held my legs as, armed with a torch, I lowered myself down. Sure enough, the main spar was badly corroded all over.

The fact was quickly reported and the spar was again inspected, this time by the Technical Officer in the same undignified fashion. The upshot was that the other Spitfire was pulled into the hangar and also inspected. Similar corrosion was found and neither of the Spitfires ever flew again with the unit: I don't know their subsequent history but one, RW 386, still exists.

Back at the Flights, the Spitfire pilots, no longer able to fly their beloved aircraft, had a few moans because the defect that had grounded them would not have been found until much later if it had not been for a carelessly dropped spanner. Not only that, they were now out of one of the best jobs in the world, flying a Spitfire.

One or two were surprisingly upset about it and would have been mad enough to happily risk their necks by continuing to fly the Spitfires.

We had several Polish pilots who were, without exception, extremely good. One in particular, a big chap called Slon who walked very stiffly, had difficulty fitting himself into the confined cockpit of a Spitfire. Once airborne, however, he could make the Spitfire fly rings round a jet fighter in a dogfight, by turning inside it.

He did this over the airfield one afternoon, after challenging an American Thunderjet to show what it could do. It was a thrilling and unusual contest. The Thunderjet could certainly outpace the Spitfire, but could not outmanoeuvre it and Slon could have shot the American down a dozen times. They finished the display with a combined beat-up of the airfield and the Thunderjet departed with a farewell waggle of its wings.

Another Polish pilot, at Christmas time, celebrated by continually looping the Tiger Moth over the airfield. He started at about 500 feet and each time he completed a loop he lost some height. The last loop brought him to within twenty five feet of the ground. At that point, an Air Traffic Controller dashed out and fired a red Very light. Fortunately, the pilot saw and complied with, the signal to stop his antics and finally landed. He was grounded for two weeks, I believe.

In summer it was most pleasant on a sunny day to be out in the open air servicing the aircraft, refuelling, or just lying on the grass yarning and joking and waiting for the aircraft to return.

In winter time there is no bleaker place than an airfield and life was much harder. We struggled and fought to crank open the hangar doors when the runners were filled with ice. Long crowbars were a necessity to both break the ice and lever the doors along, back and forth, until a final push built up sufficient momentum to overcome the resistance of the remaining ice and move the door back to its stop. Six doors at each end of the hangar could take over an hour's sweated labour to open.

Then the Ansons, Oxfords, or Spitfires would be manhandled outside as required over the rutted snow or ice. The Lincolns would be towed in or out of the hangar by the David Brown tractor, using a massive towing arm hooked on to the tailwheel, or by wire ropes shackled to the eyes on the main wheel axles. Before doing so, it was necessary to switch on the gyroscopic compass. If forgotten, it would take hours to re-orientate itself and the instrument people would get very upset.

Refuelling a Lincoln with two thousand or so gallons, during a blizzard with numbed fingers and in imminent danger of sliding off the icy wing was my worst memory.

It was necessary to turn the propellers of the Oxfords and Ansons by hand before starting to expel engine oil that drained into the lower cylinders. This prevented damage to the engine by hydraulic locking when the starters were operated. The Ansons were fitted with 24V electric starters, but the Oxfords had to be hand cranked by means of a slipping clutch and ratchet arrangement. One had to kneel on the wing and insert the starting handle through a small access hole under a hinged panel behind the engine. The Kigass hand-priming pump was also reached through the access hole. Four or five strokes of the pump were usually sufficient to prime the engine and, at a signal from the pilot, the mechanic would start to turn the handle slowly at first, to prevent the clutch from slipping and then fast as the engine went over compression.

A couple of turns of the propeller were usually enough to get the engine to fire and sometimes an extra couple of pump strokes were necessary to keep the combustion going until the engine picked up. When it did pick up, the slipstream could easily blow the mechanic off the wing. After a final check that the Kigass pump was securely screwed down, a firm hold of the edge of the access hole was required while the starting handle was removed.

With the hinged panel securely shut with an 'Oddie' fastener, there was no handhold except for two chromium-plated handles screwed to the upper fuselage side, which were used when edging back down the walkway to the trailing edge of the wing.

If the engine did not pick up, it became progressively more difficult to start and cranking it for any length of time was very exhausting. The starting handle was stowed inside the fuselage above the entrance door and secured with a strap and fastener. Once the engines were started, the pilot very often forgot that the handle had to be stowed and would open up the throttles in turn, blowing the luckless airman off the wing, or making it extremely difficult to open the entrance door to reach the starting handle stowage.

The Lincolns also had to be hand primed by two members of the ground crew, one for the two port engines and one for the two starboard engines. Each airman, by a feat of gymnastics, would swing on to the top of one of the wheels and, from there, step on to two small platforms, one on each radius rod. With legs straddled and facing forward inside the wheel bay, the engine selector valve and Kigass pump could be reached, high on the rear face of the engine bulkhead.

It was a nerve-racking position, particularly when the engines started. I had visions of the undercarriage collapsing and squashing me against the top of the wheel bay, as the wheel came up, if anybody in the cockpit accidentally operated the retraction control and I always made sure that the undercarriage locking struts were in position.

Maintenance of the Lincoln was similar to that for the Lancaster, although in some respects it seemed to give more trouble. The tailwheel strut had an external anti-shimmy damper which required frequent topping up with oil if the tailwheel was not to spin like a castoring wheel on a tea trolley. The tailwheel tyre had two treads, one on each side with a relieved area between, also for the purpose of counteracting shimmy.

The Lincoln was basically a stretched Lancaster, but did not seem to be quite as inflexible. The wings seemed to flap more in flight and also when touching down; when the engines were run up on the ground, the tail unit would waggle quite alarmingly until one got used to it. The waggling would twist the fuselage back and forth quite visibly, because the panting of the skinning was clearly shown up by the glossy black finish. As a result, small cracks in the skinning would occasionally occur in the flatter side areas of the fuselage immediately aft of the more rigid area of the bomb bay, which gave an opportunity to put my skin repairs training theory into practice.

Causes of frequent trouble were the fabric strips that sealed the gaps in the top surface of the wing between the centre section and the outer panels. The thrashing slipstream of the propellers would gradually loosen the adhesion of the strip to the wing, eventually causing the strip to be ripped away.

New fabric was applied with red dope which did not adhere very well to metal. Why a sheet metal strip, attached with screws, was not used, I can't imagine. This trouble did not occur with my particular Lancaster for the short period I worked on it. It may have had a different method of sealing.

One particular Lincoln had a spate of leaking seals on the undercarriage hydraulic jacks which had to be changed. This required a lengthy period of retraction tests to get the 'up' and 'down' locks correctly adjusted. The locks were spring loaded to engage and were released by the movement of the jack ram.

The importance of adjusting the 'down' locks correctly, lay in the fact that failure to do so could allow the undercarriage to collapse or, alternatively, prevent it from retracting. Incorrectly adjusted 'up' locks could fail to retain the undercarriage in the retracted position or, far worse, fail to release it when 'down' was selected.

During a period while the main runway was being resurfaced with a layer of tarmac several inches thick, aircraft had to use the other runway which, at one end, ran uphill to the intersection. One of the Lincolns, RF 302, was doing circuits and bumps, with some A.T.C. cadets on board for air experience. They had rather more experience than they expected on that particular flight.

One touchdown occurred at a higher speed than should have been the case, due to the upward slope of the runway. The speed was still excessive when the wheels hit the overlaid tarmac and the Lincoln bounced high into the air.

I happened to be having a mug of tea in the crew room when I glanced out of the window and saw the Lincoln poised about fifty feet up in the air in a nose-up attitude. The sound of the engines, opened up to full throttle, came across the airfield as the aircraft incredibly managed to keep going and draw away, without losing much height.

It was unfortunate that the undercarriage was then retracted, for as the Lincoln went round again for another attempt and the pilot selected 'down' again, the wheels refused to budge. No jinking of the aircraft was sufficient to release them, nor the operation of the emergency high-pressure air system and eventually the Lincoln went off to Marham to belly-land. The touchdown was effected without injury to the aircrew or the A.T.C. cadets who were flown back to Debden in Oxfords and Ansons that had accompanied the Lincoln on its last flight.

Shortly afterwards, a replacement Lincoln, RE 416 and also coded S - G, arrived at the airfield.

The three Oxfords were flown intensively, mainly for instrument rating flights for which the aircraft were specially equipped. Amber-coloured Perspex panels, stowed when not in use inside a canvas bag with compartments to protect each panel, were fitted to the cockpit windows so that only amber light entered the cockpit. The roof panel of the cockpit glazing was too awkward to cover and was itself made of amber Perspex, being a permanent fixture.

The pilot under examination was able to see through the amber screens to take off normally and when his examination began he donned special blue-tinted glasses through which he could see his instrument dials clearly. The system gave a very good simulation of night-flying conditions and was a big improvement on the hood that used to be fitted to Tiger Moths.

A curious feature of Oxfords was that two forms of undercarriage fairing were used. One Oxford might have a fairing of considerable area in front of each main wheel, which folded back as the undercarriage was retracted and another might have conventional undercarriage doors closed by bungee cords as the undercarriage retracted and forced open again as the undercarriage extended. This system was very similar to that used for the Mosquito.

Apart from this divergence, the Oxfords at Debden were identical. Another odd feature, common to all of them, was that only one jack was used on one side of each undercarriage assembly, which had a retracting mechanism similar in principle to that of the Lincoln. I would have thought that the offset pull of the jack would have twisted the assembly, but the system worked satisfactorily and gave no trouble.

The Oxfords had a smooth exterior, of pleasing appearance, on the curved surfaces of the wings and fuselage, due to the plywood skinning. The flat side areas of the fuselage, however, were in some cases noticeably rippled, although securely glued to the internal structure and quite firm. The interior, finished in cockpit green throughout, looked rather like a lightly built garden shed and somewhat frail. The plywood skin could not stand concentrated pressure and on at least one occasion a cleaning rag, carelessly left lying on the ground, was sucked up by a propeller and hurled through the skin into the cockpit.

Nevertheless, appearances were deceptive and the Oxford was, in fact, a strong lively aircraft which could do vertical banks quite safely as I was relieved to find out during one particular flight. The pilot indulged in some cloud chasing, flying around towering columns of cumulus in brilliant sunshine until the 'G' force seemed likely to rupture me. Icy conditions did not seem to bother it unduly, either. After one Oxford landed on a routine flight, I ducked under the wing to put the chocks in place and narrowly missed being hit by a solid sheet of ice, about eight feet long and one foot wide, which slid off the leading edge and crashed to the ground.

Plate 12 Airspeed Oxford LB 458

The Oxford was lighter than the Anson and made do with fixed pitch Fairey-Reed propellers of flat twisted metal, which seemed to be effective enough once the aircraft had taken off.

It was possible to fit a propeller the wrong way round and on one occasion this happened. The pilot complained that, although the revs and boost were satisfactory, the engine seemed to have no power and he barely managed to get airborne before he ran out of runway. All the plugs and harnesses were changed, but a further test flight showed no improvement and the pilot and engine experts retired, baffled, to the office to discuss the matter further.

I was driving the petrol bowser at the time and, while the aircraft was being refuelled, leaned idly against the propeller of the offending engine with my fingers around the tip of a blade. I felt a curvature at the back of the blade which struck me as being odd, so I turned and had a closer look. It was obvious that the propeller had been put on back to front. I had a quiet word with the fitter who had worked on the engine and that was the end of the matter as far as I was concerned.

Night flying was a regular monthly routine, rewarded by a late, late supper of bacon and eggs and a lie-in next morning until nine o'clock. One had to be extra careful of rotating propellers and the impatience of pilots raring to go. Once the aircraft had gone off we could relax in the crew room and wait for them to come back, an hour or two later.

One night, a returning Oxford was taxiing along the perimeter track to the hard standing, marshalled by one of the ground crew. He was using illuminated wands, which were a type of torch with sticks of frosted Perspex, which glowed when the torch was switched on. I was watching through the crew room window when I suddenly noticed the navigation lights of another aircraft approaching along the perimeter track from the other direction. The pilot of this aircraft obviously thought that the marshalling signals were for him and I realised that the two aircraft were going to meet head-on, with the unfortunate airman caught between them.

I dashed through the door and across the grass to the marshaller and shouted in his ear to put his wands out and warned him of the danger he was in. He was told to wait until I had informed the second pilot of the situation. The signal that the pilot understood that he had to wait, while the first aircraft was dealt with, would be the flashing on and off – several times – of the navigation lights.

As soon as the airman grasped this, I dashed off to the second aircraft, another Oxford, waggled the ailerons to gain the pilot's attention, climbed in and dashed up to the cockpit.

"Stop here! The signals are not for you, they are for another aircraft!" I bawled in the pilot's ear, through his flying helmet. The pilot seemed puzzled and kept edging forward, so I reached over and applied the brake by grasping the lever on the control column, an action which rather annoyed him.

I pulled his helmet away from his ear with my other hand and explained again, telling him to switch the navigation lights on and off several times. He still did not appear to have grasped the situation but, at my insistent bellowing, he finally did what he was told.

When the wands appeared again, he opened up the engines to move off again, but hastily throttled back when the red navigation light of the first Oxford began to move across his line of vision, as the aircraft was marshalled onto the hard standing beside the perimeter track. Finally, the marshalling wands beckoned us on.

"Wait until I get out and then you can go," I told the pilot and quickly made my exit. I had had to speak to him in rather a peremptory fashion, which he didn't seem to appreciate and I didn't want to be around when the aircraft finally came to rest.

Duty crew was quite interesting because of the variety of aircraft types we had to marshal in, refuel and possibly put in the hangar for an overnight stay. One day, it was a Meteor lobbing into the airfield on its last drop of fuel, with a white-faced kid of a pilot lighting up a cigarette to calm his nerves as soon as he had climbed out of the cockpit. Another time it was a Vampire which, when it was about to leave, had a wet start and flooded the engine with Avtag. We had to lean over the tail booms to tip the aircraft and let the fuel drain out of the tailpipe, then push it ten yards or so away from the spilt fuel to have another, successful, attempt to start up.

Fleet Air Arm aircraft came in occasionally. They always had an immaculate finish and even the cowling fasteners appeared to be untouched by screwdrivers. Once we had a Firefly IV stay overnight, which was the subject of much examination and admiration. On another occasion it was a Grumman Avenger that called in. It looked truly enormous for a single-engined aircraft and was immaculately finished in midnight blue. It was surprising to learn that they were still in use, seven years after the war. It had probably been pulled out of storage in the U.S.A. on account of the Korean War, which had started when I was at St Athan and which was still being waged at that time.

Another Meteor IV, VT 139 coded M - X, that was later converted to a U.15 drone, also dropped in for a visit.

I had an embarrassing few moments on the day that the A.O.C. arrived for his annual Inspection, in his personal Devon. I had previously marshalled an Anson on to the hardstanding directly across the airfield grass from the runway, to save the pilot having to taxi all the way round the perimeter track. This had been done without difficulty and when the pilot of the Devon decided to take the same route, I beckoned him on.

As soon as he left the runway I was perturbed to see that the Devon was forming three furrows in the ground as it moved. Frantically, I marshalled him on, hoping to get him to firmer ground and he obligingly opened up his throttles. Still deeper the Devon sank, until I could hardly see the nosewheel which acted more like a ploughshare.

His main wheels were throwing off thick clumps of mud and I knew that if the aircraft stopped it would require jacks and boards to extract it. I continued to energetically wave the pilot on until, as he later told me, the engines were running at full throttle, but he managed to keep the Devon moving, foot by foot.

I had a mental picture of the A.O.C. having to jump down from his bogged-down aircraft and wade through the mud to his car in his light, highly polished, shoes. It just didn't bear thinking about!

Fortunately, the pilot finally managed to reach firmer ground and taxied on to the hard standing, where the A.O.C. was able to alight with his customary dignity, to be greeted by his reception committee.

Both the pilot and the A.O.C. looked back at the three deep furrows scarring the airfield and laughed, I was relieved to note. It took some time and effort to clean up the Devon, but it could have been worse.

One bright, sunny day, a Lincoln returned to Debden after a flight, having made a detour over R.A.F. Duxford to drop some toilet rolls on that hallowed airfield, the home of a squadron of Meteors who did not take kindly to this insult.

I was on the wing of the Lincoln, helping to refuel it after its long flight and did not know about the toilet roll incident. In the distance, over Saffron Walden, a large formation of Meteors could be seen flying quite low down. They banked and turned towards

Debden, dropping even lower until they disappeared below the brow of the airfield.

It all seemed rather odd and, as the petrol continued to flow into the Lincoln's tanks, I kept an eye open for the Meteors reappearance. Just as I began to think that they must have gone off in a different direction, I saw them approaching across the airfield, towards the hangars and the Lincoln parked outside.

They were so low that no daylight could be seen between their belly fuel tanks and the airfield. Standing on the wing of the Lincoln, I was looking down on them and could see them leaving streaks of flattened grass behind them. They were heading straight for us and I would have beaten a hasty retreat down the wing ladder if there had been time. With split-second timing, the Meteors lifted their noses and shot over us, clearing the hangar and Lincoln by no more than a few feet.

One Meteor was so low that it only just cleared the Flying Control building, causing the anemometer to spin crazily and putting it out of action, as the pilot headed for a gap between two hangars. Once more they beat up the airfield before making off back to Duxford, leaving us all quite shaken.

Another aircraft seen over Debden, one Sunday afternoon, was the Handley Page 88. It was making regular flights over the airfield at high speed, passing over at an altitude of about two thousand feet. Its crescent-shaped wings, being Handley Page Victor wings to a reduced scale, could be clearly seen mounted on an Attacker fuselage, for test purposes.

It was not until later in the evening that we heard on the news that it had broken-up over the runway at Stansted, a few miles away, during a low altitude high-speed run. The pilot was killed and the news shocked us very much because the Handley Page 88 had appeared to be performing faultlessly, almost routinely, all afternoon.

It made us realise that our own aircraft were safe to fly only because courageous and dedicated test pilots had flown them first and sorted the bugs out with courage and dedication. As it was, yet another brave chap had just died endeavouring to ensure that the Handley Page Victor, that superlative and long-lived aircraft, would do all that was expected of it.

Once, travelling up to Hull, I passed by my old station, Lindholme and was quite amazed to see that the Flying Training Command Unit that was now in residence was still using old Wellingtons, with aluminium finish and yellow bands on wings and fuselages.

Technical Training Command operated a number of interesting aircraft. One was a very old Anson with a greenhouse, which arrived at the R & I on several occasions for servicing.

Another was the last Halifax in R.A.F. service, based at Henlow and presumably serviced there for it never came to Debden, except when it flew over during an exercise to simulate the dropping by parachute of infiltrators attacking Debden. The infiltrators, who were actually dropped off by lorry, managed to take over the guardroom. They captured the Orderly Officer and locked him in a cell, breaking two of his fingers in the process.

I was one of those defending the north side of the airfield opposite Brooklands Garage. Armed with rifles and blank rounds, we relieved the boredom by letting off a few rounds now and again on the pretext that we had seen something suspiciously like an infiltrator. The garage owner was not amused and threw open a window in his house – which was adjacent.

"Stop playing soldiers and buzz off!" he bellowed at us. The rest of his words were drowned with a burst of rapid fire and a few thunderflashes. When the noise died down, he tried again and threatened to report us to our superiors, which met with the same response. We were cold, wet and tired and in no mood to be apologetic. At the appointed hour that the exercise finished, we expended all our remaining ammunition and thunderflashes, just for his benefit.

One member of Flying Squadron, a chap called Lupinski, was posted on the North Gate and refused to let the Group Captain commanding R.A.F. Debden through into the camp because he did not have his identification card with him. The Group Captain was breathing fire and threatened Lupinski with incarceration for life, but Lupinski stood his ground and would not raise the barrier. The Group Captain sat fuming in his Humber Super Snipe while a call was put out for the Orderly Officer, who arrived and gave permission to raise the barrier. It was fortunate that it was later that the

Orderly Officer was locked up, or it might have been another six hours before the Group Captain could gain admittance.

Next day, Lupinski was sent for by the Group Captain. We bade him farewell and, with requests to send us a postcard from sunny Colchester, he went off, visibly trembling, for his appointment with God. To his amazement, the Group Captain greeted him with a smile and proceeded to congratulate him for obeying orders to the letter and not giving way to intimidation.

Lupinski was British and not Polish as his name might have suggested. He was a happy-go-lucky chap who, on one occasion, when his luck ran out, was awarded a few days jankers for some misdemeanour. Detailed for fatigues one Saturday afternoon, he was instructed to dig a drainage pit on the caravan site, for an officer who was posted to Debden and arriving that weekend.

The officer duly arrived that afternoon, to find Lupinski at the bottom of a deep hole still digging furiously. When the officer learned that the pit had been dug specially for his caravan, he gave Lupinski a ten-bob note, which was more than a day's pay for some airmen at that time.

On Monday, so the story went, the officer was extolling the virtues of the airmen of his new Station to the C.O.

"Splendid chaps!" he was reputed to have said. "Do you know, one of them even gave up his Saturday afternoon to dig a drainage pit for me. Well, the least I could do was slip him ten bob!"

The C.O. listened in amazed disbelief and then the penny dropped.

"Lupinski!" The call rang through the hangar.

Lupinski reported to the C.O.'s office and found that the officer with the caravan was also there.

"Is this the airman who dug your pit?" asked the C.O.

"Yes, that's the chap. Splendid fellow, salt of the earth!"

The C.O. ignored this testimonial.

"Lupinski! Give Flt. Lt. ------ his ten bob back!"

Life was never dull at Debden. One day, a reporter from Sunday newspaper *The People* came into the camp, ostensibly as an assistant to the chimney sweep. Once inside the camp, he went his own way, walking through the hangars and workshops and even being offered a cup of tea in one of them. This hospitality was rewarded with a piece in the following Sunday's edition, written by the reporter and describing how he had nosed around one of Britain's top secret airbases unchallenged.

Well, that really stirred the mire. Guards were doubled for over six months and, although sales may have been boosted nationally by this exclusive story, sales certainly plummeted on the camp and the paper lost my custom permanently.

Social life, locally, was quite good. Cambridge was not too far away, with all its city attractions and at Bishops Stortford there was Long's Restaurant, with dancing to Freddie Randall's band or Harry Gold and his Pieces of Eight – and packed out it was too! Girls even came in coaches from London, all dressed in white blouses and black skirts, to that pocket handkerchief dance floor, behind the green door of the closed café.

We usually warmed up at the Half Moon pub, across the road, where there was always a sing-song round the old joanna, even on a Sunday night and the fug was such that you couldn't see across the room, but you soon learned to be careful of the step-down in the floor, half way to the bar.

One memorable Saturday night, a bunch of us had our taxi commandeered from under our noses by a party of nurses. No other taxi would turn out at that time of night so we set off to walk back to Debden. It was a bitterly cold night, for which we were inadequately dressed and when we reached Stansted we knocked on the Police Station door to beg a cell for the night. The 'Police' sign shone brilliantly but nobody answered so, in desperation, one idiot did his best to pick the door lock, but was dragged away before he could succeed with his break-in.

A telephone box offered shelter, but not for all five of us. We tried taking turns to stand outside, but the first chap to volunteer became so cold, he chilled off the rest when he returned to the kiosk.

It occurred to me that the telephone held the solution to our problem and, after a bit of fuddled thought, I remembered that we were all members of the duty crew and there was flying on Sunday morning. I rang R.A.F. Debden and asked for the Orderly Officer, who had presumably dragged himself from his bed, for he didn't sound very pleased when he finally answered. I apologised and explained our predicament and asked for transport to be sent to pick us up. To my surprise, he accepted my sob-story and said he would send the duty driver in a truck. We would have to refund the cost but, in our situation, it was cheap at any price.

The duty driver, when he found us, was in a foul temper at being dragged from a warm bed out into a cold night, to chauffeur a bunch of well-oiled revellers. He swore that he would see to it that we were all on a fizzer in the morning, but we were too tired and cold for that to worry us.

As it turned out, he was the one to be on a fizzer, for when he reported to the guardroom on his return, the S.P. noticed that his pyjama trousers were protruding below his uniform trousers. Had the driver been less malevolent, we might have told him.

The Squadron dance was held at Saffron Walden Town Hall. We decorated the big hall and suspended various models, including the faithful Monocoupe, from the ceiling (the C.O.'s idea). Halfway through the evening, two oppos walked me round the town to work off the effects of the beer and by the time the 'do' was over I was fit enough to help load some inert bodies into the coach that took us back to camp.

It was always an enjoyable moment, after a hard day's work, when the cry rang out,

"Two-six on the bamboo bombers!" and the Oxfords were pushed off the hard-standing and down the slight slope to the hangar, coasted through the open door and, with deft use of the tailwheel steering arm, brought neatly to rest in their allotted positions with a well-timed shout of "Brakes!" and their prompt application by the chap in the cockpit.

A final call was "Chocks and driptrays!" These were placed in position; the pitot head cover, wheel covers and plugs for the instrumentation air inlets, were fitted and the hangar doors were wound shut and padlocked.

Leaving final security checks to the Duty Key Orderly, the lights were doused and we wended our way back to the welcoming lights of the barrack blocks shining through the trees and to the 'cookhouse' for tea.

B-36s of the American Strategic Air Command flew over quite regularly at this time, usually at a great height and at night. The reverberant sound, of the six piston engines and four jet engines, as the bomber passed immediately overhead, would vibrate the brick billet considerably.

To conclude this chapter, a final reminiscent look at our beloved Spitfires!

The Spitfires were a complete contrast to the Oxfords in every way, except that they also gave very little trouble. They had Packard Merlin engines, as the Lincolns did, which to the best of my memory were reliable and trouble-free. I had very little to do with the engines, except for the hydraulic and pneumatic pumps mounted at the rear, although I did, on occasions, help a fitter to time a replacement magneto. This was done by the adjustment of a Vernier type flexible coupling. The coupling had teeth on each side, with more teeth on one side than the other, so that by rotating the coupling to a different position the magnetos could be accurately timed.

The seat of the Spitfire was shaped to hold a parachute pack, which made it uncomfortable for a member of the ground crew to sit in for engine starting, etc., but otherwise, the aircraft was a pleasure to work on.

The seat could be moved down to suit the pilot's size, or up for a better view when taxiing with the teardrop hood open or on the landing approach. The rudder pedals had a two-tier arrangement to accommodate the movement of the seat, which, in the lower position used for combat or aerobatics, required the use of the bottom pedals. If the pilot flew upside-down, his feet were prevented from leaving the rudder bar by the upper pedal.

If a spanner was dropped in the cockpit, it invariably slipped under the seat where it was quite inaccessible. The only remedy was to take the seat out, complete with armour plate, which was no mean weight. The seat did not come out easily and it was necessary to remove the teardrop hood by pulling the jettison toggle, which extracted pins to release the hood from the four runners, two in each track on each side of the cockpit. Part of the track on the port side was in the edge of the small hinged panel that gave access to the cockpit and which had to be shut before the hood was closed.

The hood was closed and opened by a small cranked handle operating a sprocket and chain arrangement on the starboard side.

It was a two-man job to get everything lined up and the pins replaced when the hood was replaced. If an electrician or instrument mechanic had dropped the spanner, he had to give me a hand or he didn't get his spanner back afterwards, although, I must say, there was rarely any need to press anybody, for we all mucked in together.

The radar mechanics used to sometimes think that giving a hand to push an aircraft out was beneath their dignity and that if they did, they were really doing the rest of us a favour.

"But I'm radar!" said one to me one day, when pressed to help.

"I don't care if you're Royalty!" said I. "The exercise will do you good!"

To get back to the main subject, the flaps and brakes of the Spitfire were pneumatically operated and the undercarriage was hydraulic. When checking the operation of the flaps, it was advisable to warn other people nearby, to ensure that there was nobody under the wing, as an unsuspecting person could suffer a nasty crack on the head with the sudden movement. The flaps were either 'up' or 'down' and there was no intermediate position.

When the ram of the pneumatic cylinder extended to lower the flaps, a little spring-loaded panel in the top surface of the wing would lift up to allow room for the actuation. The raised panel also acted as a visual indication to the pilot that the flaps were fully down on each side. If only one flap was working, perhaps as a result of the Spitfire being damaged in action, the pilot had a ready indication of what was causing the aircraft to behave in an odd way and would be able to take appropriate action.

The Spitfire's undercarriage had been a source of interest to me for many years. I had built a rubber-driven Spitfire when I was an apprentice at Blackburn Aircraft Ltd. and it was Mr Kirk who fathomed out the geometry for the retracting undercarriage, which, as previously related, worked beautifully.

Earlier Spitfires had oleo legs with internal splines to prevent the wheels twizzling round, but they were very expensive to manufacture. Later versions had external torque links and, although they detracted from the previously uncluttered appearance of the oleo legs, they were not obtrusive.

The proportions of the undercarriage and elegant fairings of minimum area were just right to complement the classic lines of the Spitfire and this was true from whatever angle one looked at them. They were rather like the shapely legs of a pretty girl in that respect!

The feature of particular interest was the geometry that enabled the legs to be raked forward when extended and raked backward when retracted, so that the wheels lay behind the main spar. Within the thin wings, the wheels had to be level in the fore and aft plane—i.e. chordwise.

Each undercarriage leg was a cantilever, set at an approximate right angle to the pivot pin, or pintle, which was supported by a substantial mounting in the wing. In plan view, the pintle was angled away from the line of the wheel track, to give the back rake when retracted. In side view, with the legs raked forward, the pintle was inclined to form an angle with the wing chord line. The difficulty lay in determining precisely the angle between the pintle and the leg from the two known angles of rake.

Each leg was locked 'up' or 'down' automatically by its own spring-loaded pin which, in addition to moving in and out of its housing, could also be rotated. The tip of the pin was bevelled on one side, like a door catch and rotation of the pin through 180 degrees enabled the catch to be released.

Both pins were rotated by the undercarriage selector lever through an arrangement of sprockets, chains and cables. The selector moved through quite a large angle to rotate the lock pins and, as it did so, it also operated the hydraulic control valve which supplied pressurised hydraulic fluid to the appropriate ends of the undercarriage jacks.

When the undercarriage leg was fully down, the pin, driven by the spring, entered a close-fitting hole situated at the extremity of an angled extension above the pivot point of the oleo leg. Once the pin was fully home, the leg was securely locked in position, due to the catch action. When 'up' was selected, the pin rotated and allowed the leg extension to bear against its bevelled side. The pin was pushed back into its housing as the hydraulic jack acted on the extension and pulled it through an approximate right angle to retract the undercarriage leg.

As the undercarriage leg moved to the 'up' position, a rather flimsy-looking bracket with a hole in it, which was clamped to the leg, pressed against the bevelled side of the pin and, again, the pin was pushed back into its housing.

When the leg was fully up, the pin was then lined up with the hole in the bracket and it snapped out again to pass through the hole and lock the undercarriage in the 'up' position.

Selection of 'down' revolved the pin in the reverse direction and released the bracket as the leg moved down under hydraulic pressure to be locked automatically in the 'down' position, again by virtue of the pin. Microswitches operated lights on the control panel to indicate whether the undercarriage was locked or not, for both 'up' and 'down' positions.

A characteristic feature of the Spitfire's undercarriage was that the two legs never retracted with synchronised movement. It was not essential that they should, of course and the hydraulic system had no means of splitting the flow of hydraulic fluid equally between the two undercarriage jacks. In certain circumstances, depending on such factors as variations in tyre weights, greater pressure of air acting on one undercarriage fairing rather than the other (due to the rotating slipstream from the propeller and yawing of the aircraft as rudder was applied to counteract engine torque), meant most of the fluid could flow to one jack only. The weight of the leg acting on the other jack could possibly overcome the fluid pressure, causing the leg to drop and fluid to be displaced out of its jack. The displaced fluid would then augment the flow to the original jack, speeding up the completion of its operation. After one leg was fully retracted, maximum flow and pressure was then available to complete the operation of the other jack.

26. Happy Wanderer

Before Squadron Leader Ellis took command of the squadron, I had become a Junior Technician with one stripe upside-down. It was part of a new scheme of Technician ranks and did not constitute a promotion. However, it gave me some scope to kid girls that I was a Yank in R.A.F. uniform, but my accent usually let me down.

The previous C.O., who was a nice chap at heart, had for several consecutive weeks, pulled me up for my turnout on parade. Each week, I would be criticised for the lack of a shine on my oil-soaked shoes, for an allegedly dirty cap badge, or for some other transgression. I became so fed up, because this was all in spite of my best efforts, that I went to the clothing stores and spent all my clothing allowance and quite a lot of money in addition, to buy a complete new outfit.

It consisted of a new 'working blue' uniform: shoes, socks, tie, shirt, collars and cap. The jacket was of the old wartime battledress pattern and the last one left in the stores. Much smarter, I thought, than the new post-war version, which looked as if it had been designed for comic opera, with its long wide sleeves and short waist band.

On the next parade, the Squadron Leader looked me critically all over and said, in a terse voice:

"Report to my office after the parade, Newton!"

"Yes, sir," said I, baffled. What had he found to criticise this time?

I reported later and knocked on his half-opened door.

"Come in, Newton. What is it you want?"

"You told me to report to you after the parade, sir," I said, still baffled.

"What did I want to see you about?" he asked.

"I don't know sir, you didn't say," I replied.

"Oh..." He cogitated for a moment. "Oh, yes... I just wanted to congratulate you on your turnout. Jolly good show Newton!"

I thanked the Squadron Leader and left his office, wondering if he realised how much this accolade had cost me. However, the money turned out to be well spent when, a week or two later, I was promoted to Corporal. I realised then that the Squadron Leader had merely tried to smarten me up to justify promoting me, for I must admit that as an N.C.O. I had to set an example.

Having collected my stripes from the stores, I spent most of the evening struggling to sew them on to two uniforms and a greatcoat. I was, naturally, very pleased at this turn of events, but also rather embarrassed next day. Would my mates of yesterday treat me with new-found respect, or would they just laugh and ignore my bleated instructions? I did not have a clue how to enforce discipline, nor did I know how to put an airman on a charge if it became necessary.

I walked into the crew room and was immediately pounced upon by most of the Flight and rolled on the dusty floor for a few moments. They then helped me up and dusted me down. "That's to prevent you getting any big ideas!" they chortled. Suitably abashed, I recovered my dignity as best I could, while the chaps got on with the primary inspections. I must say, that from that day on, I never had any need to exert authority to get even the unpleasant jobs done well, for the chaps were the best and could always be relied on. In fact, they saved me from the consequences of my own ineptitude on more than one occasion.

Normally, a newly promoted N.C.O. would be posted to another unit so that he could start off on the right foot, but I remained at Debden for a further year which suited me well. Most of the happenings of interest in this year have already been mentioned, but one was the design and construction of a $1/24^{th}$ scale Handley-Page' 42 'Hannibal' airliner, for which Handley-Page Aircraft Ltd. kindly sent me, at my request, a photograph and a print of an arrangement drawing. From these, I was able to draw the various components of the model on odd pieces of paper. It was rather embarrassing, when the *Aeromodeller* magazine later asked for the plans in order to publish them, to have nothing but tatty, built-on scraps of paper to offer.

When I was finally posted, it was to 22 Group H.Q. Communications Flight, near Market Drayton in Shropshire. The C.O. arranged to have me flown to R.A.F. Ternhill in an Anson, which enabled me to take the Monocoupe, Hannibal and sundry other models, in addition to my bicycle and full kit. By the time all that was stowed in the Anson and lashed down, there would have been little room for another passenger, but I was the sole occupant of the cabin and have never since travelled in such style. This gesture by the C.O. Squadron Leader Ellis was very much appreciated, needless to say, for it would have been impossible to take all that stuff on the train.

The Comm. Flight was hangared at R.A.F. Stoke Heath, a Maintenance Unit on the other side of Ternhill airfield. It was a very large and spread out unit in those days, with various sites dotted around the countryside. Every airman at R.A.F. Stoke Heath was issued with a bicycle just to get around it.

The Comm. Flight personnel, however, were billeted in one of a number of huts in the grounds of R.A.F. Buntingsdale Hall, the Headquarters of 22 Group and reached by a path with a lot of steps through a wood. The airmen's mess was on the ground floor of the hall, but the NAAFI was adjacent to the billets. It was an unusual and pleasant place that I was posted to and I soon settled in.

A blue Bedford bus took the Flight Personnel to work each morning and brought us back each night.

The Comm. Flight had three Ansons, two Proctors and a Tiger Moth. One Anson, I remember it as being TX 160, was a Mark XIX with a wooden wing and tailplane; another, NL 247, was a Mark XII with three square windows down each side of the fuselage, which was otherwise similar to the later Marks.

The third Anson, VM 359, was a Mark XIX with metal wings and tailplane and fitted with a blue-grey carpet and comfortable seats, being the personal aircraft of the Air Officer Commanding No. 22 Group. A special boxed-in flight of steps, with a handrail, mounted on two old tailwheels, was used exclusively for this aircraft, being suitably painted in blue and white as befitted its VIP use.

I noticed, on my first day at work, that morale was not good in the Flight and I missed the cheerful atmosphere of Debden. The Sergeant in charge was due to be posted when a replacement arrived and, although I found him somewhat unpredictable, for the sake of a week or two I did my best to humour him and get on with the job.

On the second or third day I discovered that one of the Ansons had a broken cowling fastener bracket which, one of the riggers told me, had been like that for some time. A new bracket had been ordered, but the aircraft had been allowed to fly in the meantime.

This news appalled me and, as the Anson was down to fly that day, I obtained a serviceable bracket from a scrapped Anson on a dump across the road and fitted it on our aircraft.

The repair was recorded on the aircraft Form 700 and when the sergeant read the entry he went berserk.

"You don't take bits off scrapped aircraft and fit them to operational aircraft just like that," he said. "How do you know it is serviceable?"

I replied that it was in better condition than the one he had allowed the Anson to fly with. This upset him even more.

"You'll do things here according to the book," he mouthed. "Take it off and have it checked by Station Workshops."

I took it off, gave it to the Sergeant in charge of Workshops and asked him to check it.

"There's nothing wrong with it!" he said.

"Well, Sergeant ----- wants it checking, crack testing and all that," I replied. The Sergeant gave me a peculiar look when I mentioned the name.

"All right, come back for it in an hour," he said, putting it on his desk.

I went back at the appointed hour. The bracket lay on the desk exactly as I had last seen it.

"It's O.K.," said the Sergeant, handing it to me.

Sergeant ---- was still not satisfied and sent me back to get a signed certificate of serviceability. The Workshop Sergeant was not pleased, but made one out. Finally, I was allowed to refit the bracket after a strongly worded lecture on doing things by the book.

Later, another rigger came to me with a query.

"Do it by the book!" I told him, as we walked over to an Anson on which he was working.

"Well," he said, "the book states that with the oleo legs correctly filled with oil, the recommended pressures and the corresponding extensions must intersect within this shaded band on the graph." I checked the graph for correct gauge pressure and the corresponding extension. The leg was at full extension and the pressure was too high for the intersection to be within the shaded band.

"Well, according to the book, we'll have to let some air out," I said. We had to let more and more air out until the legs began to shorten and the protective gaiters began to wrinkle up like Nora Batty's stockings. After releasing more air, the plot of extension and pressure came centrally in the permitted band. Satisfied, we then repeated the procedure for the legs on the other side of the aircraft.

"We'd better check the other Ansons as well." I said.

So we did and again had to let air out for all of them. By now, the Ansons appeared to be lying down on the hangar floor.

Sergeant ---- entered the hangar, took one look at the Ansons, went back to the office and entered on each Form 700 that the aircraft was unserviceable with oleo legs requiring inflation. He then instructed me to re-inflate them, which I did. However, he expected me to sign for them as being serviceable which I declined to do, as in my opinion the aircraft were not serviceable. I suggested that if he was satisfied with their serviceability he should sign the Form 700s. His response was to order me to sign, but I had explained about the graph in the Aircraft Handbook and, knowing that I was correct to do so, I refused.

The C.O., anxious to get airborne and finding all his Ansons grounded, lost patience with this nonsense and told me to set one Anson according to the book. He rang up the Group Technical Officer, who came to the hangar and checked pressures and extensions himself. He obtained the same results that I had, so he tried again with another Turner gauge adaptor. The result was the same.

He threw up his hands and said:

"Well, it's all right according to the book!"

"But it can't be! I've never seen Ansons from other units with wrinkled gaiters," protested Sergeant ----.

The upshot of the matter was that the Command Technical Officer flew over from Brampton Hall near Huntingdon. He was in a foul mood at being called out on a fool's errand, but again the pressures and extensions were checked against the graph on the Anson I had set.

"What's the matter with you people? Can't you read a graph? The oleo legs are correct!" and he stormed off, muttering something about incompetence.

So that was the matter settled. The other Ansons were also set correctly and I signed for them as being serviceable. Shortly after, a replacement Sergeant and two or three other Corporals, were posted in. The new Sergeant was one of the best and morale improved enormously.

One day, the C.O. called me over to him and said:

"Corporal Newton, now that Sergeant ---- has gone, can you do me a favour?"

"Certainly, Sir."

"Could you pump up the Ansons' oleo legs again? They wallow like drunken pigs when they are being taxied!"

I cheerfully complied.

R.A.F. Stoke Heath had a model club and I was invited to go with them to the 1953 RAFMAA UK Championships at R.A.F. St Athan. I decided to take the Hannibal, having bought an Allbon Dart 0.5cc diesel engine and having been loaned another, to enter the Scale Model Free-flight Contest. A rather roughly constructed glider was hastily made for the Open Glider Contest.

A cheerful bunch of aeromodelling eccentrics piled on to the train at Ternhill Station, wearing hats adorned with windmills or windsocks and carrying large black model boxes marked R.I.P. From Shrewsbury we had a compartment to ourselves, most people quickly moving on down the corridor to find more respectable company. The smell of pear-drops pervaded our end of the carriage, as the opportunity was taken to catch up on some last-minute doping.

The ticket collector looked at us with disapproval, but left us in peace to continue our preparations, which included making up rubber motors and giving them a trial stretch wind in the corridor.

I managed to make, cover and dope the tailplane of the glider before we arrived at Cardiff. Having arrived at St Athan, we soon settled in and work on the models continued into the night.

Everybody who was anybody in the aeromodelling world seemed to be at R.A.F. St Athan that weekend of the 25th and 26th of July. The list of judges read like a page from an aeromodelling Who's

Who. The Chairman was Group Captain J. D. Rutherford and the members were G. Lewis, C. S. Rushbrooke, Harry Hundleby, Bill Dean, Eddie Keil, Max Coote and Eddie Cosh.

The Hannibal presented me with some difficulties in mounting the engines which, by the time they were resolved, left no time for a test flight before the contest. Being a model of a four-engined biplane airliner, mountings for four diesel engines were provided but only the two mountings on the top wing were to be used. Because of the high thrust line, I did not think that down thrust would be necessary.

On starting the engines for the first time, I found it was easier to synchronise the speeds than I had expected. The combined sounds of the exhausts resonated quite noticeably at differing speeds and it was simply a matter of adjusting the compression and needle valve of the second engine to increase its speed to that of the first engine. Synchronisation was indicated when the frequency of resonance decreased to the point of ceasing.

With the last minutes of the contest ticking away, I crossed my fingers and released the model into the wind, which was blowing across the main runway. The Hannibal rolled nicely over the smooth tarmac in an undeviating line, the tail came up and, after quite a short take-off run for a 65" wingspan model powered by a total of only 1.0 cc, it climbed steadily away.

It soon became apparent that the lack of sufficient down thrust had given the Hannibal a nose-up trim and a gentle powered stall resulted, followed by two others. These stalls caused the model to lose altitude, until it touched down gently in the long grass. There was no time to alter the thrust line before the contest time limit expired and my one flight was not good enough to obtain a place.

The following day, Sunday, the wind blew strongly off the Bristol Channel and showed no sign of abating. I decided not to risk the Hannibal by making a second flight and retired to the hangar allocated to the Championships, where most of the other competitors were sheltering. They were congregated by the main doors that were adjacent to the airfield and the rest of the hangar was quite empty.

Because of the wind, four of the hangar doors were shut and only the two centre doors were slightly ajar. Inside the hangar the air was still. The sight of the huge expanse of smooth concrete floor gave me an idea for flying the Hannibal to check out the altered thrust lines and trim settings.

I had read, many years before, in the *Aeromodeller*, that somebody, possibly D. A. Russell, had tried out his model by tying a line to the tail and allowing it to take off. By running after it and then pulling on the string to slow it up, he was able to make it land again.

A long length of string was soon obtained and tied to the tail-wheel struts at the extreme rear of the fuselage, the engines were started and the model released. It was not difficult to keep up with the Hannibal as it gathered speed down the length of the hangar and lifted off in stately fashion. Then, by slackening my pace, the string was gently tightened and the Hannibal smoothly settled back on to the hangar floor. Having proved the method, the model was returned to the starting point and a more ambitious flight was essayed. The model again performed an impressive take-off and was, this time, allowed to climb higher, but I misjudged pulling on the string, it suddenly went tight and snapped. The Hannibal carried on irresistibly, flying beautifully, down the length of the hangar until, finally, it crashed into the closed doors.

The model suffered surprisingly superficial damage, due mainly to the slow flying speed. The balsa block construction of the nose absorbed most of the shock of the impact. A couple of wing struts needed replacing, the nose was glued together again and the Hannibal was ready to fly once more.

A further flight was contemplated, but in a less dangerous fashion. Why not tie a 60 ft length of line to the undercarriage and let it fly around me? With the pendulum-controlled ailerons locked and with a touch of right rudder to keep the line tight, it was worth a try, I thought.

Willing hands started the engines, while I stood in the middle and held the string. At a signal from me, the model was released and gathered speed in an anti-clockwise circuit. It had travelled about 120 ft and I began to doubt that it would get airborne when, for some reason best known to itself, the Hannibal lifted off and commenced a slow climb to about 15 feet where it stayed, circulating in majestic flight.

Due to centrifugal force, the single fuel tank in the top wing supplied extra fuel to the starboard engine which kept it running for some 20 seconds longer than the port engine. This was a lucky turn of events that I hadn't expected, for with one engine still running as the flight terminated, the model let down gently on to the hard concrete. Without power, the glide of the Hannibal was only a slight improvement on that of a brick.

I was told to stay in the centre holding the string, while the Hannibal was tanked up and sent off again by my volunteer ground crew, flying round and round, until I was quite dizzy. I finally managed to persuade somebody else to stand in the circle for one flight, so I too could stand outside the circle for a better view.

"No skill required, old son. Just stand there and don't let go of the string! The plane will look after itself."

Standing under the flight path, the spectacle of its stately progress, with wings rocking gently as it passed through turbulent air by the hangar doors, made all the effort worthwhile.

During further flights, I found it was possible to vary the routine by running down the centre of the hangar, level with the Hannibal as it flew parallel to the hangar wall to the other end, where I stopped to swing it round and allowed it to return, in an oval-shaped flight path. Holding the string, I stood for a full hour while other people used their own diesel fuel to keep the Hannibal airborne and, in so doing, to help it earn a place in the *Aeromodeller* Plans Service.

Back at Buntingsdale Hall, the same circulatory method of flying a model in a confined space was applied to the Monocoupe on the sports field, which had a wood at the downwind end. However, I overlooked two factors; there was a slight breeze and the Monocoupe had more than twice the power of the Hannibal. Nevertheless, the first circuit was accomplished successfully. The Monocoupe took off and gained height but, as it came round for the second lap, the crosswind caused the line to slacken. The model passed downwind, the line tightened again and broke.

Freed from all restraint, the Monocoupe continued to gain height until the engine cut, too late to prevent it gliding downwind and lodging itself gently into the topmost branches of a tall pine tree.

The art of tree-climbing is a necessary attribute of any dedicated free-flight aeromodeller, but on this occasion I did not feel that the model was worth the risk. One of the spectators, a chap named Martin who was wearing his best blue in readiness for the six o'clock jankers parade – he was always on .jankers – decided otherwise and shouted out,

"I'll get it!"

In spite of protests from the rest of us not to risk his neck, including an order from me to that effect, given in my most authoritative manner, he took no notice and shinned up the tree like a monkey, reached the Monocoupe and launched it in a glide, to land safely on the playing field.

Martin slithered safely down the tree, preceded by broken bark and twigs. I was more thankful to see him safely back on terra firma than I was to have the model returned to me and I started to give him a severe rollicking but became lost for words when I saw his appearance.

His smart best blue uniform was now green and pierced with hundreds of pine needles. His hands and face were filthy and twigs were stuck in his pockets and under his crumpled, dirty, collar. And the jankers parade was due in fifteen minutes!

Martin was an ACH/GD at Buntingsdale Hall and not one of the Comm. Flight personnel, but the chaps in the Flight billet rallied round and dragged him post-haste over to the ablutions, where he was stripped of his uniform and left to wash himself. The rest of us cleaned his boots and also the buttons of a uniform that somebody kindly loaned for the emergency.

A clean shirt, collar and tie also appeared from somewhere and willing helpers tugged and pulled as they dressed him where he stood, first on one leg and then the other as his trousers and then his boots were pulled on. With a quick inspection to check that he was fully restored to the required degree of smartness, a final push through the billet door sent him running over to the Guardroom with only minutes to spare.

I spent the rest of the evening pulling out pine needles and brushing, sponging and pressing his uniform ready for the ten o' clock parade, not knowing whether to be pleased or hopping mad about it all. But, thanks to Martin, the model still exists 60 years later.

Martin was, later, posted to the R.A.F. Regiment (the 'Rock Apes'). He was just the sort of chap they needed, I am sure!

The Proctors were beautiful little aircraft, although the Mark IV was not as dainty as the Mark III which was a development of the pre-war Vega Gull. The only external difference was that the Proctor III had double curvature windscreen panels like the Proctor IV, whereas the panels on the Vega Gull were flat. The deeper and longer fuselage of the Proctor IV did not have the classic lines of the earlier model, but there was more room for the passengers.

The wings were capable of being folded by unlocking and folding upwards a section of trailing edge on each side outboard of the undercarriage legs and withdrawing two pins to release each outer wing panel and swing it back. The feature that I didn't like was that the stress of supporting the weight of each wing panel was taken solely on a hinge at the rear spar and the hinge attachment could be easily strained if, as once happened, somebody tripped over the wing tip, being close to the ground and fell on it. Luckily, no damage was done on that occasion but, thereafter, I always left the wings extended, preferring to manoeuvre the aircraft carefully in the hangar, to fit them into the limited space.

The six-cylinder Gipsy Queen engines ran more smoothly than the four-cylinder Gipsy Major of the Tiger Moth and gave little trouble. The cockpit of a Proctor was comfortable and had dual controls. Access was gained by steps let into the wing root walkways, which must have caused turbulence but probably not enough to be detrimental.

The car-like doors curved over at the tops, with upper glazed windows and short curtains on wires which could be extended forward to shade the cockpit.

Construction of the airframe was similar to that of the Oxford, being plywood skinning over a spruce framework of formers and stringers. Joints between formers and stringers were strengthened with strips of plywood, bent at right angles and glued in top and bottom corners.

The cantilever undercarriage legs were bolted to the main spar and faired, front and rear, with two-piece resin-bonded mouldings attached by quick-release fasteners to brackets on the legs.

Having a good view from the cockpit, except in a directly downward direction, the Proctor was a pleasure to fly, being light and responsive. Nevertheless, I never felt happy in tight turns, knowing what kept the wings on, but appearances are deceptive and the removable pins were stronger than they looked.

A few months after my arrival at Buntingsdale Hall, the Proctors were replaced with two Prentices. If the Proctors were as pretty as Cinderella, the Prentices were certainly the ugly sisters.

Plate 13 Percival Proctor III

Being of metal construction throughout, apart from the fabric covering on the control surfaces, the only features retained from its Proctor ancestry were the style of the undercarriage and the more powerful Gipsy Queen engine. The rest of the airframe was of a completely different design. During the process of designing it there must have been a lot of afterthoughts. The wing tips, for example, were turned up, presumably because there had not been sufficient dihedral originally and that was the easiest way to modify the wing. The elevators had the appearance of having been nibbled away to reduce the area, perhaps to make them less sensitive.

The wing itself was massive and set at a high angle of incidence to the fuselage so that the aircraft flew nose-down like a Whitley.

The effect was so pronounced that, when coming in to land, the aircraft seemed to be diving and the nose did not impede the forward view of the landing area at all.

A curious effect of the engine being throttled back for landing was that the blind-flying panel, being separately mounted from the rest of the instrument panel, would oscillate violently.

The cockpit was comfortable and had new-type seat harnesses coloured blue and attractive light-blue anodised quick release boxes. There were two seats, side by side, at the front and, separated by the radio equipment, a third seat at the rear.

This seat was located centrally, with enough floor area on each side to put a tool box on, as I found when I was flown down to Manston and other airfields, to fix one of our aircraft which had 'gone u/s'.

As a trainer, the Prentice was docile enough, but if it was fully stalled it would lose two thousand feet of altitude before pulling out. The only time I experienced this, the nose dropped so far that it went past the vertical, due to the large incidence angle and it caused the sensation that the aircraft was going into a bunt. The speed increased dramatically and quite a high G-force was experienced in pulling out. I kept my eye on the altimeter as it unwound fully two thousand feet, which seemed to me to be excessive for a trainer.

Several of the Staff officers from Buntingsdale Hall would come over to the Flight hangar and take an aircraft up to get in some flying hours and so maintain their flying pay. One was a Wing Commander who had been badly injured, probably during the war. He was reputed to be held together with gold wire, according to the ground crew who had to help him into the cockpit of the Prentice, the type he invariably flew.

He was an extremely nice chap and always asked if anybody would like to come up with him, but I was the only volunteer, more often than not and accompanied him on several flights.

He must have flown heavy bombers during the war, for he flew the Prentice in the same way: maximum take-off run, holding it down until it could go no faster and easing it off the ground gently. He usually cleared the Stoke Heath hangars by no more than fifty feet.

Once he took off over the Stoke Heath monthly C.O.'s parade, which was held on the apron outside our hangar. He was even lower than usual and had to pass between the hangar and Station Headquarters, directly over the parade. The Stoke Heath C.O., a Group Captain, was delivering a pep-talk to the airmen at the time and his words were completely drowned by the noise of the Gipsy Queen. The Group Captain was not amused.

During the flights I made with the Wing Commander, he would steadily gain height to about three thousand feet, which would take all of ten minutes and then say:

"Take over, Corporal. You have control! Keep it in Shropshire and wake me up at four o'clock!"

He would then slump back in his seat, tip his peaked cap, which he had brought for the purpose, over his eyes and go to sleep.

The first time this happened, I was amazed at his faith in my ability. I was a bit worried, too, because my watch had a habit of stopping. But I was happy to be able to wander where I chose.

Map reading was not as easy as it might have seemed and not having an intimate knowledge of Shropshire, I was soon lost. A quick 180 degrees turn to regain the last known pinpoint rarely worked and, even if it did, the necessity of keeping a sharp lookout for other aircraft meant that, as soon as I took my eyes off the countryside below, I was lost again. The only resort was to circle continuously to left or right, or make an occasional figure-of-eight, keeping a prominent landmark continually in view. When I thought that people on the ground must be wondering what I was doing, I would move away a few miles to a new landmark and repeat the process.

At the appointed hour I would awake the Wing Commander, who had slept soundly and have to admit, sheepishly, that I was lost when he asked where we were.

"Never mind." he would say. "We'll go back on the beacon." He would press a button and, by some magic I didn't understand, set course back to Ternhill which, as it turned out, was usually not far away.

27. An Encounter with the Chief of the Air Staff

No. 6 FTS at R.A.F. Ternhill was the unit that used the airfield and No. 22 Group Communications Flight was a lodger unit, which meant that Ternhill provided the administration services, stores, sick quarters, pay accounts, etc.

The Flying Training School was equipped with North American Harvard IIs, which were leftovers from the war, having serials mainly in the FT range. Nevertheless, they seemed to be in very good condition and extremely reliable. I never saw any incidents that one might have expected to see at an FTS, although I expect there were a few.

One's ears would be frequently assailed with the snarls of the ungeared engines as the Harvards took off, all day long, over the hangar, their little propellers working overtime to produce maximum thrust. It was said that the noise was produced by the propellers rather than the engines: the tip speeds, at full throttle, being close to the speed of sound.

About a year after my arrival, the Harvards began to be replaced by piston Provosts, with single-row Alvis Leonides engines. This was a new name in radial engines to me, but had been in existence since as far back as 1941, according to 'Aircraft Engines' by A.W. Judge.

Certainly, although delivering 445 max bhp, it was much quieter than the Pratt and Whitney Wasp engine of the Harvard. A popular party trick with the Provost was to take off and immediately put the nose up into a 45-degree climb, which could be maintained to about 500 feet (my guess) before having to level out.

On the Stoke Heath side of the airfield, an Aircraft Recovery Unit shared our hangar. We were separated from the Unit by a large partition, which was understandable as most of the recovered aircraft were not a pretty sight.

The cockpit of a Meteor Mk. 7 fuselage in the hangar, when I went round to have a look one day, was liberally splattered with blood and it was an unpleasant reminder to me of a less jolly aspect of aviation. I felt considerable respect, after that, for the chaps whose job it was to clear up after a plane crash.

Picking up pieces of wreckage was a vital part of their job, in order to find the cause of some catastrophic accident. There was an instance when a Canberra exploded, whether on impact with the ground or when flying, I don't know. The outline of the Canberra had been chalked on the hangar floor and the area within had been filled with bits of the aircraft, with each piece being placed in its correct relative position, as if for reassembly.

No piece was larger than a tin tray, except for the jet pipe fairings, which were the only recognisable components. I don't know if the cause of the explosion or crash was ever found but, if not, it was not for lack of a lot of effort.

Another unit at the H.Q. site of Stoke Heath renovated all types of Coles mobile cranes. Further down the road was another technical site, which I believe serviced motor transport. In later years, it was rebuilt as a Youth Custody Centre. Some National Service old-timers who did their share of jankers at Stoke Heath would probably say that nothing much has changed!

Yet another technical site, further down by Warren crossroads, had large grass-covered concrete blister hangars. A complete machine shop was housed in one of them.

Our Tiger Moth and Anson TX 160 were taken away at about the same time as the Proctors. The Tiger Moth was greatly missed, perhaps because it symbolised the passing of the biplane era in the Royal Air Force. The 'Tiggy' was replaced by a Chipmunk, which was more comfortable to fly in but did not have the 'stick and string' feeling with the slipstream tugging at one's hair. It was like the difference between a car and a motorbike.

When our genial sergeant was posted I was, as the senior Corporal on the Flight, placed in charge for several weeks until our new Flight Sergeant arrived. My period of heady authority was uneventful and remarkable only for the fact that, during one week, I signed too many leave passes so that the Flight was short-handed the following week.

However, it did the ground crew N.C.O.s no harm for them to keep in practice by helping out with the routine servicing jobs, as I explained to Flt. Lt. Besant when he asked, "Corp, where are all the troops?"

Ansons NL 247 and VM 359 soldiered on, the only remaining original Flight aircraft. When the Flight was expanded in both aircrew and ground crew, they were joined by three new Anson T 21s, so that we could operate a transport service for radio spares to Aldergrove and Wildenrath in Germany.

The three Ansons were WD 410, WJ 560 and WJ 561. Anson WJ 561, although in new condition, also symbolised the passing of an era, for it was the very last Anson to be built.

Because of my modelling interests, I was picked one day in October 1954 to go to Jurby, in the Isle of Man and pick up a collection of solid scale model aircraft which were to be taken to Hendon. With an officer and myself as passengers, Anson NL 247 took off and set course for Jurby, across the Irish Sea. We forged steadily onwards across an empty expanse of sea and I settled back in my seat to doze the time away.

I was awakened by the officer, who looked a bit worried and pointed to the starboard nacelle 'beetle back' fairing, down which black engine oil was spreading as it rippled in the slipstream. This was a routine occurrence for NL 247 so I shook my head and shouted above the roar of the engines,

"It's OK. It always does that!"

The officer looked doubtful but was reassured sufficiently to say no more.

On our arrival at Jurby, I collected the models from Flying Control. Some were damaged, but the Sergeant there knew nothing about them and was glad to be rid of them, as they were cluttering up his office. The models were in a large tray and each had to be carefully placed in the luggage compartment of the Anson, behind the cabin, through a large door on the starboard side of the fuselage. They were laid on spread-out engine covers to protect them and the large tray had to go upright on its side in the cabin. Some old curtains that were with the models were laid carefully over them to prevent them being thrown about and, satisfied that they were safely stowed, I climbed aboard the Anson. Soon after, we took off again for the flight back to England.

The aircrew decided to call in for lunch at Squire's Gate, Blackpool and we flew along the seafront to have a grand view of the town, Tower and three piers before landing.

After the meal, I took the opportunity to walk across to the hangars and was intrigued to find, between two of them, that an old pre-war De Havilland 86B Express four-engined biplane airliner had been parked out in the open air.

It appeared to be in very good condition. Engine covers were fitted, which seemed to indicate that its flying days were not yet over. Securely chocked at the front and rear of the fat doughnut tyres, the aircraft rocked gently in the strong wind as the tyres flexed.

In spite of the wires and struts of the biplane's wings, the DH 86B was very elegant in its aluminium finish. The thin, shapely wings were slightly swept back and tapered away to nothing at the tips. From its pointed nose and the trousered undercarriage nicely faired into the inboard engine cowlings, to the shapely tail unit, the aircraft could immediately be identified as a De Havilland product of the Dragon family.

The fabric-covered underside of the fuselage was unlaced along the centre line to expose the control linkages and cable runs, on which a rigger had been working before lunch. I had to get back to our Anson at the appointed hour, before he returned and so missed the chance to have a chat and learn more about this wonderful old aircraft.

Having survived the war by some miracle, the DH 86B must have been at least seventeen years old – a great age for any aircraft in those days and particularly a wooden one, because of the glue joints. I have long since lost the note I made of its registration letters, but it must have been G-ACZP, just about the last one still in existence in that October of 1954.

I returned to Ternhill where I was dropped off and the Anson continued on to Hendon. Later, I had to type a report about the broken models, their owner having lodged a complaint, but I heard no more about the matter.

In the meantime, the oil spillage was getting worse on NL 247 and something had to be done. It was finally decided by the engine N.C.O.s that excessive crankcase pressure was causing the oil to be vented from the breather of the tank and that each cylinder barrel would have to come off in order to examine the pistons and rings. Close examination of one piston led to the discovery of a small hole right through the flame face which allowed exhaust gases to pressurise the crankcase and the oil scavenge system. A new piston was fitted and the trouble was cured.

While the Anson was being worked on, the new airframe Sergeant decided to have the interior of the cabin repainted as it was decidedly scruffy. It was originally cockpit green, but the sergeant instructed the rigger to use ordinary Ground Equipment Blue paint.

The seats were removed and the rigger had nearly finished painting by the time I saw it. I was appalled that the correct specification finish had not been applied, but the sergeant just laughed and said:

"Well, you must admit it looks pretty!"

I had to admit that it was a very individual décor, but a bit too garish for me. Being gloss paint, it was easier to keep clean, which was a point in its favour, unlike the matt cockpit green which marked very easily.

Test flights occasionally had their moments of excitement. One such flight was undertaken to check the time that elapsed for the undercarriage to retract on NL 247. The Flt. Sergeant pilot maintained that the operation took too long. He was an ex-engine fitter who took pride in being able to tell which cylinder on a Cheetah had a blown exhaust gasket before the cowlings were removed. But in spite of his acknowledged expertise we were not convinced. A ground retraction test was timed at 13 seconds, the specified figure.

The Flt. Sergeant would not accept this, insisting that the airflow affected the operation in flight. So, armed with a stopwatch and flight authorisation, we took off for a test flight. At a signal from the pilot, I retracted the undercarriage and timed its operation. It took 13 seconds exactly. To make sure, the undercarriage was extended and retracted several more times and the result was always the same. I assumed that the test was over then and we would return to Ternhill. The Flt. Sgt. had other ideas and it became apparent that he intended to make the most of this opportunity for a joyride.

After cruising around for a while, he spotted a goods train puffing along towards Crewe and, without saying a word to me, proceeded to fly in a wide circle, losing height and gaining speed, until the Anson was heading directly for the locomotive. A white face at the cab window was joined by another and then both quickly disappeared as we roared over the train, clearing it by no more than 20 feet.

There was a low hill on the other side of the railway track which the pilot avoided only by hauling back on the control column. I could see individual blades of grass disappearing under our nose as my stomach endeavoured to make an exit through my posterior. Somehow we made it and rocketed up to a safer height.

I thought that that would have been enough excitement for one day, but the Flt. Sgt. was thoroughly enjoying himself and headed for Prees Heath, where the disused airfield straddled the A41 trunk road.

Too paralysed with fright to talk him out of it, I saw what his idea was as he again circled and dropped down, until he was speeding at full throttle along the length of the main runway and only a few feet above it. This particular runway was cut in two at the point where the A41 crossed it and ahead of us I could see a string of cars and lorries crossing our path in each direction.

Fortunately, some drivers must have spotted us coming, for a gap appeared in the line of traffic, just in time for us to shoot through. If a pantechnicon had been crossing at the time, we would have hit it.

Apparently satisfied with his escapade, the Flt. Sgt., at last, headed back to Ternhill. The colour had presumably returned to my cheeks by the time we landed, but when asked how the test had gone, I gave my questioner a blank stare, because I had completely forgotten the purpose of the flight.

On another occasion with the Flt Sgt., Taff Bull and I accompanied him, again in NL 247, to give air experience flights for the boy entrants at R.A.F. Cosford. Our job was to load the Anson with passengers, strap them in and hand round the 'spew bags'. Taff and

I stayed on the ground, so I didn't know what sort of flights they experienced at the Flt. Sgt.'s hands, but the spew bags were certainly needed. Finally, the last of the green-faced 'brats' were unloaded and we were about to board the Anson for the return flight to Ternhill, when Taff decided to investigate an odd noise coming from the port engine. He found a large hole in the long exhaust pipe which could have allowed exhaust flames to play on the doped fabric of the nacelle fairing.

There were no scorch marks to be seen on the fabric, but both Taff and I felt that it would be safer to leave the Anson at Cosford for repair and ring up for transport back to Buntingsdale Hall. The Flt. Sgt., however, was set on flying back regardless, as the aircraft had probably been flying in that condition all afternoon. Although he was the acknowledged expert on identifying blown exhausts, he had not noticed it and neither of us were impressed by this argument.

The Flt. Sgt. then suggested that we could take off on two engines to a safe height and then fly back on the starboard engine. This did not sound very attractive to us, but as the alternative meant that we could have been stuck at Cosford for hours, the cautious option did not appeal either.

Taff and I looked at each other, nodded assent and climbed into the Anson. We both declined to occupy the co-pilot's seat, preferring to stay in the cabin behind the main spar, just in case something went wrong!

As soon as we had taken off, the pilot cut the port engine and feathered the propeller and proceeded at a fairly low altitude towards Ternhill, some twenty miles away. I was relieved to see that the starboard engine was managing to pull us along very well on its own, burdened as it was with the deadweight of the other engine.

Ternhill could soon be seen ahead and the pilot lowered the undercarriage but found that it would not lock down. He shouted, urgently, into the cabin for me to join him in the cockpit. I scrambled forward and he explained the problem. It then dawned on me that with the port engine stopped, there was no hydraulic pressure because the pump was on that engine. A few strokes of the hand pump were hastily applied and we were relieved to see the two green lights come on, indicating that the undercarriage was finally locked down.

Next to be operated were the flaps and I frenziedly pumped away when they were selected. With seconds to spare we crossed the boundary hedge, our one valiant engine was cut and we did a perfect deadstick landing on the short runway.

Coasting along to the end of the runway, we managed to turn off on to the perimeter track before the momentum was lost. There we had to stay until the duty crew could tramp across the airfield to push us back to the hangar, not without some moaning and groaning.

Around this time, I was sent up to R.A.F. Millom for a rather unusual reason. An Anson had crashed into Snaefell, the highest mountain on the Isle of Man, killing the crew, which, I believe, consisted of a number of Group Captains. The funeral was to be held near Millom and attended by Air Staff Officers including Air Chief Marshal Sir Dermot Boyle, the new Chief of the Air Staff.

I was sent there to attend to the V.I.P. aircraft flying in for the funeral and was flown up with another airman, on the previous day. We were dropped off at the end of a disused runway, on a bleak and windswept wartime airfield. After we had tramped across to the wooden huts of the Station, booked in and organised a meal and a bed, there was just time to go down into the town for a pint. It was the drabbest town I had ever been to and it appeared to exist on work provided by the old ironworks. The pubs were depressing in the extreme, but the beer was all right.

Next day, we scouted round to see what equipment there was that we could use. The camp was a School of Technical Training – for firemen, I believe, but apart from an old fire tender, which we commandeered and some foam extinguishers purloined from some empty billets and transported to the airfield on the tender, there was nothing.

The exposed airfield was cold and wet and the murky skyline was dominated by the mountain of Black Combe. On a day like that, the name seemed appropriate. The whole of the airfield was given over to sheep and, shortly before the V.I.P.s were due, we had to tear up and down the runway on the fire tender to chase them away. We also removed some of the larger rocks and stones, for use as makeshift chocks and we cleared other debris that had littered the runway.

There were no trolley-accs or CO_2 extinguishers on that Station, so I could only hope that the aircraft would all start on their internal batteries without trouble, when they left after the funeral.

We had brought our marshalling bats with us, fortunately, as there were a few hectic minutes as the several VIP aircraft arrived in rapid succession and taxied up the runway to be parked on the adjacent grass, near the pile of collected stones.

A car had been laid on to convey the V.I.P. mourners to the funeral, but it was late in arriving. When Air Chief Marshal Sir Dermot Boyle jumped down from his Devon, it was obvious that he was in a hurry, for he did not wait for us to get out the aircraft steps.

When he learned that the car had not arrived, he expressed some impatience and was definitely not impressed with the arrangements. I felt that it was ironic that the supreme officer of the Royal Air Force, with all his authority, was, if only temporarily, quite powerless to alter the train of events and was reduced to kicking his heels on a remote, abandoned airfield, half frozen in the penetrating wind.

Thankful that I was not responsible for the transport arrangements, I apologised for the lack of normal airfield equipment, explaining that in the circumstances it was the best I could organise and proceeded to place the rock chocks in position before his Devon blew away.

We had to stay with the aircraft to ensure their safety and went round them putting in the flying control locks to prevent the rudders flapping about and causing loss of air pressure. We had to shelter from the wind in one of the aircraft and were not sorry when the party returned.

There being no Air Traffic Control, I took this duty upon myself and asked the pilots not to start engines until they had the signal, because the rocks had to be removed from the wheels first. It would have been impossible to move them afterwards. They would have to start without chocks, using just their brakes and I had no intention of having impatient pilots tearing about, creating a hazard.

This meant that they had to wait in turn while the engines warmed up and so space out their take-offs. They were not very pleased about this, but I let it be known that I expected my instructions to be followed and, rather to my surprise, there was no argument.

In the event, all the engines were started successfully in turn as each preceding aircraft taxied to the far end of the runway, turned and took off. Finally, right on time, our own aircraft touched down, picked us up and returned to Ternhill in time for tea.

The Anson was a strange mixture of airframe construction, particularly the earlier versions of the Mk XIX, of which TX 160 had been an example. The wings and tailplane were of wooden construction, glued with Aerolite 306 and covered with madapolam fabric, the mainplane being in one piece.

The main portion of the fuselage was of welded tubular steel construction, faired with light formers and stringers to form a streamlined shape and covered with doped Irish linen fabric. The nose section alone was of semi-monocoque, all-metal, riveted construction in light alloy.

A large removable inspection panel was situated under the fuselage, immediately behind the nose section and secured with quick release fasteners. Due to the curvature of the panel, which was a wooden frame covered also with linen fabric, the heads of the fasteners were set inside quite deep holes and it was difficult to tell if they were correctly fastened. On one occasion, on VM 359, it fell off as the aircraft was about to taxi out. The panel gave access to the flying controls and trim cabling. Bicycle-type chain was much in evidence. We used to tell curious clerks from Stoke Heath, who were in the hangar to book a seat down to Hendon in the weekly Anson, that when there was a full load of passengers they were expected to assist at take-off by pedalling hard. It was surprising how many were not sure that we were pulling their legs.

It seemed to me that the Anson was derived, by the construction of its wing and fuselage, from the Fokker VIIB/3m which Avro used to build under licence. Known as the Avro 618 Ten, later developments were the Avro Five and Six; and the same constructional methods were used for the forerunner of the Anson, the Avro 652. With engines of greater power and a requirement for a retractable undercarriage, it was an obvious solution to move the wing from the top to the bottom of the steel tube fuselage and delete the centre engine. This was the basis of the Anson Mk I. The final development was to fit a new metal wing and tailplane.

The low wing made it easier to fit a simple retracting undercarriage, which was similar in principle to the DC2, an aircraft of the same vintage and a forerunner of the Dakota, with the wheels partly exposed. Such an aircraft could land safely if the undercarriage failed to extend, although the Anson would have lost its pitot head.

To take the landing shock, round rubber buffers were fitted to the Anson wheel axles outboard of the oleo legs which, when the undercarriage was retracted, fitted into shaped receptacles attached to the main structure of the nacelles.

The metal wings, of slightly less area, of later Ansons and some Anson XIIs, NL 247 being one, had detachable sections outboard of the engines. The metal tailplane had rounded tips, whereas the wooden tailplanes had a larger radius at the tips from the leading edge, which terminated sharply at the trailing edge to give a chopped-off appearance.

Alone of our Ansons, NL 247 had an earlier 12v electrical system instead of the normal 24v and there was no ground/flight switch, the rotation of the power socket cover serving as one when the cable plug was pulled out after starting. When parked in the hangar, the only way to isolate the battery of the aircraft was to fit a dummy plug.

NL 247 also had an earlier pneumatic system with a BTH compressor and an oil seal which had to be topped up regularly with castor oil. The oil, forced back to the compressor by the system air pressure, lubricated the air outlet valve. If the oil level dropped, the outlet valve would leak air back through the compressor, so that there would be no pressure to operate the brakes after standing for a while.

The brakes themselves, on NL 247, were operated by an earlier type of dual relay valve of quite massive construction, which was connected to the rudder pedals for differential braking. Later Ansons had a smaller dual relay valve, in the shape of a cube, which was commonly used on other types of aircraft as well.

It was neat but seemed to give more trouble than the older type. In consequence, the first thing one did on entering the cockpit was to check the air pressure gauge. When the aircraft was parked in the open, the rudder lock was usually fitted to prevent the rudder flapping in the breeze and causing air to be exhausted from the system.

Another quaint leftover, from earlier Ansons, on NL 247 was the brake lever protruding from the centre console, below the throttle levers. It was intended as a parking brake, but was often used for taxiing because more precise control could be obtained than with the brake levers on the control column 'spectacles'.

On later Ansons, parking was effected by an over-centre locking device on the control column brake lever.

The flaps on the metal-winged Ansons projected beyond the blunt trailing edge of the wing structure and had quite a sharp edge. It was easier to push hard when the aircraft was being moved out of the hangar if the flaps were lowered first. Flaps on other aircraft were also often lowered in the hangar for servicing access and to relieve stress on the hydraulic system by exhausting the hydraulic pressure stored in the accumulator.

On the ground, the fabric-covered 'beetle-back' nacelle fairings of the Anson had flat areas between the stringers due to tautness. In flight, the fabric was belled out by the suction of the airflow so that the ridges, formed by the stringers underneath, virtually disappeared and the result was a perfect double curvature of the surface area of the fairing.

If a model was built of an Anson with completely smooth fairings, without any representation of stringers and fabric, it would therefore be quite correct as a model of an Anson in flight. It is an interesting point, if one is a stickler for accuracy.

Most weekends, NL 247 was flown down to R.A.F. Hendon, on Friday afternoons, by the 22 Group Senior Air Staff Officer (SASO), pushed into a hangar over the weekend and flown back to Ternhill on Monday morning. There was always a waiting list of airmen from Stoke Heath, eager for a 48-hour leave in London, to occupy the spare seats.

I used to travel down to London quite frequently, but found the train fare expensive. Other means of transport were therefore sought. A lift on the back of Phil Hearne's motorbike was too much for me, it was three hours of pure fear, because I could not get myself used to leaning into the bends. I expect Phil was relieved when I said I would return on the train. He was a first-class motorcyclist, but had an accident when he returned early on Monday morning. A cat ran into his front wheel but luckily his crash hat saved his life, twice in fact, the second time being when a following motorbike hit him as he lay in the road. He suffered slight concussion and a broken bone or two in one hand.

I visited him in the Sick Quarters ward, which was mainly occupied with motorcycle accident cases. Another good friend of ours was not so lucky. He was a pleasant, modest, fellow Corporal, who entered for the Isle of Man Junior T.T. We listened on the radio in the crewroom and heard his name mentioned as he completed the first lap, but his name was not mentioned again. A report came in that a rider had been killed and, sadly, it was our friend. He had collided with a wall.

I decided that motorbikes were not for me and opted for flights down to Hendon when I could. I enjoyed these opportunities for executive-style travel, for a Flight member was always sent as a crew member to assist the S.A.S.O. with map reading, in addition to the usual duties of issuing spew bags and checking that the passengers were strapped in.

Hendon was quite a busy airfield and there were several interesting aircraft based there that belonged to Air Attachés of various countries. They were kept in one of the original hangars that still had the words: 'GRAHAM WHITE COMPANY LIMITED', painted on an end wall.

The duty crew would refuel the Anson for us and hangar it over the weekend. At eight o'clock on Monday morning I had to be back at Hendon, to remove the control locks from the Anson, give it a pre-flight inspection. and warm the engines up before the SASO arrived. After all the passengers were accounted for, we would take off and arrive back at Ternhill at about 10 o'clock.

Each passenger paid a nominal sum of 2/- which went into the Flight fund. Money thus accumulated was used for the Flight annual outings by coach to Rhyl, Blackpool, or wherever else was chosen.

A few airmen from R.A.F. Stoke Heath, which included myself, were sent for a week on an exercise to R.A.F. Acklington, which was a pretty bleak spot in Northumberland, near Ashington. I remember that on the way there we were quizzed by a stout lady in the train compartment as to whether or not we were married. None of us were and we were subjected to a sharp lecture about doing some poor girl out of marriage!

Basically, we were sent to be ground crews to some Meteor NF 11s on scrambles at any time of the day or night. They were parked on hard standings at the side of the runway, with the crew already in the cockpit when on standby and with the trolley-acc plugged in. When the telephone rang, two men to each aircraft would rush out of the mobile office, which was our shelter in the biting cold and the engines would be wound up. As soon as they were running, it was advisable to switch the ground/flight switch to 'flight', remove the trolley-acc plug and fasten the access flap as soon as possible. The pilot rarely waited for a signal to go, but opened up the throttles and moved off onto the runway and took off immediately. Fortunately, a low bank of earth gave us some protection, as we and the trolley-acc were blown over it by the blast from the jet engines. It didn't do the trolley-acc any good, or us for that matter. We were quite glad when the exercise was over. One thing that interested me at Acklington, was that there were large yellow-painted towed gliders for target practice, with tricycle undercarriages. I wondered how it was controlled in the air, because in my experience from using model gliders towed by the Monocoupe, once directional stability was lost, the glider would oscillate increasingly from side to side until it was quite out of control.

28. Final Two Years

Preparing one of the Ansons for its flight to Germany, I was in the process of checking the dinghy which was stowed in the luggage compartment – I don't know how it was supposed to be got at if the aircraft ditched – when I smelt petrol. There were no petrol tanks in the fuselage, so I looked around and found it was trickling down the underside of the fuselage fabric from the trailing edge of the port wing. I took off a couple of inspection plates and found a pinhole leak in the inboard aluminium tank.

Rushing into the office, I grabbed the Form 700 from the startled pilot and wrote the details in the Change of Serviceability and Repair Log, effectively grounding the aircraft. One crew member asked if it was necessary. I reminded him of the Dakota, which only a week before had blown up in flight and pointed out that it was probably a petrol leak that caused it. He went very quiet, then. We had to work over the weekend to change the tank, because the cargo was urgently needed.

One of our Ansons flying to Germany had become unserviceable at Manston, where it had to land for Customs clearance and I was sent down there with a Flight Sergeant pilot to fix it. We had to call in at Aston Down, for some reason, on the way there and set off in a Prentice.

Visibility was very poor and the pilot followed the course of the river Severn, flying down the valley to keep under the low cloud. My impression from the back seat, where I was ensconced with my toolbox, was of flying along a winding grey tunnel from the moment we rounded the Wrekin all the way past Bridgnorth, Kidderminster and Worcester until, at Tewkesbury, visibility improved and we headed for Aston Down.

From Aston Down our course took us over Epsom racecourse and the huge grandstand, which the pilot pointed out to me.

When we finally arrived at Manston, with its enormously wide runway that was used by crippled aircraft returning home during the war, I found that the Manston duty crew had already fixed our

Anson and it had taken off to continue on its way to Germany just before we landed. There was nothing else to do but have lunch and wend our way home.

The Americans were in residence at Manston and had a Grumman Albatross, for air-sea rescue purposes, standing at readiness. It was a very large amphibian and it rocked gently on its retractable tricycle undercarriage in the strong wind. I had a close look at it and it seemed to exude an air of solid dependability, being beautifully made and finished.

The Americans never flew anywhere without filing a flight plan with Air Movements, apparently and the clerk at the desk appeared to be a bit dubious when told that we didn't have one. My Flt. Sgt. pilot preferred to map-read his way home, making detours if necessary to avoid bad weather.

After a good lunch, we took off and headed out over the Thames Estuary, the area where Amy Johnson went missing. Having only a single engine, I found the thought a bit perturbing, but the Gipsy Queen, dependable as ever, pulled us along at a slow but steady pace. Periodically, we would pass over groups of long-abandoned anti-aircraft gun platforms, mounted on fabricated towers sticking out of the sea and interconnected by catwalks. I wondered if Amy Johnson was accidentally shot down by one of them, for it was common practice to shoot first and argue about it afterwards, during the war. As each group of towers appeared, one after the other, out of the haze, it was easy to imagine nervous gunners doing just that.

Leaving the Estuary behind us, we crossed the mudflats of Foulness – well named, I thought – and headed back across England in leisurely fashion, for you couldn't hurry a Prentice! I had time to observe a phenomenon I had noticed before, during other flights; that England was covered in an industrial haze, which extended upwards to an altitude of around 2000 feet. The limit of haze was sharply defined and, above it, the air was crystal clear. The ground, even directly below, was hardly visible, however, although it was a beautiful sunny day, as it was when we finally landed back at Ternhill at the end of a long, wasted, but totally enjoyable round trip.

Shortly before Christmas 1954, I had an opportunity to fly over to Wildenrath in Germany as a passenger on one of our regular runs with radio spares. The flight, via Manston, was uneventful, although I found it interesting to fly over the coast of Belgium and across part of Holland, the scene of so much action during the war. The countryside appeared to be flat and highly cultivated, but otherwise unremarkable. There was no indication of the moment we crossed the border into Germany and we arrived at Wildenrath sooner than I expected.

Plate 14 De Havilland DH 88 Comet

There was no sign of war damage on the airfield that I could see. It was bounded to the east by pine forests and had permanent barrack blocks, built for the Luftwaffe before the war and offering good accommodation to its new occupants. The Station was a hive of activity, with Volkswagen vans and cars very much in evidence.

We were transported to the billet area in a Volkswagen minibus which had a German driver. There appeared to be a large number of Germans employed for general work in the running of the Station.

Here I bumped into an old friend, Paddy Delaney, whom I had last seen at Mauripur. He shared a small comfortable room, in one of the barrack blocks, with three other airmen. I was soon shown the ropes and was able to change some pounds into marks and 'Baffs'. Baffs were paper money in British denominations and was the only currency one could use in the NAAFI or the Malcolm Club, i.e., threepence, sixpence, etc.

I was stopping for only one night and the marks were to be used to buy some wine and a cyclamen plant from Wildenrath village. After tea, I set off out of camp and turned left down the road. Night had fallen and it was a strange feeling being alone in Germany, for the war was still fresh in my memory, although it had been over for nine years.

I passed a farm worker, still working by the lights of his tractor, with typical German diligence, loading beet onto a trailer. Shortly afterwards, I came to the village.

The houses looked to be quite substantial, but did not have gates or front gardens. Bright neon lights at intervals indicated the availability of 'Pils' at the village's two or three pubs. There were also three brightly lit shops, two of which were closed. One was full of BMW motorbikes and another appeared to sell nothing but television sets in ornate cabinets. The third shop, a general store, was open and I was able to buy a cyclamen and a bottle of wine. They were not cheap and I had a feeling I was being ripped off but I had enough left, I calculated, for a glass of beer in a pub. I picked one with a bright 'Pils' sign and entered.

There were a few regulars leaning on the bar, farmworkers by the look of them, talking to the tall landlord. To me, he appeared to be typically German with his rimless glasses, close-cropped grey hair and cigar. I spoke the only appropriate German word I knew – "Pils!" – and he proceeded to serve me.

At this point his frau entered the bar, spotted me and commenced a tirade at the top of her voice, aimed at everybody in general. I was in uniform and it was obvious that she objected to my presence, making the fact known in no uncertain manner. I turned to go but the landlord motioned me to stay and ordered his wife back up the stairs. She finally did so, still shouting loudly.

I was highly embarrassed at being the cause of domestic strife, but the landlord said something, which one of the regulars translated as:

"Sit down and enjoy your beer!"

"Jarmin beer guit?" the regular added.

I took a sip, said "Yah!" and, as our respective vocabularies were then exhausted, took myself off to a seat by the television and watched the German news, which appeared to be identical to the news I had watched at Buntingsdale Hall the previous evening.

The apparent affluence, to judge from what little I had seen, of a previously impoverished, war-torn country surprised me. The Germans had obviously worked hard to bring about their country's recovery and I felt respect for their abilities if not their past history. Without the help of America, who had supplied Britain long before they entered the war themselves, we would probably have lost the war after Dunkirk.

I returned to the airfield and my bed in the transit billet. Next morning we returned, uneventfully, via Manston for Customs clearance, to Ternhill.

Travelling by train in those days left a lot to be desired, what with late arrivals and missed connections, for there was little time to waste if you were going on leave with a 48 hour pass.

The last straw, in a forgettable day's travel back to camp one Sunday night, was to miss my connection to Market Drayton at Crewe and to be charged excess fare to Nantwich, from where I had to walk through the night to be back at 0800 hrs.

I resolved to stop smoking and to use the money that I saved to buy a car. Down in Little Drayton was a car breaker's yard which had for disposal a 1926 Austin 7, a 1930 Austin 7 with a special body in ash and aluminium and an SS 100. The 1930 Austin 7 seemed to be the best buy at £20, but it was in a bad state, as were the other two cars.

This was at a time when one could buy a complete Spitfire for £50. There were dozens up for disposal, parked in the fields around R.A.F. Lyneham, which I saw one day when we called in, en route to Manston. Had I known what I know now, I would have bought all three cars and a couple of Spitfires too and found a place to keep them. That was another of my many lost opportunities!

The Austin 7 that I chose had been on a farm and was full of hen muck; the steering column was loose and the electrics consisted of a wire from the battery to the coil and another from the coil to the distributor. To stop the engine one pulled the wire off the battery terminal. The carburettor needle was from another type of carburettor and did not fit properly. It took a whole gallon of petrol – which the chap had put in the gravity petrol tank for me – to drive, on trade plates, the mile or two to Buntingsdale Hall. It was a wonder that the car did not set on fire, for the petrol had dripped onto the exhaust pipe as it leaked away. The petrol finally ran out at the top of a hill and I had to push the car for the last half mile to the car park.

My oppos hooted with laughter and waggled the steering wheel up, down and sideways, as they forecast that the Camp Commandant, Flt. Lt. Minchinton, would tell me to get it off Air Ministry property, immediately. However, when I asked him for permission to keep it on the camp, he was extremely helpful and suggested that I should keep it in an old barn and rebuild it there.

I gratefully accepted the offer and lost no time in pushing it to the barn. After a bit of work removing bolts, etc and enlisting the help of the billet, the body was soon removed and laid on the ground beside the chassis, to bag enough working space, for when everybody else with cars heard about my permission to use the barn, they naturally assumed that if I could, they could too!

The car was quickly stripped down to its component assemblies, each of which was, in turn, refurbished and painted. The Model Club, which had been formed at Buntingsdale, had the use of a Nissen hut for a club room and this was festooned with freshly painted suspension and chassis parts which had been cleaned, brazed or welded as necessary, re-bushed, re-pinned and reassembled.

The chassis had a small crack radiating from one of the engine mounting bolt holes, but it presented no difficulty to carry the chassis to the Flight bus one morning, to transport it up to Stoke Heath where my friend, the workshops sergeant, arranged to have it welded.

It is strange, but unofficial private jobs – "foreigners" – are usually treated with top priority, perhaps to get them out of the way and official jobs have to wait their turn. I was certainly very pleased to be told that the chassis was ready for collecting the same day and it was back at Buntingsdale that evening, beautifully welded.

While in Station Workshops, I had an opportunity to study a fully sectioned Junkers Jumo jet engine. Not for the first time, I had to give the Germans their due, to even my unqualified eyes it was apparent that they knew their stuff when it came to jet engines. This was the engine that powered the Messerschmitt ME 262.

The Junkers Jumo was an axial-flow engine that had been in full production. Most equivalent British jet engines had centrifugal compressors using existing technology, which were simple and sure but not exactly in the mainstream of progress. The Germans were on the right track, but did not have the right materials to extend its rather short service life. The feature that really fascinated me was the beautiful, miniature, flat four-cylinder petrol engine that was the jet engine starter motor. It was mounted centrally in the air intake, inside a streamlined fairing.

Bit by bit, the car was rebuilt. I knew little of electrical charging and ignition circuits, or engines and had to learn fast. In four months, it was complete and British Rail had lost another customer. I ran it for five years and every journey was an adventure. I have written a book about these times called *'Life with an Austin Seven'*.

The possession of a car to go to, and from, work gave me a strange immunity from the attentions of Service Police in the guardroom at Stoke Heath. It was just as well, for the car was held together with A.G.S. parts gleaned from the junk box, half of my toolkit was under the seat and an old Anson engine cover (rescued from the annual clearout for the A.O.C.s inspection and used to protect the body and hood from the elements), was stowed behind the back seat.

By contrast, my oppo, later to be my best man, was pulled in and searched when handing in the hangar keys one night. The SP found a 2BA spanner in my oppo's breast pocket and charged him with attempting to take it off the worksite, although it was signed for as part of his toolkit. Being an N.C.O. my oppo received a reprimand, which upset him somewhat for he knew about my successful record of undetected crime.

The possession of a car must also have demonstrated to the C.O., Flt. Lt. 'Jimmy' Besant, that I could actually drive safely, for he entrusted his pre-war Ford Anglia to me, when he was away for the day flying the A.O.C., so that I could take his wife to the pre-natal clinic. I found that job to be more nerve-wracking than being on a test flight. When the C.O. was posted I asked him for a reference, as my demob was drawing closer and I received a most excellent one.

The personal Assistant to the A.O.C. was a Polish Flt. Lt. who had been a Count in his own country. I think he looked on Buntingsdale Hall as a substitute for his lost estate in Poland, for he ruled the place with strict discipline. It was he who had Martin charged for his many misdemeanours, more often than not, but it was also he who told the SP in the guardroom that he was not to charge Martin any more until the following year because Martin had exceeded his allowable quota of jankers – he had completed 120 days, I believe.

The first words I had heard, when I arrived at Buntingsdale, were:

"Watch out for the Count!"

"Watch out for—who?" One soon learned who!

There were so few N.C.O.s at Buntingsdale that instead of having Orderly Sergeants and Orderly Corporals the Station duties were combined and called Duty N.C.O. So it came about that, when it was my turn, one of my duties was to take the six o'clock jankers parade. The Officer that day happened to be the Count and it was also the day my watch decided to take a five-minute rest.

I arrived late at the guardroom to find the Count pacing up and down, breathing fire, in front of the jankers parade who were, no doubt, watching developments with interest.

I saluted him, expressed surprise that the parade had started and feigned disbelief that my watch could possibly be wrong. As the Count, oddly enough, had only the ancient yard clock to go by, I managed to persuade him that the yard clock must have been at fault.

The Count dropped the subject, to my considerable relief and proceeded to inspect the disappointed janker-wallahs. I managed to carry through the remaining routine and finally dismiss the parade, my knowledge of the correct procedure having been gained through experience, being an ex-janker-wallah myself!

Next morning, it was one of my duties to raise the R.A.F. ensign on the flagpole at the front of Buntingsdale Hall, while the Orderly Officer saluted it. While it was being hoisted, any passing airmen or officers were supposed to stand to attention.

I waited patiently for the Count to put in an appearance, but there was no sign of him. According to my watch he was five minutes late. And even later if the watch had been playing up again. I then hoisted the ensign without him.

Just as I was securing the halyard, he came puffing round the corner of the Hall and demanded to know why the flag had been pulled up in his absence. He was told that I had waited but, as the A.O.C. was due to arrive shortly, I felt it was prudent not to delay further.

The Count must have known that he was late, but did not admit the fact. However, he said no more about the matter and for the rest of my time at Buntingsdale we got on very well. In fact, he turned out to be quite human after all.

The Count's office was right at the top of Buntingsdale Hall and, one summer's evening, he was working late, sustained by some sandwiches. He sent for the duty clerk who was on call in his billet. The clerk had to traverse the wood, go down the steps, walk along the path and up the steps at the other end, cross the road and the Hall yard and, finally, climb three flights of stairs to the office. Having knocked on the door, the Count bade him enter and ushered him over to the window.

"Do you see those sparrows on the lawn down there?" asked the Count.

"Yes, sir," said the clerk.

The Count thereupon gave the clerk the paper bag that had held the sandwiches and said:

"Well, take this bag down there and throw the crumbs out for them to eat."

The clerk took the bag of crumbs, down the three flights of stairs, onto the lawn, distributed them to the sparrows and then returned to his billet. A few minutes later he had another call to report to the Count's office. Back he went, along the path and the steps, through the wood, back across the road and the Hall yard and again climbed the three flights of stairs to the office.

The Count again took the clerk over to the window.

"Do you see that big black crow on the lawn down there?" asked the Count.

"Yes, sir," replied the clerk.

"Well, go down there and shoo him away! He's taking all the crumbs from the little sparrows!"

How do I know all this? I know because everything was duly recorded in the Duty Clerk's Occurrence Report Book.

Aeromodelling took a back seat for a time, but I managed to build another Southerner Mite, powered by the Allbon Dart from the Hannibal. The Hannibal had been sent down to Debden at the request of Johnny Dumble, so that it could be flown during that year's Battle of Britain Open Day.

I was told that it performed well at Debden, as a control-liner, which was more than it did for me when I tried it out with a bell-crank, but in Johnny's capable hands almost anything could be made to fly. I once watched him knock together a model in a quarter of an hour, in order to enter an Open Glider Contest on the spur of the moment. He took a spare wing and a spare tailplane and, with a length of ¼" x ½" balsa for a fuselage and a scrap of sheet for a fin, it was completed in time to enter and win the contest.

The Southerner Mite performed as well as the previous one and one day it, too, flew off and lodged in the far end of the pine wood that had so nearly claimed the Monocoupe. An extensive search failed to locate the model and I gave it up for lost. My new C.O. came to hear of my loss and offered to fly me over the area in a Prentice so that I could try to spot it.

It turned out to be a more hair-raising flight than I expected. We made several low, steeply banked, turns over the area and must have pulled several 'G's, for I had to hang on to anything handy to avoid being spread-eagled on the floor of the rear seat. The trees rushed past the widow in a blur of green, as I strained my eyes to spot the lost model. However, I failed to do so and it was never found.

In the meantime, the *Aeromodeller* model aircraft magazine had written to me asking for the design of the Hannibal and I sent them the scraps of paper on which it was drawn, as previously related. The model itself was sent down to them so that they could cut it open to measure the hidden details. An Anson crew bound for Hendon agreed to drop it off at Hendon guardroom. It was picked up from there by somebody from the *Aeromodeller* staff and taken to their offices at Watford, the location of the magazine at that time.

To return to the full-sized models – I always liked to think of our aircraft as full-sized models of perfect construction and finish, for when one has cosseted and cared for, serviced, pulled apart, repaired, reassembled, cleaned, started up and marshalled out what one looked upon as one's own aircraft, it was easy to imagine it as the ultimate in scale models.

A flight to Northolt in an Anson gave me an anxious half hour. On the way there, cloud increased considerably and we found ourselves flying over a solid blanket of the stuff which, as it turned out, extended down to the ground. Above us, there was a higher level of solid overcast giving the effect of flying through a grey and unattractive never-never land. Approaching Northolt, the Anson sank down into the cold, dark and damp sea of cloud rather like a submarine submerging. Streaks of water were driven across the windows and the wing tips disappeared into the gathering murk.

It became noticeably colder in the previously warm cabin as the aircraft sank lower and lower for minute after minute and the murk outside became steadily darker. Through the opening to the cockpit I could see the pilot watching the two crossed needles on the beam approach instrument, which was situated centrally above the coaming. As the needles moved, the pilot made appropriate corrections to our heading and rate of descent and for the first time I knew what it meant to trust and have blind faith in a delicate instrument, in order to return safely to terra firma. 'The more firma, the less terra', was the motto of most of my fellow airmen, but not one I had subscribed to until then. It crossed my mind that it was a most sensible point of view that I should have heeded more often.

Our pilots used to practise beam approaches at Halfpenny Green and on the one occasion I went along for the trip, being daylight with blind-flying amber panels fitted, there was nothing desperate to distinguish the beam approach from an ordinary landing approach.

By contrast, the approach to Northolt was a very claustrophobic experience, shut in a little world of our own, as we groped our way down. I swallowed several times to relieve the pressure on my eardrums and felt that we must surely land on somebody's roof. In fact, I believe one of our Ansons actually did land on a factory roof but this happened some months after I left the R.A.F. and I don't know the circumstances.

My belief that we must have been running out of altitude was suddenly confirmed as black and white stripes flashed past under the Anson, quickly followed by a large white-painted number. A gentle bump announced that we had touched down in exactly the right place along a runway, now reassuringly visible as it streaked from the wing to the tailplane. There was nothing to be seen beyond the wings, however, the thick fog obliterated even the edge of the runway; and once we finished the landing run we had to wait helplessly until a Land Rover edged gingerly out of the gloom, displaying an illuminated sign stating "Follow me" and led us towards the hangars.

We stayed at Northolt for an hour. All that could be seen of the place was the corner of a hangar looming eerily out of the murky air, so I stayed in the aircraft and dozed until it was time to go. The Land Rover guided us back to the runway and left us to our own devices. The fog had lifted slightly and the full width of the runway was now visible as the Anson lifted easily and climbed steadily away towards the clearer skies above.

One winter's day, Anson VM 359 developed an oleo leg leak at R.A.F. Wyton and was parked in a hangar to await attention. A spare oleo leg was soon obtained from stores and I was detailed to go down and fix it. The weather forecast predicted snow over eastern counties and, sure enough, during the flight to Wyton, in another Anson, one could see the dividing line where the snow-covered countryside commenced. It ran from north to south in a straight and undeviating line. The transition strip from clear to snow-covered ground was no more than a mile or so wide.

Arriving at Wyton at tea time, I put my toolbox in the hangar stores, fixed myself up with a bed for the night and retired to it, early in the evening, to escape the boredom of the N.A.A.F.I.

Down at the hangar next morning, I found the Anson parked by the partly open hangar doors. A minor blizzard drove swirls of snowflakes through the opening and around the Anson, which was looking rather pathetic with a list to port and a pool of oil on the hangar floor under the defective oleo leg. There was no possibility of moving the aircraft on my own and nobody seemed willing to help, being pre-occupied with Hawker Hunters. An ancient Avro Anson excited no interest at all.

It was necessary to jack the aircraft up to remove the leg, but no suitable jack was available. I settled for a large adjustable wing trestle, which a sympathetic airman helped me to drag the length of the hangar. After that, I was on my own.

Placing the trestle at a suitable position under the wing, I gingerly screwed up each end of the trestle, bit by bit in turn, as high as it would go until the port wheel was just off the ground.

Examining the port undercarriage, I discovered that the job was not going to be as easy as I had thought. The oleo leg was secured at the top by a pivot tube held in position by four large taper pins and the small ends of the pins were peened over to secure them. To extract them would require the undercarriage to be partially retracted to provide access space between it and the bulkhead. The hydraulic jack was disconnected and the down lock released and, by dint of much effort, I managed to lift the wheel high enough to kick a chock under it. Having gained enough room to use a junior hacksaw, I carefully sawed off the end of the first taper pin, filed it smooth and endeavoured to punch it out. There wasn't enough room to line up the punch, let alone hit it with a hammer, so the undercarriage had to be retracted a bit further, not without a lot more effort.

I wasn't happy with the security of the Anson on the trestle, as every gust of wind that came through the gap in the hangar doors gave rise to strange creaking noises. The wing trestle was intended only for the purpose of steadying an aircraft that was supported on jacks and to expect it to hold up half an Anson was asking a lot of it. I wasn't happy, either, at the thought of being squashed in the undercarriage if the trestle collapsed. However, I was so numb with cold I would probably have not felt anything.

After considerable profanity and the letting of some blood, I finally persuaded the first pin to give up and get out. At this point, the C.O. rang up, asking when I was likely to be finished. It was difficult to explain over a bad telephone line why it was taking most of the working day to do a five minute job, not to mention the fact that another quarter of an hour had just been wasted because the telephone was in the next hangar to the one that housed the Anson.

Back on the job, the second taper pin proved even more difficult to remove and the C.O. rang again before it was extracted by which time, after snatching a quick lunch, it was 14.00 hours. It occurred to me that, if I was not to be stuck at Wyton for most of the week, some other way had to be found to remove the leg. Close examination showed that short of removing the whole undercarriage assembly from the aircraft there was no easy way to remove the taper pins.

Looking again at the oleo leg, it could be seen that the top end consisted of a socket with a hole through which the pivot pin fitted. The socket could only be held with a screw thread because the two ferrules connected by a screwed rod were large enough only to prevent the socket unscrewing. The ferrules were quickly unscrewed and removed from the u/s leg which, in turn, was unscrewed and removed from the socket with surprising ease, leaving the socket still attached to the rest of the undercarriage. This is the answer, I thought; take the socket off the new leg, screw the leg on to the old socket and Bob's your uncle! Driven by a sense of my own brilliance and not a little desperation, I set to work with renewed purpose.

There was just one snag. When the leg was fully screwed on, the ferrule holes did not line up. To make them do so, I had to unscrew the leg nearly half a turn, producing a gap of about 20 thou between leg and socket. This meant that on landing, the full weight of the aircraft would be taken on the screw threads instead of through the abutting faces. However, the screw thread appeared to be more than adequate to take the stress, so I took the plunge and decided to leave the leg as it was.

There remained only the telephone call to the C.O. to send somebody to fly the Anson back to Ternhill and, while I waited, to replace the two taper pins. This was a much easier job, because I could stand up in the wheel bay to hammer them in and peen them over, using a riveting dolly as a reaction block. After relocking the undercarriage down and reconnecting the jack, a final check was made before the Anson was lowered and the trestle dragged away. I had just enough time for a cup of Naafi tea and a smoke, after cleaning myself up and giving the Anson a pre-flight inspection, before the crew arrived to fly it back.

The pleasure of sitting in the comfortable chair normally occupied by the A.O.C., as we taxied out for the take-off, was rather spoiled for me by every bump. My nerves jangled as I imagined the threads stripping under the load. The landing at Ternhill seemed rather heavy, but nothing untoward happened. For days after, I surreptitiously checked the gap with feeler gauges but it never closed up. The other legs also developed leaks after a few months and it was with some relief that I saw VM 359 off to an MU for a Major Inspection, during which the entire undercarriage was replaced.

Occasionally, it was necessary to collect a spare aircraft part from whatever unit happened to have one. Our Chipmunk had lost a jettisonable panel from its sliding 'green house' canopy while on a flight one day and, for some reason that I can't remember, a replacement panel would not have been available for another week through the normal channels. The Chipmunk was urgently required for use, so I was sent to do the rounds of the local M.U.s to beg, borrow or steal one. In fact, I was virtually told not to come back without one and off I went in a Prentice with a pilot to chauffeur me around.

The first call was to 27 MU at Shawbury where I drew a blank. Next was 29 MU at High Ercall where the result was the same.

The Chipmunk was comparatively new in R.A.F. service and spares of any sort were uncommon. Therefore, when we took off again for 9 MU at Cosford, we had a feeling we were wasting time.

At Cosford I left the pilot, who was getting a bit fed up by this point, to his own devices once again, while I went to find the stores. Arriving there, I asked for the person in charge and was told it was tea-break time. As I have never believed that other people's tea-breaks are sacrosanct if I can't have one myself, I asked to be directed to his office and tapped on the door.

On entering, I was confronted with what was, to me, an odd scene. At a desk, mounted on a dais, sat the boss, a middle-aged, bespectacled gentleman. Around him were some two dozen ladies, presumably his clerks and typists, sitting on tables, chairs and the dais itself and all drinking tea. Perhaps it was the official Civil Service tea-break procedure. However, I was courteously received and told that if there was a spare panel lying about on the unit I could have it. A thorough search of the stores failed to unearth one, so I went down to the M.U. hangar where a number of interesting aircraft, including a Boulton Paul Balliol, were being serviced.

The foreman, to whom I introduced myself, was quite helpful, saying that he had seen a panel somewhere and he showed me where he thought it was. It was not there, but the foreman was adamant that there was one and gave me leave to search every corner of the hangar.

I was about to give up when I came upon it, half hidden by other bits and pieces, propped up against a bench. I pulled it out and examined it closely. The Perspex was in good condition and I could see no defects, so I tucked it under my arm. Just then a chap came dashing up.

"Hey! You can't have that!" he said.

I looked around the hangar for a Chipmunk that it might have belonged to. There was no Chipmunk.

"Why not?" I asked.

"It's mine!" he replied.

"What do you mean – it's yours?" I queried.

"So-and-so said I could have it!"

"What for?"

"It's for a cold frame," he admitted.

I gently explained to him that the panel happened to be Air Ministry property and it was needed for a Chipmunk and there was no further argument, although there was no proof that I didn't want it for a cold frame, too!

Without further ado, not even having to sign for it, I carried the panel out to the waiting Prentice and we set off, to the pilot's relief, back to Ternhill. The Chipmunk was soon fitted with the new panel and adjustments were made to ensure that it would not also be accidentally released.

We had a jettisonable panel go adrift from an Anson one day. It was made of Perspex, situated centrally in the cockpit canopy and held at the corners, like a photo in an album, by brackets. The panel was sealed with doped fabric strip connected by a loop to a wire with a release toggle. When the toggle was pulled, the fabric strip was peeled off the canopy. A push was all that was then needed to release the Perspex panel from the corner brackets. On this particular occasion the pilot was in a hurry to get home and was pushing the Anson along as fast as it would go when the panel suddenly popped out like a cork from a bottle. The pilot's maps and various other sundry bits and pieces were also sucked out by the slipstream.

Returning to the subject of the Chipmunk, I had a few flights in it and found it to be very pleasant, although rather claustrophobic in the back seat with the cockpit canopy closed. The only way to get out if the canopy jammed was through the jettisonable panel.

Slight buffeting, to warn that a stall was impending, was generated by angle strips riveted to the wing leading edges, from the fuselage outwards as far as the undercarriage legs. The angle strips were positioned on the leading edges so that they turbulated the airflow only at high angles of attack.

The wing walkways extended onto the flaps which used to deflect slightly under my weight. I never felt very happy about putting my full weight on it and used to step directly on and off the wing, but it was rather a stretch. It was the first and only aircraft I had seen with disc brakes and they were very effective. They used to make a clicking noise when the aircraft was pushed backwards, but I never found out the reason why.

All too soon, the months slipped by to my demob. I was offered the opportunity of signing on again but by this time I was married and my idea was to settle in one place and put down roots, perhaps even to start a business. A letter to a local firm at Newport brought an offer of an interview, which I arranged to attend. At the last minute, the voltage regulator and cutout on the Austin 7 gave up the ghost and, too late, I discovered that the local bus and train services were totally inadequate.

Before I could make other arrangements, an airman at Stoke Heath offered me the use of his immaculate 1932 Austin 7 tourer to motor the 24 miles round trip. I scarcely knew the chap but the only proviso that he made was that I should replace the petrol and oil that I used. Thanks to his good-hearted and trusting gesture, so typical of my fellow airmen, I attended the interview feeling fresh and confident and got the job. I was also able to get a new VR/CO from the Lucas agent at Newport and so my own car was soon back on the road.

I was given two days off to travel down to Woking to collect my demob outfit of civvies and elected to travel down in the Austin with my wife. The car was running well and reliably but I underestimated the time the journey would take. We started at six o'clock in the morning to arrive at Woking for midday, but were defeated by the traffic lights at Slough and arrived half an hour late.

Fortunately, there was an issue of civvies in the afternoon and I collected mine without difficulty. While I was there, I met a chap who had been a fellow recruit at Cardington and whom I had not seen since. He had been an M.T. driver and I asked him what he was going to do in Civvy Street.

"Going back to the mines," he said, which surprised me. He was an ex-miner who had managed to qualify for a more congenial job after deciding to leave the mines. Perhaps working down a pit was not as hard as it was made out to be. After working in the fresh air for ten years, it certainly did not appeal to me. Working in a factory would be bad enough.

My wife and I decided to stop overnight in Windsor and take the opportunity to visit Runnymede and Windsor Castle. Wearing my Karachi sports jacket, (which was still as good as new and far removed in quality and cut from my demob suit still reposing in the cardboard box it was packed in at Woking), I must have looked smarter than usual. A sentry gave me a butt salute every time I passed him, which made a good impression on my wife, who thought all Corporals were entitled to a salute after that, until I explained that the sentry was merely following the golden rule:

If it moves, salute it; if it doesn't, paint it!

So it was advisable to keep moving!

On the journey back to Shropshire we called at the *Aeromodeller* offices, which were then at Watford, to pick up the Hannibal and have a chat with Ron Moulton before wending our way up the A5 (no M1 or M6 in those days!).

At last the day came when I collected my clearance chit and made the rounds for the last time. At the Sick Quarters the M.O. looked at my records.

"It says here that you suffered from anaemia before you joined up," he said.

"Never suffered from it in my life." I replied.

"Well, that's what you stated on your form listing previous illnesses," he rejoined.

I wondered why the Royal Air Force was worried about my having anaemia after ten years of excellent health and thought hard. Perhaps they weren't going to let me out! Then I remembered.

There had been a formidable list of illnesses and you had to state which ones you had contracted. The list ranged from flat feet to beri-beri, but none of them applied to me. Somebody had once said that I looked anaemic, so I put myself down for that, for I thought nobody would believe that I had not suffered from one of them at some time or another.

I explained this to the M.O. who looked a bit incredulous. Anyway, he signed my chit and shook hands.

"Good luck, Newton," he said. "You'll need it!"

Epilogue

Now my story is ended. They say that it doesn't matter how you finish a book; if your reader is still with you at that last page, you've already won! If you have, indeed, read this far, dear reader, thank you for making the effort of writing it worthwhile. For me, it has been a strange experience to be transported back in time, to rummage through old memories and recall events that I had forgotten for over thirty years.

I never fully appreciated at the time what a wonderful life it was in the Royal Air Force and never thought to keep a diary or other records. It seemed that life would go on as it was forever and changes were so imperceptible that they made little difference.

Is it still the same R.A.F. today? Is there still the same comradeship? Does it still have characters in its ranks, or have they all been weeded out by political correctness in the selection processes?

I only know that ten years of my life could not have been spent more enjoyably, or to better purpose and I wouldn't have missed it for a gold clock.